Leadership and teams in educational management

COMPANION VOLUMES

The companion volumes in this series are:

Educational Management: Strategy, Quality and Resources, edited by Margaret Preedy, Ron Glatter and Rosalind Levacic

Organizational Effectiveness and Improvement in Education, edited by Alma Harris, Nigel Bennett and Margaret Preedy

Professional Development for Educational Management, edited by Lesley Kydd, Megan Crawford and Colin Riches

All four of these readers are part of a course, Effective Leadership and Management in Education, that is itself part of the Open University MA Programme.

THE OPEN UNIVERSITY MA IN EDUCATION

The Open University MA in Education is now firmly established as the most popular postgraduate degree for education professionals in Europe, with over 3,500 students registering each year. The MA in Education is designed particularly for those with experience of teaching, the advisory service, educational administration or allied fields.

Structure of the MA

The MA is a modular degree, and students are therefore free to select from a range of options the programme which best fits in with their interests and professional goals. Specialist lines in management and primary education are also available. Study in the Open University's Advanced Diploma and Certificate Programmes can also be counted towards the MA, and successful study in the MA programme entitles students to apply for entry into the Open University Doctorate in Education programme.

COURSES CURRENTLY AVAILABLE:

- Management
- Child Development
- Primary Education
- Curriculum, Learning and Assessment
- Special needs
- Language and Literacy
- Mentoring

- Education Training and Employment
- Gender
- Educational Research
- Science Education
- Adult Learners
- Maths Education

OU supported open learning

The MA in Education programme provides great flexibility. Students study at their own pace, in their own time, anywhere in the European Union. They receive specially prepared study materials, supported by tutorials, thus offering the chance to work with other students.

How to apply

If you would like to register for this programme, or simply to find out more information, please write for the *Professional Development in Education* prospectus to the Central Enquiry Service, PO Box 200, The Open University, Walton Hall, Milton Keynes, MK7 6ZS, UK (Telephone 01908 653231).

Leadership and teams in educational management

Edited by
MEGAN CRAWFORD, LESLEY KYDD
AND COLIN RICHES
at The Open University

OPEN UNIVERSITY PRESS
Buckingham · Philadelphia

Open University Press
Celtic Court
22 Ballmoor
Buckingham MK18 1XW

email: enquiries@openup.co.uk
world wide web: http://www.openup.co.uk

and 325 Chestnut Street
Philadelphia, PA 19106, USA

First published 1997
Reprinted 1998 (twice)

A catalogue record of this book is available from the British Library

ISBN 0 335 19842 2 (hb)   0 335 19841 4 (pb)

Library of Congress Cataloging-in-Publication Data

Leadership and teams in educational management/edited by Megan
    Crawford, Lesley Kydd, and Colin Riches.
        p.   cm. – (Leadership and management in education)
    Includes bibliographical references and index.
    ISBN 0-335-19841-4(pb)   ISBN 0-335-19842-2(hb)
    1. Educational leadership–Great Britain.   2. School management
teams–Great Britain.   3. School management and organization–Great
Britain.   I. Crawford, Megan, 1957–   .   II. Kydd, Lesley, 1950–
.   III. Riches, Colin R.   IV. Series.
LB2900.5.L43   1997   96-42218
                                                                                                   CIP

Typeset by Type Study, Scarborough, North Yorkshire
Printed and bound in Great Britain by Redwood Books, Trowbridge

Contents

Part 2 Working in teams

Acknowledgements

The chapters listed below come from the following sources, to whose publishers grateful acknowledgement is made.

1 Ogawa, R. and Bossert, S. (1995) 'Leadership as an organizational quality', *Educational Administration Quarterly*, 31(2): 224–43.
2 Beare, H., Caldwell, B. and Millikan, R. (1992) 'Leadership', Chapter 13 in M. Preedy (ed.) *Managing the Effective School*, London, Routledge.
3 Southworth, G. (1995) 'Primary headship and leadership' (commissioned article).
4 Grace, G. (1995) 'Critical leadership studies' (commissioned article).
5 Hall, V. (1993) 'Women in educational management: a review of research in Britain', Chapter 3 in J. Ousten (ed.) *Women in Educational Management*, Harlow, Longman.
6 Riches, C. R. (1994) 'Motivation', Chapter 10 in T. Bush and J. West-Burnham (eds) *The Principles of Educational Management*, Harlow, Longman.
7 Crawford, M. (1995) 'Managing stress in educational organizations' (commissioned article).
8 Walton, R. E. (1987) 'Introduction', in *Managing Conflict: Interpersonal Dialogue and Third-Party Roles*, 2nd edn, (pp 2–12, 15 and 16). © 1987 Addison-Wesley Publishing Company Inc. Reprinted by permission of Addison-Wesley Longman Inc.
9 Bell, L. (1992) 'Staff teams and their management', Chapter 4 in *Managing Teams in Secondary Schools*, London, Routledge.
10 Wallace, M. and Hall, V. (1994) 'Team dynamics', Chapter 4 in *Inside the SMT: Teamwork in Secondary School Management*. Reprinted with permission from the author, © 1994 Paul Chapman Publishing Ltd, London.
11 Johnston, J. and Pickersgill, S. (1992) 'Personal and interpersonal aspects of effective team-oriented headship in the primary school', *Educational Management and Administration*, 20(4): 239–48.

12 Hargie, C., Tourish, D. and Hargie, O. (1994) 'Managers communicating: an investigation of core situations and difficulties with educational organizations', *International Journal of Educational Management*, 8(6): 23–8. Reprinted by permission © MCB University Press Ltd, http://www.mcb.co.uk
13 Riches, C. R. (1994) 'Communication', Chapter 12 in T. Bush and J. West-Burnham (eds) *The Principles of Educational Management*, Harlow, Longman.
14 Adair, J. (1986) 'Teambuilding', Chapter 11 in *Effective Teambuilding*, London, Pan.

Introduction

MEGAN CRAWFORD

During any discussion on managing people, there is an inevitable focus on how people work together most effectively. Both leading and team working are pervasive activities in Human Resource Management (HRM) in education, and are part of the process through which successful teaching and learning takes place in educational settings. The prime importance of leadership in creating and maintaining effective schools and colleges is also being given increasing prominence in research, policy and practice. Leadership, of course, cannot be exercised except in relation to the other people in an organization. This book concentrates on the way leadership is practised organizationally and within teams of one sort or another, and how these depend on leadership for their overall effectiveness. Thus the book argues that leadership and team working are at the core of managing people, the most important resource in the whole field of educational management or indeed any other sort of management. The rationale of this book is to give centrality to both topics in a way that practically all existing readers and texts on educational management fail to do.

The interrelatedness, interactions and symbiosis of leadership and teams is crucial. In the last few years we have seen educational management increase in complexity as more and more management activities are devolved to individual institutions. In this climate of multiple changes, more delegation of tasks to individuals and teams within schools and colleges is called for. The importance of leading and team working within educational organizations thus increases. This book takes the view that managers, as never before, need to develop skills both in leading and in being effective members of teams. This could range from leading from within a management team to being a member of a year or course team. All these teams call for effective leading and following at every level. Thus leading is not a one-dimensional activity but a process in which more than one person is engaged, whether this is within a whole organization or specific team setting. Proficient leading and team working is, therefore, central to effective performance within schools and colleges.

Part 1: Leading and leadership

In this part the ways in which people might exercise leadership for more effective organizational performance in a variety of contexts are discussed. Kakabadse *et al.* (1988: 188) observed: 'There has probably been more research, discussion and controversy on the topic of leadership than most other areas of management.' It can be a confusing concept, and each definition seems to emphasize one aspect of leadership more than another. Whichever view of leadership is discussed, there is general agreement that leadership involves influencing others to go in a particular direction. No matter what the definition is, leadership plays such an important part in educational institutions that its importance cannot be ignored. This book's definition of leadership is wide and is to be expressed in terms of leading within a wide variety of roles, whether formal or assumed, at a variety of levels and in teams of different sizes and complexity. Included in this is one central tenet: that when thinking of leading, the corollary is following.

Many people have strong views on what makes an effective leader, and assume that the leader will have a position of some power or authority. In the literature of leadership studies this can be defined as the *trait theory* approach whereby researchers have tried to identify the common personality characteristics of individual effective leaders. Often these characteristics will depend on the leadership situation at the time, and the group context will make a great difference to a leader's effectiveness. *Style theorists*, on the other hand, have tried to identify the most effective management style that a leader should choose in order to influence their followers effectively. For example, participative management styles have gained in popularity as they are seen to be a way in which team members may have greater commitment to the team purpose. Another view is that of *contingency theorists*, who suggest that what is appropriate will depend on the leader, the led, the task and the wider context. These leadership theories have a narrowness about them that invites critical comment. They seem to concentrate too much on just one aspect of leadership – that of using authority or power within a group to make their followers take up a specific course of action. These theories also stress the importance of the one person as leader. Leadership, it can be argued, is more than this. It also depends on the organizational context. Leadership can be viewed as a process with leaders being identified as those who make particular contributions to leading and leadership. Leadership can therefore have its origins in more than one member of a team. The first part of the book aims to help the reader understand that leadership can be looked at in very different ways, and as a particular type of process within teams. Formal position within a team may give a person influence over the way that team reaches decisions, but a well-run team may have more than one leader. An effective leader will want to recognize that s/he may not have to perform all the functions of a leader in a particular context.

So, this part of the book first considers leadership as an organizational quality. It then goes on to discuss some valuable strands in thinking about leadership and its expression in different sectors of education, followed by a critical look at the whole notion of leadership. Gender differences in management style are explored as is the importance of motivating not only in decision making, but also in all aspects of professional life. When thinking about motivation a number of issues concerning stress arise both for those leading and those following. Such stresses, tensions and conflicts require resolution through negotiation. Effective leadership involves the successful handling of issues of this kind, and this book endeavours to discuss them within a framework of team working.

In the opening chapter, Ogawa and Bossert suggest that leadership should be conceptualized as an organizational quality. They argue that leadership flows through the networks of roles that go to make up organizations. People are therefore central both to the way that leadership shapes the systems that produce patterns of interaction and also to the meanings that others attach to organizational events. This approach focuses attention on the ethics of leadership, and the symbolic dimension of organizations. Ogawa and Bossert recognize that there have been moves in this direction recently, but there needs to be more emphasis in the literature on the organizational qualities of leadership.

Beare *et al.* in a wide-ranging chapter look at the major features of current knowledge about leadership in outstanding schools. They argue the importance of influence, and place the emphasis firmly on transforming rather than transactional leadership. Leadership is at the heart of the culture of the school, and the chapter gives school managers some ideas about what this might actually involve in practice. Geoff Southworth then takes up a critical review of the literature that involves leadership in primary school management, and finds that this is still largely focused on the headteacher. He suggests from his own research that for some primary headteachers, headship is neither a matter of style or role, but part of their occupational identity. From his study of the literature, he concludes that there are many deficiencies in current awareness of primary school leadership that still need to be tackled.

Gerald Grace's chapter looks at what he terms 'critical leadership studies', and the arguments for developing a new approach to the study of leadership. Grace suggests that this is not only a new framework for the understanding of educational leadership, but also a new way of framing what such leadership should be. He argues that it is necessary for those who lead to demonstrate some understanding of underlying moral values and to make explicit the relationship between values and actions in institutions. As part of this discussion, Grace looks briefly but interestingly at gender issues. For women in educational management, Valerie Hall's review of the research literature reveals a picture of an overall failure to discuss gender issues in a sustained and coherent manner. She suggests that research in this area falls well behind that in the United States and that which is done concentrates either on the concept of career or looks for evidence of 'female' management style. Research that exists is generally descriptive and based on small samples; she argues for further work that will include gender as a fully relevant concept for understanding educational management.

The study of motivation, as discussed by Colin Riches, arises from the increasing emphasis in education on HRM. He argues that motivating people to get results through them is central to the purposes of management. The chapter discusses various theories of motivation, and their implications for school and college managers. However, he recognizes that sometimes motivation fails and cites stress as one of the causes. The Crawford chapter which follows looks more closely at this much-discussed concept, and argues that both a personal and an institutional knowledge of stress management is crucial to effective performance. Managers need to learn what causes stress and how to manage their own stress levels before they can look at how their organization deals with stressed employees.

Finally, on a wide canvas, negotiation is an important aspect of leading within an organization to enhance performance. Walton's introduction to conflict management proposes a framework for diagnosing a conflict, and suggests the options that managers have for either controlling or resolving it. The chapter presents the view that better management of conflict involves making sure that all the parties involved are engaged in a well-managed dialogue. This may at times involve a third party in the negotiations.

Part 2: Working in teams

At the start of this introduction, I stated that leading and following is by definition a group or team activity. Many kinds of groups make up educational organizations, both formal and informal, but teams have a special place in the discussion. They are a particular kind of group, and one way that they can be distinguished from an informal grouping is that they work together for a common goal or purpose. As a formal grouping they will also have regular, perhaps timetabled opportunities to interact with other members of their team. Parsloe (1981) has suggested that teams are 'soaked in positive values', so that writers tend to give the word 'team' very positive overtones. Of course, if the team is functioning well, team members will be able to give each other mutual support, increase the team's motivation, and use many differing skills in the fulfilling of the team's function. But if the team is not working well, there may be many problems to solve ranging from the internal (e.g. group conflict) to the external (e.g. where the team's values have become distanced from those of the rest of the organization). For effective interpersonal interactions in teams, group dynamics are important. When teams are discussed readers must also be aware that naming a group 'team' does not necessarily mean that the group functions as a team. Riches (1993: 13) summarized the indicators of successful and effective teams from the literature. Such a team:

- is value driven;
- has good communications;
- is collaborative in its dealings;
- maximizes the use of the abilities of its members;
- has the ability to listen to others in an effective way;
- has a willingness to solve problems;
- offers enjoyment of membership;
- has well motivated people in the team;
- has dynamism;
- has flexibility;
- has the ability to cope with confrontation and conflict;
- relates to other teams; and, of course
- has effective quality leadership.

    Part 2 discusses some of these in relation to working in teams.

Part 2 includes an empirical study of team dynamics in a senior management team in a secondary school and a study of teams at the primary level. What emerges from these studies is that team effectiveness is largely the result of applying interpersonal skills, some of which have already been considered. Successful communication is central to team performance, but so are motivation, negotiation and leadership, as discussed in the previous part. Team-building skills for the process and achievement of task performance can be developed if closer attention is paid to our knowledge of how people operate in teams.

Les Bell discusses how educational teams should be managed, and suggests that there needs to be a greater emphasis on sustaining good, professional working relationships. The chapter looks at the four key elements in effective team management – individual team members, task, team, and leadership – and suggests ways of building team resources. Wallace and Hall's study of Senior Management Teams (SMTs) examines team dynamics and the process of team working. It discusses whether shared decision making is the norm in the teams studied, and looks at the criteria that people inside and outside the SMT can use to judge team effectiveness. Johnston and Pickersgill examine headteachers' perception of themselves as role holders who are being stretched to the limit, undervalued, undersupported and underresourced. They point to the propensity for heads to interpret the majority of organizational problems as a reflection of their personal failure. The authors wonder whether a team-oriented approach to headship would alleviate some of the difficulties.

Hargie *et al.* consider how managers communicate, and in particular which situations cause educational managers the most difficulty. They suggest the communication skills that they believe are necessary to overcome these common problem areas. Such personal communication skills are seen as necessary to effective team working. Riches' chapter also focuses on this important area of communication, focusing on the wide range of concepts and theoretical positions that are involved, and their relevance to school and college management. He argues that managers in education need to examine carefully the stages, content and process of communication in order to establish a positive communications policy.

Finally, Adair's chapter concentrates on team building, and how leaders need to be committed to both the project and the team in order for teams to work to their maximum potential. Although he states that it is difficult to attribute anything directly to team building, if it doesn't exist the team will not function well.

Summary

In this introduction, I have argued that leadership is central to creating effective teams. The readings collected together in this book will help you to become more knowledgeable about the leaders and teams in your educational setting.

References

Kakabadse, A., Ludlow, R., Vinnicombe, S. (1988) *Working in Organisations*. London: Penguin.
Parsloe, P. (1981) *Social Services Area Teams*. London: Allen and Unwin.
Riches, C. (1993) *Managing Change in Education*. E326. Milton Keynes: The Open University.

PART 1

Leading and leadership

1 | Leadership as an organizational quality*

RODNEY T. OGAWA AND STEVEN T. BOSSERT

Joseph Campbell (1988) recalled the words of Black Elk, the great shaman of the Sioux: 'I saw myself on the central mountain of the world, the highest place, and I had a vision because I was seeing in the sacred manner of the world. But the central mountain is everywhere' (p. 111). Campbell explained, 'The center of the world is the *axis mundi*, the central point, the pole around which all revolves' (p. 111).

Background

There are concepts in our society on which much seems to turn. Because they are important, we look for them in special places. Leadership, it seems, is such a concept. It is important, most would agree. We expect it of elected officials, look for it in outstanding students and athletes, and admire those who have it. Moreover, leadership matters. We know that it affects how organizations – from social clubs and athletic teams to corporations and armies – perform.

Following these beliefs, scholars in the field of educational administration have sought to determine how leadership affects school organizations. They have focused their search for leadership on a particular organizational corner, but they have had little success finding it. In this chapter we offer a view of leadership that does not treat it as the province of a few people in certain parts of organizations. Rather, we treat leadership as a quality of organizations – a systemic characteristic. To find it, we submit, one must not look in one place or another but must step back and map leadership throughout organizations.

Our central purpose is to argue that leadership is an organizational quality. Our argument extends beyond the obvious point that individuals throughout organizations lead by suggesting the following: Leadership flows through the networks of roles that

---

* This material has been edited.

comprise organizations. The medium of leadership and the currency of leadership lie in the personal resources of people. Leadership shapes the systems that produce patterns of interaction and the meanings that other participants attach to organizational events.

In making this argument, we build outward from the concept of leadership as an organizational quality. We begin by acknowledging and tracing the roots of this conceptualization. We then briefly review four assumptions that have guided previous theorizing and research on leadership. We discuss how different theoretical perspectives on organizations lead to very different treatments of leadership. We demonstrate this point first by reviewing how the dominant perspective on organizations has contributed to a narrow treatment of the four assumptions on leadership. We then examine the implications of an alternative view of organizations for conceptualizing leadership, noting that it offers an expanded, or organizational, treatment of the four assumptions. Finally, we close by offering some thoughts on the implications of conceptualizing leadership as an organizational quality for future research.

The conceptual roots

In this chapter we treat leadership as a quality of organizations – a systemic characteristic.

This perspective on leadership is not new. It simply has been overlooked. The conceptual antecedents can be traced to some of the earliest writings in the modern literature on administration and organization. Barnard (1968) observed that the 'authority of leadership' is not confined to those in executive positions, thus acknowledging that leadership may be exerted by anyone in an organization. Similarly, Thompson (1967), while describing administration rather than leadership, asserted that it is something that flows throughout an organization, spanning levels and flowing both up and down hierarchies.

This perspective was given its fullest expression to date by a group of scholars associated with the Institute for Social Research of the University of Michigan. Viewing leadership as a form of control exerted over organizations' members (Cartwright 1965), several members of that group treated leadership as a phenomenon that can be found throughout organizations (Tannenbaum 1962; Cartwright 1965; Katz and Kahn 1966). They concluded that leadership is a variable that is measurable at the organizational level. On the basis of Tannenbaum's (1962) empirical work, they established that organizations have different levels of leadership, that leadership varies across organizations and even within organizations over time. Moreover, they claimed that under some conditions a positive relationship exists between the level of organizations' total leadership and their overall performance (Tannenbaum 1962; Cartwright 1965).

Thus the notion of leadership as a quality of organizations has been expressed in the past but lost in later discussions. For example, recent reviews of the treatment of leadership in the educational administration literature (Immegart 1988; Hoy and Miskel 1991) never mention it. Only very recently has this conceptualization begun to re-emerge (Bolman and Deal 1994).

Four underlying assumptions

Arguably, four basic assumptions underlie most treatments of leadership. They attend to four dimensions of leadership: function, role, the individual, and culture. The first assumption is that leadership *functions* to influence organizational performance (Pfeffer 1978). A second assumption holds that leadership is related to organizational *roles*. A third assumption indicates that leaders are *individuals* who possess certain attributes, act in certain ways, or both. A fourth assumption that has recently found its way into the literature is that leaders operate within organizational *cultures* (Pfeffer 1981; Smircich and Morgan 1983; Daft and Weick 1984; Schein 1985).

Underlying conceptions of organization

Selznick (1957) suggested that how we conceptualize organizational leadership is necessarily rooted in how we conceptualize organizations. Organization theory offers many competing perspectives. Several authors note that these perspectives emphasize different organizational features and thus offer varying explanations of organizational phenomena, including leadership (Burrell and Morgan 1979; Foster 1986; Scott 1992).

Here, we confine our discussion to the implications of two perspectives on organizations for understanding leadership. The first is drawn from a technical-rational theory of organizations; the second is taken from institutional theory. The former rests leadership in certain organizational corners; the latter distributes leadership throughout organizations. We adopt an institutional perspective because we believe that, among emerging conceptualizations, it provides a promising viewpoint for examining the many facets of school organization, including leadership. We encourage others to explicate the views of leadership offered by other emerging theories of organization.

The dominant view: a technical-rational perspective

Most theories and research on leadership do not explicitly reveal the organizational perspectives from which they are derived. However, an examination of the literature suggests that it has been dominated implicitly by one perspective. That perspective depicts organizations as technically rational systems and thus emphasizes two organizational features: goals and formal structure (Scott 1992).

From the technical-rational perspective, organizations exist to attain specific, predetermined goals. All else springs from organizations' efforts to reach goals efficiently: they adopt or develop technologies to attain goals; they generate formal structures to enhance the efficient operation of their technologies.

Formal structures are the organizational rules and procedures that govern the behavior of members by precisely and explicitly prescribing roles and role relations (Scott 1992). Typically, managers located at the top of organizations' hierarchies are authorized to develop formal structures, because they possess the requisite competence and are positioned to comprehend their organizations' overall operations. They develop structures that enhance their organizations' efficiency by rationalizing internal operations and managing relations with external environments.

The technical-rational view of organizational leadership

The dominance of the technical-rational perspective in the leadership literature is reflected in the treatment of the four assumptions of leadership. Working from this perspective, scholars confine leadership to the narrow corridors of power that exist in the uppermost levels of organizations' hierarchies and emphasize goal attainment as its ultimate product.

The function of leadership

One assumption about leadership is that it functions to influence the performance of organizations by affecting the minds and behaviors of participants. This perhaps is the most fundamental assumption, for it reveals the reason for widespread interest in the phenomenon of leadership. It provides a cause of an important effect: organizational performance (Pfeffer 1978).

From the technical-rational perspective, performance means goal attainment. Thus successful leaders are those whose organizations reach their goals. This emphasis on goal attainment is evident in mainstream scholarship on leadership. Theories ranging from the work generated by the Ohio State leadership studies and by the University of Michigan Survey Research Center to Fiedler's contingency model and House's path goal theory purport to capture those dimensions of leadership that are linked to organizational performance (Yukl 1989). In educational administration, research has sought to determine the extent to which leadership affects perceptual and independent measures of school performance, including students' performance on standardized achievement tests (Hoy and Miskel 1991).

Organizational roles

A second assumption holds that leadership is related to organizational *roles*, or offices. The technical-rational perspective on organizations locates the competence and hence authority for making strategic decisions in managerial positions at the top of organizations' hierarchies. As a consequence, theories and research usually treat leadership as the province of certain roles in organizations. Widespread adherence to this particular expression of this assumption is evident in the designs of leadership studies. Studies of organizational leadership with rare exceptions are studies of top-level managers. For example, studies of leadership in school organizations usually have principals and superintendents as their subjects.

Traits and behaviors of individuals

A third assumption is that leaders are *individuals* who possess certain attributes, act in certain ways, or both. Some of the earliest research on leadership attempted to identify the traits that set leaders apart from other group members (Bass 1981; Yukl 1989; Hoy and Miskel 1991). More recent studies sought to chart the behaviors of effective leaders (Bass 1981; Yukl 1989; Hoy and Miskel 1991).

The technical-rational perspective on organizations emphasizes two basic ways in which managers lead: they establish and fix attention on goals, and they develop formal structures to enhance the efficiency with which those goals are attained. These two components are reflected in mainstream theory and research on leadership. For example, House's (1971) path-goal theory emphasizes the role of leaders in affecting subordinates' perceptions of both organizational and personal goals.

The Ohio State leadership studies that produced the Leader Behavior Description Questionnaire, perhaps the most broadly cited conceptualization of leadership in the educational administration literature, highlights two dimensions of leader behavior. One, which is labeled 'initiating structure', concerns those behaviors of leaders that define organizations' formal structures (Halpin 1966). Spurred by the availability of easily administered surveys, numerous studies of the leadership behaviors of educational administrators were conducted (Hoy and Miskel 1991).

This perspective on leadership is also reflected in the field of educational administration's conceptualization of instructional leadership (Ogawa 1992). A major component of instructional leadership concerns the development of mission and goals (Murphy 1989). Scholars also characterize instructional leaders as managing the educational production function by setting schedules and establishing policies and procedures.

The cultural context

A final assumption about leaders is that they operate within organizational *cultures* and affect how other participants interpret organizational events and thus influence how they behave (Pfeffer 1981; Smircich and Morgan 1983; Daft and Weick 1984; Schein 1985). Resulting from the recent emergence of the cultural metaphor in organization theory, this view of leadership has gained increased attention. This is reflected in the educational administration literature, where scholars have argued that administrators lead by shaping the cultures of their school organizations and thus affect the meanings that other participants fix to organizational events (Sergiovanni and Corbally 1986; Deal and Peterson 1990; Bolman and Deal 1994).

Despite this focus on symbolism and the shaping of meaning, cultural treatments of leadership typically have not escaped the technical-rational emphasis. This is evident in the persistent focus on both high-level managers and goal attainment. For example, the management literature has generally been concerned with how managers frame meaning for subordinates (Pfeffer 1981; Smircich and Morgan 1983; Schein, 1985) and how culture is linked to organizations' performance (Deal and Kennedy 1982). In educational administration, the same tendencies are present. Recent treatments of cultural leadership in schools have continued to focus on principals (Deal and Peterson 1990; Reitzug and Reeves 1992; Reitzug 1994) and have examined the relationships between leadership, school culture, and productivity (Deal and Peterson 1990).

As Smircich (1983) argued, this reflects but one view of organizational culture. It treats culture as 'something an organization has' (p. 347) and thus emphasizes how culture can be manipulated to enhance the efficiency with which goals are attained. Smircich identifies another view, one that treats culture as 'something an organization is' (p. 347). It focuses on patterns of symbols and meanings that arise consensually from social interaction and hence focuses on how organization itself is accomplished. This view, then, seems to broaden the scope of inquiry to include the entire organization and escapes the technical-rational emphasis on goal attainment.

Integrated models of leadership

Scholars have made several efforts to link these four assumptions about leadership in comprehensive, integrated models – models intended to exceed the limitations of past treatments of leadership. Yukl (1989) offered an 'integrating conceptual framework' that focuses explicitly on managerial leadership and that includes such factors as 'leader traits and skills', 'leadership behavior', and 'criteria of unit effectiveness'. Similarly, Immegart's (1988) review of leadership research in the educational adminis-tration literature includes culture, activities and outcomes among other factors in his 'model of a broad conceptualization of leadership'. Hoy and Miskel (1991) included leadership traits, leader behavior, situational characteristics – including leader role and effectiveness, organizational and personal – as elements of their schema for the study of leadership.

Clearly, the assumptions regarding function, role, individuals' traits and behavior, and culture are evident in these models. And, although comprehensive, they remain bound to the technical-rational perspective on organizations. That is, they concentrate on the leadership of people in certain roles, namely, those in the highest levels of organizations' hierarchies, and their impact on organizational goal attainment. How might leadership look from a different perspective on organizations?

An institutional perspective on organizations

Institutional theory provides an alternative to technical-rational conceptions of organ-izations. This perspective on organizations flows from a general institutional theory of social organization, which explains that the behavior of actors, both individual and collective, expresses externally enforced institutions rather than internally derived goals. Institutions are general, societal rules that take the form of cultural theories, ideologies and prescriptions (Meyer *et al.* 1987). An example of an institution is the belief that human development occurs in a fairly linear, sequential order, which is reflected in the age-graded structure of the vast majority of elementary schools in the United States. From an institutional perspective, then, action is the enactment of broad institutional scripts.

Accordingly, when applied to organizations, institutional theory emphasizes the impact of the institutional environment on the structure of organizations. It explains that in the external environment some structural elements of organizations are insti-tutionalized, or imbued with value (Selznick 1957). This occurs, in part, because the elements reflect society's cultural theories.

In the absence of clear technologies and competitive markets, some organizations are not well suited to adopting structures to enhance the efficiency of their operations. Instead, they develop structures that reflect institutions to gain social legitimacy (Meyer and Rowan 1977; DiMaggio and Powell 1983; Scott 1987; Zucker 1987). For example, numerous school districts have adopted school-based management despite the absence of evidence that it affects the academic performance of students, suggesting that school-based management has been adopted in at least some instances to gain legitimacy.

Public schools are clearly marked by the characteristics of highly institutionalized organizations (Meyer and Rowan 1977): their technology – teaching and learning –

has been characterized as unclear (Cohen *et al.* 1972). For the most part, they do not compete for clients (Carlson 1964).

Some institutional theorists argue that legitimacy contributes to organizational effectiveness (DiMaggio and Powell 1983). They suggest that legitimacy enhances the ability of organizations to attract resources from the environment. Thus it contributes to organizational survival and hence to the attainment of organizations' ultimate, albeit implicit, goal. For example, school districts will cite recently adopted programs, such as the development of site councils, in their campaigns to gain support for bond measures.

The pursuit of legitimacy leads organizations to decouple administrative structures in two ways. First, organizations horizontally decouple structural elements from one another (Meyer and Rowan 1977). This enables organizations to adopt structures that reflect conflicting or even contradictory values in their environments. For example, school districts may adopt strict discipline policies aimed at removing disruptive students, while also providing alternative programs for students who cannot conform to the norms of conventional educational settings.

Second, organizations vertically decouple administrative structures from activity (Meyer and Rowan 1977). Because organizations adopt structures to reflect institutionalized rules rather than to enhance internal efficiency, their activities may depart markedly from their adopted structures. Thus they decouple to reduce the likelihood that inconsistencies between structure and activity will be discovered. For example, after a new instructional program is adopted by a school district, it is common for administrators not to monitor its implementation.

Despite the decoupling of structure from activity, institutional theory suggests that the structures may have an indirect impact on the work of organizations in two ways. First, institutions, once adopted by organizations, can serve as the focus of symbolic activity. These symbolic activities can facilitate the development of shared meaning and values among organizations' members (Meyer and Rowan 1977; March and Olsen 1984). Shared meaning and values, in turn, can produce commitments to engage in coordinated, or organized, action. Thus individuals at any organizational level can structure work formally or informally. School-based management may provide an example of symbolic action that may have indirect, substantive consequences. There is little empirical evidence that decisions made by school councils affect schools' instructional programs, suggesting that participation on councils is largely symbolic. However, some research suggests that principals, teachers, and parents view opportunities to participate in decision making with enthusiasm, which may carry over to activities that have instructional consequences.

Second, because administrative structure can be decoupled from activity, individuals engaged in the work of highly institutionalized organizations enjoy a great deal of discretion. In fact, Meyer (1983) posited that new structures, or innovations, introduced by individuals at lower, technical levels of organizations are more likely to affect their substantive performance. For example, when school districts adopt reading series that employ particular instructional approaches, teachers have been known to use quite different approaches, while using the materials provided by the adopted series.

We return to the four assumptions about leadership and examine them from the perspective provided by institutional theory. The view, we submit, is quite different.

The parameters of leadership

Whereas the function of leadership from the technical-rational perspective is organizational performance and goal attainment, the function of leadership from the institutional perspective is social legitimacy and organizational survival. Rather than the technical-rational focus on affecting the 'minds and behaviors of participants', the institutional perspective requires affecting the minds and behaviors of external constituents.

As noted earlier, it is widely assumed that leadership functions to affect the overall performance of organizations. From an institutional perspective, performance involves the survival of the organization. This exceeds the technical-rational emphasis on goal attainment, because survival transcends other, more specific goals. In fact, attaining the wrong specific goals does not contribute to organizations' survival.

This view of the first assumption, then, clearly fixes the parameters of leadership at the organizational level. If leadership affects the survival of organizations, then it is a phenomenon of nothing less than organizational proportions. This is hardly a startling revelation, but one that is missed by many conceptualizations of leadership – particularly those that treat it as a quality that individuals possess apart from a social context.

Assuming the organizational goal of survival also suggests that leadership is systemically causal, March (1955) and Simon (1957) observed and Cartwright (1965) reminded scholars that social influence, including leadership, is a special instance of causality: 'the modification of one person's responses by the actions of another' (p. 3). However, causality, in the case of leadership from the institutional perspective, exceeds the individual level. Survival, after all, depends on both the adoption of institutionalized structures at the administrative level and the development of coordinative mechanisms at the technical level.

Thus leadership must affect more than individuals' actions; it must influence the system in which actions occur. This point has been recognized previously. Early research by Hemphill and Coons (1950) noted that leadership defines patterns of organization. Similarly, Katz and Kahn (1966) observed that leadership changes organizational structure, interpolates structure, and uses structure.

[. . .]

The social web of leadership

A second assumption links leadership to organizational roles. A role is the set of activities expected of the incumbent of a particular social position or office (Gross *et al.* 1958; Katz and Kahn 1966). This does not seem to square with the institutional perspective, according to which individuals at different levels can exert leadership by affecting how their organizations are structured: individuals working in upper management develop formal structures in response to the institutional environment; individuals working at the technical level develop informal structures to coordinate work activities and adopt new work techniques.

Role theory resolves this potential contradiction and reveals the symmetry of the conceptualization of leadership as an organizational quality. Role theory suggests that role, *per se*, is not the critical concept in understanding organizations. Rather, the important unit of analysis is the network of relations among roles, because it is the network that comprises the organizational system (Katz and Kahn 1966; Scott 1992). Leadership, then, lies in the system of relations among the incumbents of roles and affects organizational legitimacy. Consequently, leadership enhances the likelihood of organizations' survival by affecting their structures, which have been defined as 'the regularized aspects of the relationships existing among participants in an organization' (Scott 1992: 16).

Katz and Kahn (1966) suggested that 'the essence of organizational leadership [is] the influential increment over and above mechanical compliance with the routine directives of the organization' (p. 302). Thus it is not leadership when individuals gain the compliance of others simply by virtue of the organizational roles they occupy. Barnard (1968) referred to this as authority of position.

It is leadership, however, when organizational members gain compliance by deploying resources needed by others to enact their roles. Here, again, the system of roles is crucial to organizational leadership because different roles provide access to different resources. For example, information, a staple of modern organizations, is distributed across organizational roles: the incumbents of some roles have greater access to information about external environments (Bass 1981), whereas the incumbents of other roles have greater access to information needed by others to operationalize their roles effectively, are in a position within the network of roles to exercise influence, or leadership.

In school organizations, district superintendents use their knowledge of state guidelines to influence school boards, principals and teachers. Principals employ their knowledge of budgets to influence the decisions of both district superintendents and teachers on school councils. Also, teachers use their knowledge of effective instructional techniques to affect principals and district curriculum directors.

From the institutional perspective, the assumption that ties leadership to organizational roles and offices provides conceptual specification concerning leadership as a systemic quality of organizations. It reveals that leadership is embedded not in particular roles but in the relationships that exist among the incumbents of roles. By shifting attention to relationships, this assumption now suggests that organizational members can draw on resources to which their roles provide access to influence others who require those resources to enact their roles successfully. That success, from the institutional perspective, takes the form of social legitimacy and, consequently, organizational survival.

The currency and medium of leadership

A third assumption about leadership is that it involves individuals' attributes and actions. When viewed from the institutional perspective, both the traits and actions of individuals take on added significance. Traits, rather than simply marking leaders, are resources on which individuals draw in attempting to exert influence. This is consistent with the systemic interpretation of the assumption regarding leadership and organizational roles that leadership is influence that exceeds routine compliance with organizational structures.

Thus leadership requires that organizational actors draw on personal resources. Katz and Kahn (1966), for example, focus on expert and referent power (French and Raven 1959). Both are based on personal traits of individuals who exert influence. Expertise concerns the possession of task-relevant knowledge. Referent power is based on one's capacity to engender feelings of loyalty. Other traits identified by studies of leadership also provide resources that can be deployed in efforts to exert influence. They include self-confidence, tolerance of stress, creativity, high energy, persistence, willingness to assume responsibility, and cooperation (Yukl 1989).

Katz and Kahn (1966) claim that, because organizational members possess individual resources regardless of their formal positions and roles, all potentially can lead. In addition, this means that leadership is not a zero-sum game. Depending on the extent to which organizational members use personal resources to exert influence, or leadership, organizations' overall levels of leadership can vary. Tannenbaum (1962) empirically verified this and linked the overall levels of influence in organizations to their performance.

[. . .]

Individuals' behaviors, or actions, also take on new meaning when leadership is seen as an organizational quality. According to the first two assumptions, leadership is systemic and relational. Thus focus shifts from people's isolated actions to their social interactions. The interact, not the act, becomes the basic building block of organizational leadership. Interaction is the medium through which resources are deployed and influence is exerted. And, because leadership affects organizational structure, it affects the interactions of individuals in organizations. In essence, leadership through interactions influences the system of interactions that constitute an organization.

Treating social interaction as the building block of leadership has another implication for examining leadership, one that is consistent with the systemic view of leadership. It underscores what many theorists have observed: leadership is relational. Consequently, both the leader and followers are important components. As Cartwright (1965) suggested, it is important to consider the parts played by both the agent and subject of influence.

Moreover, because leadership occurs through interaction, influence cannot be assumed to be unidirectional. The agent of influence is, to some degree, also a subject. Coupled with the notion that leadership is not the province of certain roles, the third assumption indicates that leadership can flow, as Thompson (1967) argued, both up and down levels and between organizational components, including roles, regardless of formal prescriptions. In school organizations, teachers can be affected by students, even as they influence their charges. What teacher does not take cues from students as a lesson progresses? Similarly, principals take their lead from teachers on instructional matters, and teachers leave it to their principals to organize work by setting class schedules and introducing instructional initiatives.

Thus the assumption that focuses on the traits and actions of individuals identifies the currency and medium of leadership. Individuals draw on personal qualities as resources to influence organizations. The medium by which leadership is exerted is social interaction. And, ultimately, leadership affects the systems that produce the patterns of interaction that comprise organizations – their structures, which can produce social legitimacy for organizations. Finally, the interactive nature of leadership means that leadership is reciprocal.

The context of leadership

A fourth assumption treats leadership as a cultural phenomenon. Although scholars do not agree on what specifically constitutes organization culture (Smircich 1983), they acknowledge that organizations have or are cultures and that culture produces patterned behaviors and interactions. Leadership, then, involves shaping organizations' cultures (Deal and Kennedy 1982; Schein 1985) and influencing the meanings that people attach to organizational events (Smircich and Morgan 1983).

This cultural treatment of organizational leadership is congruent with the institutional perspective at two levels. First, institutional theory suggests that organizations erect structures to reflect cultural rules in their external environments. Second, it indicates that organizations conduct activities around those structures to facilitate the development of shared meaning and values among organizations' members, that is, to develop culture.

Sergiovanni (1986), reflecting on the treatment of culture in the educational administration literature, concluded, 'Underlying the cultural perspective is the concept of community and the importance of shared meanings and shared values' (p. 8). This interpretation of culture shares much with Durkheim's (1933) concept of mechanical solidarity. Solidarity is the social cohesion and cooperative action directed toward the achievement of collective goals that characterizes groups. Durkheim (1933) identified two bases of solidarity: organic and mechanical. Organic solidarity is based on the interdependence of highly specialized roles in a complex system of a division of labor. Mechanical solidarity is based on similarity of values and behavior and loyalty to tradition and kinship. Institutional theory embraces both types of solidarity, suggesting that leaders at different hierarchical levels may effect different forms of solidarity.

[. . .]

An institutional perspective on organizational leadership

Much is revealed by institutional theory when it is used to examine the four assumptions on which theories and studies of organizational leadership have been based. It sets leadership's parameters at the level of organization. It reveals the almost contradictory relationship between leadership and organizational roles. It suggests the nature of both the resources on which leadership is based and the social element on which leadership is built. Finally, it embeds leadership in a cultural context. Together, these assumptions reintroduce a perspective on leadership that has been lost by scholars. They reveal that leadership is an organizational quality.

From this perspective, leadership functions to enhance organizations' social legitimacy and their chances of survival. This sets leadership's parameters at the organizational level. Moreover, it treats leadership as causal – a form of social influence. By combining the organizational and causal parameters, we learn that leadership goes beyond influencing individuals; it affects organizations' structures. In a word, leadership is organizing.

The relationship between leadership and organizational roles reveals that leadership is not confined to certain roles in organizations. Rather, it flows through the networks of roles that comprise organizations. Moreover, leadership is based on the deployment of resources that are distributed across the network of roles, with different roles having access to different levels and types of resources.

Thus the currency on which leadership is based lies in the resources possessed by individuals. The medium of leadership is, however, not individual action but social interaction. Leadership affects the systems that produce the patterns of interaction that occur among organizational members; that is, it affects organizations' structures.

The context of leadership from an institutional perspective is largely cultural. Administrators are instrumental in adopting structures to mirror cultural rules in the environment. They then engage other members of their organizations in symbolic activities that focus on these structures. These activities, in turn, shape and reinforce shared values and beliefs, which can produce commitment, or solidarity, leading to coordinated activity.

Implications for inquiry

The conceptualization of leadership as an organizational quality has implications for how leadership in school organizations is studied. They fall into three rough categories: general research strategies, focus on new dimensions, and promising developments in theory and research.

General research strategies

To capture leadership as an organizational quality will require adopting rather paradoxical research strategies that increase the unit of analysis and reduce the focus of inquiry. If leadership is treated as an organizational quality, then studies of leadership must have as their unit of analysis the organization. On the one hand, this will mean taking approaches similar to those employed by researchers at the University of Michigan's Institute for Social Research. Several studies produced by the institute measured the total influence exerted throughout organizations (Tannenbaum 1962). On the other hand, this will require researchers to trace leadership throughout organizations. They will have to track its flow up and down organizations and within levels. Moreover, institutional theory suggests that leadership may respond to different contingencies and thus produce different outcomes at various levels of organizations' hierarchies. Thus researchers must be sensitive to the variations in leadership's form and substance.

Tracing leadership throughout school organizations will also require researchers to examine micro-organizational events. Data on the network of interactions that occur in organizations must be compiled over time. That will mean recording at least samples of actual interactions that occur between organizational members. The importance of the dimension of time must be emphasized. If leadership involves influencing organizational structures, then time is important. Only time will tell if attempts at leadership affect organizational solidarity. Also, the time that is required for such effects to occur and the duration of the persistence of the effects may be important variables.

Focus on new dimensions of leadership

If researchers adopt an institutional perspective for examining leadership, they will necessarily have to focus on organizational dimensions that are underemphasized in existing research. Three come to mind. The first concerns the outcomes of leadership. As we have argued, research conducted from the technical-rational perspective has focused on the impact of leadership on organizational goal attainment. This focus will broaden from an institutional perspective, which depicts organizations as seeking legitimacy, rather than technical efficiency, and ultimately survival. Research might examine how individuals employ social influence to develop structures that do not affect their core technologies but nonetheless enhance external constituents' assessments of their school organizations.

In addition, such research might be forced to address the ethics of this form of leadership. If, as we have suggested, the technical-rational conceptualization of organizations and leadership is itself deeply institutionalized, then what ethical issues may be involved when leaders knowingly direct their organizations to adopt structures that appear substantive but, in fact, are merely symbolic efforts to gain legitimacy?

The symbolic dimension of organizations is a second and related area that should command the attention of researchers seeking to examine leadership from an institutional perspective. Research might explore how organizational actors adopt symbolic structures and use them as the focus of events aimed at building solidarity among participants. In addition, research could closely scrutinize the possible links between the solidarity born of ceremonial activity and efforts by organizational members to coordinate or directly engage in substantive activity, or the work of their organization.

Researchers who attempt to capture leadership as an organizational quality might also examine how varied organizational contingencies evoke leadership from various organizational corners. If leadership does flow throughout organizations, research might begin to tease out the sets of problems, both symbolic and substantive, to which organizations respond and the sets of roles whose incumbents possess the requisite resources to develop routine ways, or structures, for handling these problems.

Promising developments

Finally, we recognize that the dominant, technical-rational conception of organizational leadership is deeply institutionalized. Following the cultural script, educational researchers focus their studies of leadership on administrators, and practitioners place the responsibility for leadership on the incumbents of administrative offices. Thus efforts to introduce other conceptualizations of leadership will be met with resistance.

However, there are signs of change. Recent research on the leadership of teachers and efforts to implement reforms aimed at empowering teachers and others associated with the educational enterprise mark the change. Similarly, discussions on the development of educational communities and the shared responsibility that characterizes them reflect the change (Sergiovanni 1994). Perhaps a different conception of leadership is emerging, one that sees it everywhere.

References

Barnard, C. I. (1968) *Functions of the Executive*. Cambridge, MA: Harvard University Press.

Bass, B. M. (1981) *Stodgill's Handbook of Leadership: A Survey of Theory and Research*. New York: Free Press.

Bolman, L. G. and Deal, T. E. (1994) Looking for leadership: Another search party's report. *Educational Administration Quarterly*, 30: 77–96.

Burrell, G. and Morgan, G. (1979) *Sociological Paradigms and Organizational Analysis*. Portsmouth, NH: Heinemann.

Campbell, J. (1988) *The Power of Myth*. New York: Doubleday.

Carlson, R. O. (1964) Environmental constraints and organizational consequences: The public school and its clients, in D. E. Griffiths (ed.) *Behavioral Science and Educational Administration* (pp. 262–76). Chicago: University of Chicago Press.

Cartwright, D. (1965) Influence, leadership, control, in J. G. March (ed.) *Handbook of Organizations* (pp. 1–47). Chicago: Rand McNally.

Cohen, M. D., March, J. G. and Olsen, J. P. (1972) A garbage can model of organizational choice. *Administrative Science Quarterly*, 17: 1–25.

Daft, R. L. and Weick, K. E. (1984) Toward a model of organizations as interpretation systems. *Academy of Management Review*, 9: 284–95.

Deal, T. E. and Kennedy, A. A. (1982) *Corporate Cultures*. Reading, MA: Addison-Wesley.

Deal, T. E. and Peterson, K. (1990) *Symbolic Leadership and the School Principalship: Shaping School Cultures in Different Contexts*. Washington, DC: US Department of Education.

DiMaggio, P. J. and Powell, W. W. (1983) The iron cage revisited: Institutional isomorphism and collective rationality in organizational fields. *American Sociological Review*, 48: 147–60.

Durkheim, E. (1933) *The Division of Labor in Society*. New York: Free Press.

Foster, W. (1986) *Paradigms and Promises: New Approaches to Educational Administration*. Buffalo, NY: Prometheus.

French, J. and Raven, B. H. (1959) The bases of social power, in D. Cartwright (ed.) *Studies of Social Power* (pp. 150–67). Ann Arbor, MI: Institute for Social Research.

Gross, N., Mason, W. and McEachern, A. W. (1958) *Explorations in Role Analysis: Studies of the School Superintendency Role*. New York: Wiley.

Halpin, A. W. (1966) *Theory and Research in Administration*. New York: Macmillan.

Hemphill, J. K. and Coons, A. E. (1950) *Leadership Behavior Description*. Columbus, OH: Ohio State University, Personnel Research Board.

House, R. J. (1971) A path-goal theory of leadership effectiveness. *Administrative Science Quarterly*, 16: 321–38.

Hoy, W. K. and Miskel, C. G. (1991) *Educational Administration: Theory, Research and Practice* (3rd edn). New York: Random House.

Immegart, G. L. (1988) Leadership and leader behavior, in N. J. Boyan (ed.) *Handbook of Research on Educational Administration* (pp. 259–78). New York: Longman.

Katz, D. and Kahn, R. L. (1966) *The Social Psychology of Organizations*. New York: Wiley.

March, J. G. (1955) An introduction to the theory and measurement of influence. *American Political Science Review*, 49: 431–51.

March, J. G. and Olsen, J. P. (1984) The new institutionalism: Organizational factors in political life. *American Political Science Review*, 78: 734–49.

Meyer, J. W. (1983) Innovation and knowledge use in American public education, in W. R. Scott and J. W. Meyer (eds) *Organizational Environments* (pp. 233–60). Beverly Hills, CA: Sage.

Meyer, J. W., Boli, J. and Thomas, G. M. (1987) Ontology and rationalization in Western cultural account, in G. M. Thomas, J. W. Meyer, F. O. Ramirez and J. Boli (eds) *Institutional Structure: Constituting State, Society, and the Individual* (pp. 12–38). Newbury Park, CA: Sage.

Meyer, J. W. and Rowan, B. (1977) Institutionalized organizations: Formal structure as myth and ceremony. *American Journal of Sociology*, 83: 340–63.

Murphy, J. (1989) Principal instructional leadership, in P. W. Thurston and L. S. Lotto (eds) *Advances in Educational Administration* (pp. 163–200). Greenwich, CT: JAI.

Ogawa, R. T. (1992) Institutional theory and examining leadership in schools. *International Journal of Educational Management*, 6: 14–21.

Pfeffer, J. (1978) The ambiguity of leadership, in M. W. McCall, Jr. and M. M. Lombardo (eds) *Leadership: Where Else Can We Go?* Durham, NC: Duke University Press.

Pfeffer, J. (1981) Management as symbolic action: The creation and maintenance of organizational paradigms, in B. Staw (ed.) *Research in Organizational Behavior* (pp. 1–52). Greenwich, CT: JAI.

Reitzug, U. C. (1994) A case study of empowering principal behavior. *American Educational Research Journal*, 31: 283–310.

Reitzug, U. C. and Reeves, J. E. (1992) 'Miss Lincoln doesn't teach here': A descriptive narrative and conceptual analysis of a principal's symbolic leadership behavior. *Educational Administration Quarterly*, 28: 185–219.

Schein, E. H. (1985) *Organizational Culture and Leadership*. San Francisco: Jossey-Bass.

Scott, W. R. (1987) The adolescence of institutional theory. *Administrative Science Quarterly*, 32: 493–511.

Scott, W. R. (1992) *Organizations: Rational, Natural, and Open Systems* (3rd edn). Englewood Cliffs, NJ: Prentice-Hall.

Selznick, P. (1957) *Leadership in Administration*. New York: Harper and Row.

Sergiovanni, T. J. (1986) Cultural and competing perspectives in administrative theory and practice, in T. J. Sergiovanni and J. E. Corbally (eds) *Leadership and Organizational Culture: New Perspectives on Administrative Theory and Practice*. Urbana, IL: University of Illinois Press.

Sergiovanni. T. J. (1994) Organizations or communities: Changing the metaphor changes the theory. *Educational Administration Quarterly*, 30: 214–26.

Sergiovanni, T. J. and Corbally, J. E. (eds) (1986) *Leadership and Organizational Culture: New Perspectives on Administrative Theory and Practice*. Urbana, IL: University of Illinois Press.

Simon, H. A. (1957) *Models of Man*. New York: Wiley.

Smircich, L. (1983) Concepts of culture and organizational analysis. *Administrative Science Quarterly*, 28: 339–58.

Smircich, L. and Morgan, G. (1983) Leadership: The management of meaning. *Journal of Applied Behavioral Science*, 18: 257–73.

Tannenbaum, A. S. (1962) Control in organizations: Individual adjustment and organizational performance. *Administrative Science Quarterly*, 7: 236–57.

Thompson, J. D. (1967) *Organizations in Action*. New York: McGraw-Hill.

Yukl, G. A. (1989) *Leadership in Organizations* (2nd edn). Englewood Cliffs, NJ: Prentice-Hall.

Zucker, L. G. (1987) Institutional theories of organization. *Annual Review of Sociology*, 13: 443–64.

2 | Dimensions of leadership*

HEDLEY BEARE, BRIAN CALDWELL AND ROSS MILLIKAN

Outstanding leadership has invariably emerged as a key characteristic of outstanding schools. There can no longer be doubt that those seeking quality in education must ensure its presence and that the development of potential leaders must be given high priority.

[. . .]

The purpose of this chapter is to describe and illustrate the major features of what is now known about leadership in a way which should provide a guide to action in the school setting. Emphasis is given to the broader, emerging view although attention is given to some products of the earlier 'theory movement' which, while of limited utility, are nevertheless part of the larger picture. Prominent in this larger picture is vision in leadership: outstanding leaders have a vision for their schools – a mental picture of a preferred future – which is shared with all in the school community and which shapes the programme for learning and teaching as well as policies, priorities, plans and procedures pervading the day-to-day life of the school. The major part of the chapter is devoted to ten generalizations about leadership which have emerged from recent studies. Illustrations in the school context are offered in each instance. The final section of the chapter gives special attention to description and illustration of vision in leadership and the ways in which vision may be articulated. [. . .]

Leader and leadership defined

A useful starting point is to clarify the concepts of 'leadership' and 'leader'. The view taken here is that there is no one 'correct' meaning and that differences in definition reflect different contexts as well as different perspectives.

---

* This material has been abridged and was originally published as 'Leadership'.

Dubin (1968: 385) saw leadership as 'the exercise of authority and the making of decisions' while Fiedler (1967: 8) considered the leader to be 'the individual in the group given the task of directing and co-ordinating task-relevant group activities'. According to these definitions, principals, headteachers and other senior staff who have formal authority by virtue of their appointments are leaders and may exercise leadership. Dubin and Fiedler offer a view which is constrained by the source of power (authority), scope (task-relevant) and function (decision-making, directing, co-ordinating). Stogdill (1950: 4) had a broader context in mind when he defined leadership as 'the process of influencing the activities of an organized group toward goal setting and goal accomplishment'. While this view includes the contexts envisaged by Dubin and Fiedler, it acknowledges that people without formal authority may exercise leadership. The source of influence or power may be their expertise, or their capacity to bring rewards or benefits, or their capacity to apply sanctions, or their personal qualities which make them liked or respected as people. Such leadership may emerge in many contexts in a school and may involve people other than the principal and senior staff.

Stogdill's view also included the setting of the goal itself as well as the influence of activities associated with the accomplishment of the goal. This aspect of leadership is important in effecting change. Lipham (1964: 122) focused exclusively on change when he defined leadership as 'the initiation of a new structure or procedure for accomplishing an organization's goals and objectives'. In this view, a principal will not be a leader at all if activity is limited to the maintenance of existing means and ends. Management rather than leadership may be a more appropriate description of such an activity.

More recent attempts to explain the concept of leadership penetrate more deeply than 'the organization' and the activities associated with goal setting and goal accomplishment. Attention now is also given to meanings and values. Pondy (1978: 94), for example, considers that the effectiveness of a leader lies in 'ability to make activity meaningful . . . not to change behaviour but to give others a sense of understanding of what they are doing'. The exercise of leadership by the principal thus involves making clear the meaning of activity in the school by posing and securing answers to questions such as the following. What are the purposes of our school? How should we as teachers work with students to reflect our purposes? What should be the relationship between our school and its local community?

To Greenfield (1986: 142) 'leadership is a willful act where one person attempts to construct the social world for others'. He suggests that 'leaders will try to commit others to the values that they themselves believe are good. Organizations are built on the unification of people around values' (p. 166). Greenfield challenges us to think of leaders in terms very different from those in the traditional view. For example, debate on a school's discipline policy may be seen as a contest of values reflecting different beliefs about 'what ought to be'. Those representing each set of values are leaders in that debate. The outcome of the contest is reflected in the words of the policy. The principal may be a leader in debate and, once policy is determined, becomes a leader in another sense. The policy is presented to all parents and students as an expression of the values of the school and an attempt is made to build commitment to that policy: an attempt to bring about 'unification of people around values' and to 'construct the social world for others'.

An example of each definition of leader and leadership can thus be found in the school setting. Concise definitions and descriptions are difficult, if not inappropriate. As Duke (1986: 10) observed, 'Leadership seems to be a gestalt phenomenon; greater than the sum of its parts'.

Leadership traits and theories: part of the picture

Studies until the late 1970s and early 1980s yielded useful but limited information about leaders and leadership. Attempts to identify the traits of leaders led to a relatively small list of attributes to guide the selection process. A quarter-century of careful research focused on two dimensions of leadership behaviour, generally concerned with tasks and people, with some measure of success in determining which particular behaviours or styles are the more effective in different situations.

Traits of leaders

Studies in the first half of the century compared the physical and psychological characteristics of leaders and non-leaders. An analysis of many of these studies by Stogdill (1948) found little consistency in their findings. The search for traits in leadership continued, however, with different approaches to measurement and an effort to distinguish among leaders on the basis of their effectiveness. Analyses of these later studies by Stogdill (1974) revealed a number of traits which consistently characterize more effective leaders. These include:

- sense of responsibility;
- concern for task completion;
- energy;
- persistence;
- risk-taking;
- originality;
- self-confidence;
- capacity to handle stress;
- capacity to influence;
- capacity to co-ordinate the efforts of others in the achievement of purpose.

While these characteristics may be used with a relatively high degree of confidence in the selection and development of leaders, they are but a small part of the picture and provide little to guide the day-to-day activities of leaders in the school setting. More detail was added as attempts were made in the 1950s and 1960s to develop theories of leadership.

Theories of leadership

Some major findings of the 'theory movement' in leadership are briefly summarized here.

Research has consistently revealed the importance of two 'dimensions' in describing the behaviour of leaders. These behaviours reflect a concern for accomplishing the tasks of the organization and a concern for relationships among people in the organization. It is generally accepted that both kinds of behaviour are required for successful leadership. Attempts to develop theories have involved the careful study of situations in which leadership is exercised, acknowledging that there is no one best way to lead in all situations, but that in any particular situation one approach to leadership may be more effective than another. The challenge has been to identify particular attributes of leadership and circumstances which are important in establishing these situational contingencies. Two well-regarded contingency theories (Hersey and Blanchard 1982; Fiedler *et al.* 1977) are summarized briefly, with illustrations of their utility in the school setting.

Hersey and Blanchard (1982) proposed in their situational theory that leadership behaviour should be varied according to the maturity of subordinates or followers. The situation in this theory is thus defined by maturity, with two dimensions proposed: professional maturity and psychological maturity. There are also two dimensions of leadership behaviour: task behaviour, in which the leader emphasizes or specifies the task; and relationship behaviour, in which the leader invests time in developing good interpersonal relationships with and among the group. The theory proposes four general types of leadership behaviour, each of which is appropriate to a particular level of maturity. With increasing maturity, the leader should move through styles designated 'telling' (high task, low relationship); 'selling' (high task, high relationship); 'participating' (low task, high relationship); and 'delegating' (low task, low relationship).

Application of the Hersey and Blanchard theory calls for a highly personalized approach to leadership behaviour. In the school setting, for example, there may be high variability among staff in terms of maturity so that different behaviours will be required for different people. Particular members of staff may have different levels of maturity for different tasks. Furthermore, maturity levels will change from year to year as staff acquire professional and psychological maturity.

Surprisingly, the Hersey and Blanchard theory has not been subjected to rigorous validation. However, its propositions are intuitively well received and have become the focus of widely used management training programmes. The capacity carefully to diagnose maturity levels of staff and then to select matching leadership behaviour according to these propositions would appear to be a worthwhile addition to the repertoire of the school leader.

To understand the contingency theory of leadership formulated by Fiedler (see Fiedler *et al.* 1977, for more detailed explanation and illustration), we need to distinguish between leadership style and leadership behaviour. To Fiedler, leadership style is an innate, relatively enduring attribute of our personality which provides our motivation and determines our general orientation when exercising leadership. Leadership behaviour, on the other hand, refers to particular acts which we can perform or not perform if we have the knowledge and skills, and if we judge them appropriate at the time (this is the sense in which leadership behaviour is used in the Hersey and Blanchard theory).

Fiedler found that task-motivated leaders (those whose primary, driving motivation is to ensure that the task at hand is addressed) tend to be best suited to situations which are either highly favourable or highly unfavourable according to the extent to which tasks are structured, where there are good leader–member relations and when the leader has position power. Relationship-motivated leaders (those whose primary, driving motivation is to ensure that there are good relations with and among members of the work group) are best suited to situations which are moderately favourable on these dimensions. The Fiedler theory has implications for matching leaders to situations and for encouraging leaders to modify their situation where possible to ensure consistency with style. These applications rest on such fine distinctions, and represent such a small aspect of all that must be considered, that the theory seems unlikely to have major impact, despite its validation through research in a variety of settings.

Hodgkinson summed up the theory movement in leadership as embodied in what he judged to be the finest of its products:

> I am prepared to acknowledge that the general productive effort of this type of research, particularly as it is embodied in Professor Fiedler's work, yields us the best theory we have to date in the domain of psychological discourse. I would suspect, however, a paradox. The closer such theory approaches the truth, the more incomprehensible it will become.
>
> (Hodgkinson 1983: 200)

[. . .]

Emerging generalizations

Emerging from these studies are several generalizations which can shape leadership in schools where excellence is valued. Ten are offered here, with acknowledgement of their source in the literature described above. A summary with brief illustration is contained in Table 2.1. Guidelines and further illustrations are provided in the next section [. . .].

1 Emphasis should be given to transforming rather than transactional leadership

This important distinction was made by James McGregor Burns (1978) in his study of leadership and followership. According to Burns, leadership is transactional in most instances, that is, there is a simple exchange of one thing for another: jobs for votes in the case of a political leader and the electorate; a congenial working atmosphere and security in return for keeping central office, parents and students happy in the case of a principal and teaching staff. The transforming leader, while still responding to needs among followers, looks for potential motives in followers, seeks to satisfy higher needs, and engages the full person of the follower. The result of transforming leadership is a relationship of mutual stimulation and elevation that converts followers into leaders and leaders into moral agents (Burns 1978: 4).

The transforming leader may motivate citizens to make new commitments to help those in need (Mother Teresa) or to achieve a breakthrough in civil rights (Martin Luther King Jr) or to achieve independence (Mahatma Gandhi). The principal who is a transforming leader may secure substantial commitments of time and energy from teachers in a drive to change attitudes of students and parents to school in a community where previously there were low levels of achievement and little value was

Table 2.1 Generalizations and illustrations reflecting recent advances in knowledge about leadership

Generalization	Illustration
1 Emphasis should be given to transforming rather than transactional leadership	Principal takes action to change community attitudes towards school
2 Outstanding leaders have a vision for their organization	Principal envisages school as a learning centre for whole community
3 Vision must be communicated in a way which secures commitment among members of the organization	Principal seeks commitment of teachers in devoting time and energy to change community attitudes towards school
4 Communication of vision requires communication of meaning	'Community' is metaphor for school; principal rewards related teacher activities
5 Issues of value – 'what ought to be' – are central to leadership	Principal has strong commitment to equity in terms of access to schooling
6 The leader has an important role in developing the culture of the organization	Principal involves members of community in all ceremonies at the school
7 Studies of outstanding schools provide strong support for school-based management and collaborative decision-making	School policy is determined by group representing parents, teachers, students and community at large
8 There are many kinds of leadership forces – technical, human, educational, symbolic and cultural – and these should be widely dispersed throughout the school	Planning for the various programmes in school carried out by teams of teachers, each having its own leader
9 Attention should be given to institutionalizing vision if leadership of the transforming kind is to be successful	The vision of the school as a learning centre for the community is reflected in goals, policies, plans, budgets and activities
10 Both 'masculine' and 'feminine' stereotype qualities are important in leadership, regardless of the gender of the leader	Principal is sensitive and caring about personal needs ('feminine' stereotype); principal fosters competitive, team approach in raising school's academic standing ('masculine' stereotype)

placed on education. Illustrations of this thrust in transforming leadership are contained in Table 2.1.

2 Outstanding leaders have a vision for their organization

Providing a vision was one of four strategies or themes in the study by Bennis and Nanus (1985) of 90 transforming leaders in a variety of settings. A vision is

> a mental image of a possible and desirable future state of the organization . . . as vague as a dream or as precise as a goal or mission statement . . . a view of a realistic, credible, attractive future for the organization, a condition that is better in some important ways than what now exists.
>
> (Bennis and Nanus 1985: 89)

The vision of Martin Luther King Jr was captured in his stirring 'I have a dream' speech on the steps of the Lincoln Memorial in Washington. The vision of John F. Kennedy concerning space exploration was precise: a man on the moon before the end of the decade.

The importance of vision is a recurring theme in studies of excellence and leadership in education. [. . .]

3 Vision must be communicated in a way which secures commitment among members of the organization

Bennis and Nanus highlight the compelling nature of what is involved:

> Their visions or intentions are compelling and pull people toward them. Intensity coupled with commitment is magnetic . . . [Leaders] do not have to coerce people to pay attention; they are so intent on what they are doing that, like a child completely absorbed in creating a sand castle, they draw others in. Vision grabs.
>
> (Bennis and Nanus 1985: 28)

Starratt (1986) includes the same requirement in his theory of leadership, emphasizing that the shared vision must pervade day-to-day activities. One facet of this theory is that 'the leader articulates that vision in such compelling ways that it becomes the shared vision of the leader's colleagues, and it illuminates their ordinary activities with dramatic significance' (p. 116). In a school, for example, a vision of high levels of self-esteem for every child in a community marked by severe disadvantage requires the shared commitment of all teachers. This commitment must shape every interaction of teacher and student; every word and every action must reflect that vision. Vaill (1986) coined the term 'purposing' to describe what is required of leaders in helping to achieve commitment. Purposing is 'that continuous stream of actions by an organization's formal leadership which have the effect of inducing clarity, consensus and commitment regarding the organization's basic purposes' (p. 91). One can imagine the very careful attention to 'purposing' in a school where the achievement of self-esteem is part of the vision, since that achievement is dependent on 'clarity, consensus and commitment' among the staff as they carry out their 'ordinary activities'.

4 Communication of vision requires communication of meaning

According to Bennis and Nanus (1985: 33) 'the management of meaning, [the] mastery of communication, is inseparable from effective leadership'. In reviewing the significant changes which have occurred over a decade of study in leadership, Sergiovanni asserted that

> At the heart of these changes is the view that the meaning of leadership behaviour and events to teachers and others is more important than the behaviour and events themselves. Leadership reality for all groups is the reality they create for themselves, and thus leadership cannot exist separate from what people find significant and meaningful.
>
> (Sergiovanni 1987: 116)

Particular attention has been given in recent years to the use of metaphors and symbols in the communication of meaning. Spoken and written words have always been regarded as important in the sharing of purposes and intentions, but the choice of metaphors takes on special significance, not only in expressing a vision but also in shaping the climate of the school and the meaning of ordinary activities. Some of the metaphors employed in describing a school are familiar: factory, hospital, family, community, war zone, or even a prison. The student is portrayed, respectively, as a worker, patient, family member, young citizen, soldier or prisoner. Teachers may be seen as factory supervisors, doctors, parents, community leaders, sergeants or warders. There will be debate and conflict about the choice of metaphors since they reflect values and views about the nature of people, society, schooling and education. Gaining consensus and commitment to the particular metaphors which will shape the ordinary activities of the school is thus an important concern for the principal and other leaders in the school.

Symbols are also important for the communication of meaning by leaders. A recent study of the management of symbols by school principals led Kelley and Bredeson (1987: 31) to describe symbolic leadership in terms of integrated messages 'communicated through the patterned use of words, actions and rewards that have an impact on the beliefs, values, attitudes and behaviours of others with whom the principal interacts'. The principal who seeks commitment among teachers to a vision which includes raising the levels of self-esteem will give careful thought to words, actions and rewards. For example, verbal interaction with students will be characterized by praise and encouragement. The principal will choose to attend and, where appropriate, participate in a wide variety of activities involving students with low levels of self-esteem. The presence of the principal will communicate to teachers, students and parents that these activities are valued. Rewards will come in the form of praise and encouragement of teachers who use similar words and engage in similar activities.

5 Issues of value – 'what ought to be' – are central to leadership

Greenfield (1986: 166) asserted that 'organizations are built on the unification of people around values. The business of being a leader is therefore the business of being an entrepreneur of values.' For transactional leadership, where there is a simple exchange between leader and followers ('votes for jobs'), these values will be what Burns (1978: 426) called modal values or values of means such as honesty, responsibility, fairness and the honouring of commitments. For transforming leadership, where the pursuit of higher goals calls for full engagement and commitment, he suggests that the leader must be more concerned with end values such as liberty, justice and equality (p. 426).

Much of the principal's work will involve transactional leadership. The aforementioned values of honesty, responsibility, fairness and the honouring of commitments are a basic requirement if the support of teachers is to be gained. If excellence is the goal, then transforming leadership and associated end values are needed. Excellence, however conceived, is itself an end value and, along with other end values, will be the subject of debate. Sergiovanni et al. (1987: 7) recognized this when, writing in the American context, they stated that 'at the heart of educational policy debates are four widely held but conflicting values: equity, excellence, efficiency and liberty'. Similar debates occur in other countries. Managing conflict over basic values will be as much part of the principals' role as it will be of leaders at local, state and national levels. For example, the value of excellence, conceived in terms of high levels of achievement in a relatively narrow range of academic studies, may conflict with the value of equity, conceived in terms of access to a range of educational programmes for all students, regardless of social and economic circumstance. Alternatively, substantial investment in resources with the intention of achieving excellence and equity might conflict with the value of efficiency. These conflicts, however resolved, will be followed by leadership acts designed to achieve what Greenfield (1986: 166) described as the 'unification of people around [these] values'.

6 The leader has an important role in developing the culture of the organization

[. . .] As with the management of meaning, 'cultural leadership' has emerged as a major theme in studies over the last decade. Indeed, generalizations offered thus far are all embodied in the special attention which is accorded this aspect of leadership. While acknowledging that technical and managerial conceptions have their place, Sergiovanni believes that

> Cultural leadership – by accepting the realities of the human spirit, by emphasizing the importance of meaning and significance, and by acknowledging the concept of professional freedom linked to values and norms that make up a moral order – comes closer to the point of leadership.
>
> (Sergiovanni 1987: 127)

The opportunities for cultural leadership in the school may be briefly illustrated. While definitions of culture are as varied as the definitions of leaders, there is general agreement that shared values and beliefs lie at the heart of the concept. There is also agreement that the extent to which values and beliefs are shared cannot be easily measured or directly observed. We can only rely on what Deal (1987: 6) called 'tangible cultural forms' or Sathe (1985: 17) described as 'manifestations of culture' in making inferences about culture in an organization.

Deal listed six tangible cultural forms, each of which can be developed by the principal: shared values as reflected in shorthand slogans ('we care for every child in this school'), heroes in the life of the school or in society at large who embody the values which are held to be important ('former teacher Beth Hanson visited the home of every child she taught in 20 years of service'), rituals in the form of repetitive activities in which shared values are experienced ('new students are made welcome each year at a party where they are served by teachers'), ceremonies where values and heroes are highlighted and celebrated ('every child has the opportunity at least once each year to be recognized in some way at the Monday morning assembly'), stories illustrating, for example, where values and heroes triumphed in adversity ('the principal recounted to beginning teachers how Beth Hanson visited the parent of one of her students, the father, who was in prison at the time'), and cultural networks of people ('gossips, spies, storytellers') who in a variety of ways serve to protect the ways things are done.

7 Studies of outstanding schools provide strong support for school-based management and collaborative decision-making within a framework of state and local policies

While acknowledging that much research remains to be done, Purkey and Smith (1985: 355) believe that existing research on school effectiveness 'is sufficiently consistent to guide school improvement efforts based on its conclusions'. They offer a model for creating an effective school, with implications for school leadership among its 13 elements. One strategy for the development of school culture is the adoption of collaborative planning and collegial relationships. Another in the same vein is school-site management wherein

> The staff of each school is given a considerable amount of responsibility and authority in determining the exact means by which they address the problem of increasing academic performance. This includes giving staffs more authority over curricular and instructional decisions and allocation of building resources.
>
> (Purkey and Smith 1985: 358)

These recommendations are consistent with those of scholars such as Theodore Sizer and John Goodlad, following their respective studies of schooling in the USA. Sizer (1986: 214) believes that one 'imperative for better schools' is to give teachers and students room to take full advantage of the variety among them, a situation which 'implies that there must be substantial authority in each school. For most public and diocesan Catholic school systems, this means the decentralization of power from headquarters to individual schools.' Goodlad (1984: 275) proposed 'genuine decentralization of authority and responsibility to the local school within a framework designed to assure school-to-school equity and a measure of accountability'. He noted that 'the guiding principle being put forward here is that the school must become largely self-directing' (p. 276).

School-based management calls for approaches to school leadership which encourage and support high levels of collaboration among teachers and, where appropriate, parents and students.

8 There are many kinds of leadership forces – technical, human, educational, symbolic and cultural – and these should be widely dispersed throughout the school

Symbolic and cultural aspects of leadership have been a feature of recent studies as reflected in most of the generalizations offered thus far. However, other aspects which have been part of more traditional perspectives must also be sustained. Sergiovanni (1984: 6) provided a useful classification of what he called 'leadership forces', each of which 'can be thought of as the means available to administrators, supervisors and teachers to bring about or preserve changes needed to improve schooling'. Technical leadership forces include the capacity to plan, organize, co-ordinate and schedule. Human leadership forces include building and maintaining morale, encouraging growth and creativity and involving people in decision-making. Educational leadership forces include the capacity to work with staff to determine student needs and develop curriculum and to provide supervision.

The technical, human and educational aspects of leadership in the Sergiovanni classification encompass the task and relationship dimensions of leadership behaviour used in earlier attempts to develop theories of leadership. Sergiovanni suggested that these three forces alone may ensure an effective school but, if excellence is desired, symbolic and cultural forces should also be evident.

It will be rare for a single leader such as the principal to exercise all of the leadership forces. Consistent with evidence of benefit from collaborative approaches, Sergiovanni (1987: 122) suggests that highly successful leaders recognize the importance of 'leadership density' which refers to 'the extent to which leadership roles are shared and the extent to which leadership is broadly exercised'. There will thus be many leaders in an excellent school.

9 Attention should be given to institutionalizing vision if leadership of the transforming kind is to be successful

This generalization takes up implications of those listed previously that point to the importance of what Burns (1978) called 'transforming leadership', with the principal having a vision for the school, and being able to articulate that vision in such a way that others become committed to it and day-to-day activities are imbued with its meanings and values. It is necessary, of course, that the vision be sustained or 'institutionalized', with its meanings and values embedded in the culture of the school. Starratt (1986) combined all of these perspectives in a simple, eloquent model for leadership as the 'communal institutionalizing of a vision':

- The leader's power is rooted in a vision that is itself rooted in something basic to human life.
- That vision illuminates the ordinary with dramatic significance.
- The leader articulates that vision in such compelling ways that it becomes the shared vision of the leader's colleagues, and it illuminates their ordinary activities with dramatic significance.
- The leader implants the vision in the structures and processes of the organization, so that people experience the vision in the various patterned activities of the organization.
- The leader and colleagues make day-to-day decisions in the light of that vision, so that the vision becomes the heart of the culture of the organization.
- All the members of the organization celebrate the vision in ritual, ceremonies and art forms.

This model may be shaped further by other generalizations related to collaborative decision-making as well as to density of leadership and the variety of leadership forces (technical, human, educational, symbolic, cultural). The principal should work with others to establish the vision for a school. The principal should work with others to implant the vision in the structures and processes of the school, something that calls for the technical and human skills of policy-making and planning. The making of day-to-day decisions in the areas of curriculum and instruction in a manner which reflects the vision will call for density of the educational leadership force; that is, a number of teachers will be leaders as the purposes, policies and priorities of the school are reflected in the various areas of the curriculum and in approaches to teaching and learning.

*10 Both 'masculine' and 'feminine' stereotype qualities are important in
leadership, regardless of the gender of the leader*

The shortcomings of research and theory on the basis of their limited focus on males
has been documented (Shakeshaft and Nowell 1984). A cultural bias toward leadership by males is also evident, with Burns (1978: 50) noting that 'femininity has been
stereotyped as dependent, submissive and conforming, and hence women have been
seen as lacking in leadership qualities'. Burns believed that 'male bias is reflected in
the false conception of leadership as mere command or control'. He sees promise of
a shift in bias as other conceptions of leadership take hold, especially those which
deal with the relationship between leader and followers. An examination of this
relationship was central to his own study of leadership which led to the important distinction between transactional and transformational leadership. Burns concluded that
as 'leadership comes properly to be seen as a process of leaders engaging and mobiliz-
ing the human needs and aspirations of followers, women will be more readily recognized as leaders and men will change their own leadership styles'.

Some valuable insights on this issue were provided by Lightfoot (1983) in her investigation of 'the good high school'. She described her studies as 'portraits' because
'I thought it would allow us a measure of freedom from the traditions and constraints
of disciplined research methods, and because I thought our work would be defined by
aesthetic, as well as empirical and analytic, dimensions' (p. 13). This approach enabled
her to capture aspects of leadership which may have eluded the researcher who
employed a more constrained methodology. She found that the six principals in her
investigation, all of whom were male, were stereotypically male in some respects
(images included 'the raw masculinity of the coach', 'the paternalism of the father-
principal', 'the imperial figure'). Yet, she observed, 'in all cases, the masculine images
have been somewhat transformed and the arrangements of power have been adjusted.
In the most compelling cases, the leaders have sought to feminize their style and have
been aware of the necessity of motherly interactions with colleagues and staff'. Lightfoot concluded that the 'people and context demand a reshaping of anachronistic
patterns':

> The redefinition includes softer images that are based on nurturance given and
> received by the leader; based on relationships and affiliations as central dimen-
> sions of the exercise of power; and based on a subtle integration of personal
> qualities traditionally attached to male and female images.
>
> (Lightfoot 1983: 333)

While the need for further research is evident, a generalization which acknowledges
the importance of both masculine and feminine qualities in leadership can be offered
with confidence. It seems especially relevant to leadership in a shift toward more
autonomy for schools, with school-based management characterized by collaborative
approaches.

Vision in school leadership: guidelines and illustrations

The final section of the chapter provides guidelines and illustrations of three generalizations related to vision in school leadership:

- Outstanding leaders have a vision for their organization (see generalization no. 2 above).
- Vision must be communicated in a way which secures commitment among members of the organization (generalization no. 3).
- Communication of vision requires communication of meaning (generalization no. 4).

In most instances, these guidelines and illustrations are for the school as a whole, with the principal as leader. The same guidelines and similar illustrations may be developed for units within the school and their leaders.

The nature of vision

Bennis and Nanus considered vision in broad terms to mean

> a mental image of a possible and desirable future state of the organization . . . as vague as a dream or as precise as a goal or mission statement . . . a view of a realistic, credible, attractive future for the organization, a condition that is better in some important ways than what now exists.
>
> (Bennis and Nanus 1985: 89)

Some writers would prefer to distinguish between a vision, a mission and an objective, but the broader view is adopted here. It is acknowledged, however, that the term 'vision' as it now appears in the literature on leadership has the same or similar meaning as has been usually ascribed to words like 'goal'. Sheive and Schoenheit (1987), for example, wrote about vision and leadership after interviewing 12 educators, including five principals, who were widely regarded as leaders. These interviews began with a question which asked about the leader's goals as an educator, after which the subject was asked 'Is your vision, then, to . . .?' (p. 96). In this chapter we are not ascribing to the term 'vision' any special characteristic which has recently been discovered, although we accept its usefulness in describing a 'mental picture' which is shaped by one or more goals.

The study by Sheive and Schoenheit is a useful starting point for providing illustrations of visions for schools. Those interviewed shared two kinds of vision, one related to their own organization and the other to the world beyond their own organization; the former embodied a vision of organizational excellence, the latter centred on the issue of equity and was concerned with 'righting a wrong'. It would seem that the specific vision for the school is shaped in part by a more general vision which reflects some basic values and beliefs held by the leader. This is consistent with the model for leadership proposed by Starratt (1986) which suggested that 'the leader's power is rooted in a vision that is itself rooted in something basic to human life'. At the broadest level, these basic values and beliefs seem to fall into constellations which are often in conflict. These 'competing visions' in society as a whole were described by Sowell (1987).

[. . .]

Drawing together this research and writing, we offer the following as a guide to the nature of vision for a school:

- The vision of a school leader includes a mental image of a possible and desirable future state of the school.

- The vision will embody the leader's own view of what constitutes excellence in schooling.
- The vision of a school leader also includes a mental image of a possible and desirable future state for the broader educational scene and for society in general.
- The vision of a school leader also includes a mental image of a possible and desirable process of change through which the preferred future state will be achieved.
- Each aspect of the vision for a school reflects different assumptions, values and beliefs about such matters as the nature of humankind; the purpose of schooling; the roles of government, family and church in schooling; approaches to teaching and learning; and approaches to the management of change.
- There will be competing visions of schooling reflecting the many, often conflicting differences in assumptions, values and beliefs.

[. . .]

Summary

Our purpose in this chapter has been to demonstrate how recent advances in knowledge about leadership can contribute to the achievement of excellence. Earlier views about the nature of leadership itself were rather constrained and superficial, tending to emphasize the exercise of formal authority in achieving the goals of the school. This view gave way to recognition that leadership involves influence and that many who are not formally designated as such may serve as leaders. More recently, we have gained a deeper appreciation of leadership by examining the relationship between leaders and other members of staff, noting the importance of meanings which are derived from leadership acts.

So theories of leadership have provided only a small part of the total picture. We know, for example, that it is important for leaders to give attention to two dimensions: accomplishment of the tasks at hand, and establishing good relationships with and among members of staff. So-called 'contingency theories' offer refinements which are helpful but are somewhat narrow in their potential for application and impact. For example, the situational theory of Hersey and Blanchard reminds us of the importance of varying leadership behaviour according to the maturity of staff for the task at hand; the more mature in a personal and professional sense, the less directive and more participative the leader should be. Fiedler's contingency theory tells us that the relatively unchanging, somewhat innate aspects of our leadership style make us better suited to some situations than to others.

However, it is the larger picture which has resulted from leadership studies which will prove most helpful to the leader who wishes to make a contribution to excellence in the school. It seems that emphasis should be given to transforming rather than transactional leadership, with the intent being to change attitudes and bring about commitment to 'a better state' which is embodied in a vision of excellence for the school. We know that outstanding school leaders have such a vision and that they succeed in communicating it in a way that secures the commitment of others in the school and its community. The most important aspect of communication is the meaning it conveys. So it is important for the school leader to decide on the meanings which are intended and then to choose acts which will ensure the intended outcome. Leadership is concerned with gaining commitment to a set of values, statements of 'what ought to be', which then become the heart of the culture of the school. Gaining this commitment can be achieved in a number of ways, especially with collaborative approaches to decision-making and with placing at the school level high responsibility and authority for making decisions related to the allocation of resources in the school. We know that there is a variety of what Sergiovanni called 'leadership forces' – technical, human, educational, symbolic and cultural – and all should be present and widely dispersed in the school ('leadership density') if excellence is to be attained. Having a vision and securing commitment to that vision is just the starting point. That vision must then be 'institutionalized' so that it shapes the everyday activities in the school. All of these approaches call for masculine and feminine qualities of leadership, regardless of the gender of the leader.

This chapter also contained some guidelines and illustrations for forming and communicating a vision. The vision should be concerned with a possible and desirable future state for the school, should embody a view of excellence and a view of a preferred future for education and society in general, should incorporate a picture of the process of change through which the vision for the school will be achieved, and will reflect different assumptions, beliefs and attitudes which are basic to life and education. There will be competing visions of what is preferred, reflecting a variety of assumptions, beliefs and values. In communicating the vision, the school leader should use a wide range of symbolic leadership acts, broadly classified as words, actions and rewards, with consistency in their use being important.

References

Bennis, W. and Nanus, B. (1985) *Leaders*. New York: Harper and Row.

Burns, J. M. (1978) *Leadership*. New York: Harper and Row.

Deal, T. E. (1987) The culture of schools, in L. T. Sheive and M. B. Schoenheit (eds) *Leadership: Examining the Elusive. 1987 Yearbook of the Association for Supervision and Curriculum Development*. Arlington, VA: ASCA.

Dubin, R. (1968) *Human Relations in Administration* (2nd edn). Englewood Cliffs, NJ: Prentice-Hall.

Duke, D. L. (1986) The aesthetics of leadership. *Educational Administration Quarterly*, 22(1).

Fiedler, F. E. (1967) *A Theory of Leadership Effectiveness*. New York: McGraw-Hill.

Fiedler, F. E., Chemers, M. M. and Mahar, L. (1977) *Improving Leadership Effectiveness: the Leader Match Concept*. New York: John Wiley.

Goodlad, J. I. (1984) *A Place Called School*. New York: McGraw-Hill.

Greenfield, T. B. (1986) Leaders and schools: willfulness and non-natural order in organizations, in T. J. Sergiovanni and J. E. Corbally (eds) *Leadership and Organizational Culture: New Perspectives on Administrative Theory and Practice*. University of Chicago Press, Urbana and Chicago.

Hersey, P. and Blanchard, K. (1982) *Management of Organizational Behavior: Utilizing Human Resources* (4th edn). Englewood Cliffs, NJ: Prentice-Hall.

Hodgkinson, C. (1983) *The Philosophy of Leadership*. Oxford: Blackwell.

Kelley, B. E. and Bredeson, P. V. (1987) Principals as symbol managers: measures of meaning in schools. Paper presented at the annual meeting of the American Educational Research Association. Washington, DC: AERA, April.

Lightfoot, S. L. (1983) *The Good High School*. New York: Basic Books.

Lipham, J. (1964) Leadership and administration, in E. E. Griffiths (ed.) *Behavioral Science and Educational Administration*. Chicago, IL: University of Chicago Press.

Pondy, L. R. (1978) Leadership is a language game, in M. W. McCall Jr and M. M. Lombardo (eds) *Leadership: Where Else Can We Go?* Durham, NC: Duke University Press.

Purkey, S. C. and Smith, M. S. (1985) School reform: the district policy implications of the effective schools literature. *The Elementary School Journal*, 85.

Sathe, V. (1985) *Culture and Related Corporate Realities*. Homewood, IL: Richard D. Irwin.

Sergiovanni, T. J. (1984) Leadership and excellence in schooling. *Educational Leadership*, February.

Sergiovanni, T. J. (1987) The theoretical basis for cultural leadership, in L. T. Sheive and M. B. Schoenheit (eds) *1987 Yearbook of the Association for Supervision and Curriculum Development*. Alexandria, VA: ASCA.

Sergiovanni, T. J., Burlingame, M., Coombs, F. S. and Thurston, P. W. (1987) *Educational Governance and Administration* (2nd edn). Englewood Cliffs, NJ: Prentice-Hall.

Shakeshaft, C. and Nowell, I. (1984) Research on theories, concepts, and models of organizational behavior: the influence of gender, *Issues in Education*, 2.

Sheive, L. T. and Schoenheit, M. B. (eds) (1987) Leadership: examining the elusive, in *1987 Yearbook of the Association for Supervision and Curriculum Development*. Arlington, VA: ASCD.

Sizer, T. R. (1986) Rebuilding: first steps by the coalition of essential schools. *Phi Delta Kappan*, September.

Sowell, T. (1987) *A Conflict of Visions*. New York: William Morrow.

Starratt, R. J. (1986) Excellence in education and quality of leadership. Occasional Paper No. 1. Southern Tasmanian Council for Educational Administration.

Stogdill, R. M. (1948) Personal factors associated with leadership: a survey of the literature. *Journal of Psychology*, 25: 35–71.

Stogdill, R. M. (1950) Leadership, membership and organization. *Psychological Bulletin*, 47.

Stogdill, R. M. (1974) *Handbook of Leadership*. New York: The Free Press.

Vaill, P. B. (1986) The purposing of high performing systems, in T. J. Sergiovanni and J. E. Corbally (eds) *Leadership and Organizational Culture: New Perspectives on Administrative Theory and Practice*. Urbana and Chicago: University of Chicago Press.

Primary headship and leadership

GEOFF SOUTHWORTH

This chapter provides a critical review of the literature focusing on primary school headteachers. Although leadership in primary schools is not confined to headteachers, most of the literature concentrates upon them and not on deputy heads, coordinators and others who exercise leadership. Indeed, the first point to emphasize about leadership in primary schools is the paucity of information about the work of deputy heads and other school leaders. Despite a growing belief in the need for leadership to be widely distributed across a school, studies of leadership in primary schools generally remain fastened to regarding the headteacher as the principal leader. This trend has existed for some time.

This chapter will therefore focus most strongly upon headteachers. It will note weaknesses and inadequacies in the literature, as well as identify the emerging and common themes. The chapter is divided into two sections. The first and longest section reviews the literature concerned with primary headship. This section is subdivided into five parts. In the second section the issues arising from the literature will be noted.

Review of the literature

Some general observations

No major study into primary school headteachers has been undertaken in this country (Coulson 1988: 3). Primary heads therefore lack a data base which would enable them to relate their work to a large sample of heads.

By contrast, secondary school headteachers have been studied in greater detail (e.g. Morgan *et al.* 1983; Hall *et al.* 1986; Weindling and Earley 1987). International comparisons also show that in this country our knowledge of primary heads is shallow. In Australia *A Descriptive Profile of Australian School Principals* (Chapman 1984) has been produced which presents detailed factual information concerning school principals (e.g. personal backgrounds, formal education, work experience). No such comparable data base exists for heads in England and Wales. In the USA the wealth of research into school leadership is reflected in the published literature (e.g. Wolcott 1973; Kmetz and Willower 1982; De Bevoise 1984; Sergiovanni and Corbally 1984; Blumberg and Greenfield 1986; Greenfield 1987; Sheive and Schoenheit 1987; Burdin 1989).

Given the sparseness of material available on primary headship in England and Wales and the lack of large-scale research investigations into the work of these heads, 'writing and research on the topic remains the province of individuals, mainly heads themselves' (Coulson 1988: 3). Consequently, such research as has been undertaken is limited in scope and time-scale. Although there are exceptions to this pattern, few attempts have been made to develop a comprehensive survey of headteachers, or a holistic view of primary headteachers at work.

The literature can be divided into four categories. These categories are of unequal size and are not discrete. They are:

- leadership style
- prescriptions
- descriptions
- headship and school effectiveness.

Each will be examined in turn.

Leadership style

According to Coulson (1988: 3), in the 1960s and 1970s much of the discussion of headship relied on Lewin's autocratic–democratic dimensions, the Ohio State leadership studies or role analysis, while later work continued to explore heads' authority and their leadership styles. Coulson (1980) drew attention to the close identification between head and school and described the characteristic (male) headteacher style as 'paternalistic':

> At the root of the primary head's paternalism lies the ego-identification which he normally has with the school. He tends to think of it as 'his' in a very special way and therefore to feel a deep sense of personal responsibility for everything and everyone in it.
>
> (p. 286)

Nias (1989) interviewed 99 graduates who had taken jobs in infant and junior schools. The questions these teachers were asked in interview were designed to chart their views on teaching as a career. So strongly were these teachers' views affected by their present satisfaction with teaching, which, in turn, they associated with their headteachers' success as managers, that Nias elected to examine their views on school leadership and job satisfaction (p. 255). Her analysis employs a threefold typology of leadership styles developed from Halpin (1966) and Yukl (1975): initiating structure, consideration, and decision centralization, each being an independent dimension along which leadership can be distributed (Yukl 1975: 162). Nias's study confirms Yukl's typology. However, Nias also proposes three 'leadership types' since individual leaders can be differently positioned, in respect of different characteristics, along each of the three dimensions of leadership style. The three 'types' are passive, positive and Bourbon. Positive-type heads were the most favoured by the teachers in her sample: they established a sense of cohesion in the school, gave support and encouragement to individuals and displayed high standards of personal commitment and professional competence.

Winkley (1983) introduces another variable to the discussion. While utilizing autocratic–democratic dimensions of leadership he suggests that these are not fixed styles but, rather, stages of development in school leadership. The idea is advanced as a firm hypothesis although in places Winkley is engaged in a very speculative exercise. Nevertheless, the idea is not without merit. He suggests that there are three stages to headship (autocracy, democracy, the autonomy of the group), each of which is an advance on its predecessor, in terms of the head's tenure and maturity). It is an interesting idea which others have touched upon (Craig-Wilson 1978; Lloyd 1985; Nias *et al*. 1989). Southworth (1995a) suggests that changes in a headteacher's approach to the role may be part of a process of headteacher maturation. As a result of time in post, greater professional knowledge, increased confidence and personal development, heads, over time, alter how they lead 'their' schools (pp. 146–7).

Lloyd (1985) examined the role perceptions of 50 primary heads. Starting with Yukl's three-dimensional theory of leader behaviour and drawing upon interview data, Lloyd proposes six headship types: nominal, coercive, paternal, familiar, passive and extended professional. The last he regarded as the most effective and, within his sample, the single largest group, prompting him to suggest that there was a trend away from the 'head-centred' approach to leadership:

> Although the primary school head clearly remains a potentially influential and powerful figure, with the capacity to impose a very personal and egotistical regime in the school, this is no longer perceived desirable by over half the heads in this sample. The evidence suggests that the paternal and coercive headship types, which may once have been the most common approaches to primary school leadership, are now in decline.
>
> (p. 304)

Lloyd suggests that the 'extended professional' approach, whereby teacher collaboration and development are actively encouraged and where the school moves forward in a jointly agreed way (p. 304), is replacing the head-centred paternalistic style. However, such a claim was perhaps over-confident, given his acknowledgement that over half the heads who comprised the 'extended professional' group found it difficult to combine high levels of initiating structure with high levels of decision decentralization. The difficulty of achieving such a combination led Lloyd to note that there was a strong likelihood of those heads who were enthusiastic for initiating structures to adopt a style in which the head played a more dominant role and which began to assume the characteristics of the paternal approach to leadership (p. 304). In other words, 'extended professional' leaders also lean towards paternalistic leadership and the differences might not be sufficiently significant to warrant Lloyd's claim.

One feature of the above analyses is the predominance of a male role conception (e.g. paternalism). This has been noted and explored by Johnston (1986). He investigated, using a questionnaire approach and factor analysis, the gender differences in teachers' preferences for primary school leadership. The teachers were drawn from eight primary schools and his analysis highlights five dimensions of headship: director, coordinator, controller, authoritative leader, facilitative leader. He argues that different expectations for leadership arose from the gender preferences of teachers (p. 224):

male heads are expected by their staff groups to be more directive, authoritative and task-oriented and female heads more facilitative, considerate and example-setting. Moreover, his findings 'reflect the continuance of traditional societal assumptions about males as authority figures and of the paternalism which is traditionally associated with the male head in the primary school who is working with a preponderance of female staff' (p. 224).

Together these articles and studies provide some valuable insights into primary headship. They suggest that although primary school heads may adopt a range of styles there is some evidence for saying that one particular style is relatively common. This is the 'paternalistic' style which Coulson (1980: 276) argues is a blend of personal control and moral authority. Moreover, 'although most heads now affect a benevolent image and have made some moves towards "democratizing" their schools, the traditional, centralized pattern persists' (p. 285).

Centralized personal control also stems from the way some heads are high on initiating structure and low on decision decentralization. Such an approach appears to be acceptable to the 'followers' and in particular may be a preference of teachers who are led by male headteachers. The lack of decision decentralization has caused some researchers to advocate greater delegation by heads, although not at the expense of them 'abrogating their responsibilities' (Boydell 1990: 22), or reducing their power (see Hellawell 1991: 335).

However, these studies assume that style is an unproblematic notion. Yet style 'does not go very far in recognising the dynamic complexity of leadership behaviour in real life' (Hughes 1985: 265). Also, the value connotations of terms such as 'autocratic' and 'democratic' are not explored. Nor is the applicability to educational settings of categories generated in commercial contexts questioned, or their relevance to primary schools examined. Instead these studies are forms of category analysis, and since the categories are taken as given, headship may be tailored to fit the categories rather than the reverse. In short, there is a danger that these studies are Procrustean analyses.

Critics of leadership style theorizing emphasize the abstract character of the categories, or argue that style is not the important factor in leadership (Viall 1984: 102). Indeed, Southworth (1995a: 150) suggests that primary headship is for some heads not a matter of style, but of occupational identity.

There is one further difficulty to note. These studies are based upon data collected from interviews and questionnaires. Therefore, the interpretations are based upon what heads and teachers believe heads do (Coulson 1988: 5). These ideas are not based upon observation of heads in action.

Prescriptions

This section of the literature is broadly concerned with school management issues. Most of the material is published in book form, thus being easily accessible to headteachers who wish to read about school management and leadership. The books are basically 'how to do headship' texts (Holtom 1988: 55) and focus upon the issues heads need to be aware of and the skills they need to discharge their responsibilities. They offer ways of approaching or dealing with problems common to primary headteachers (e.g. internal communications, staff selection, financial management, delegation). Many are written by practising heads or LEA advisers/inspectors with experience of primary headship (e.g. Whitaker 1983; Craig 1987; Dean 1987; Kent 1989; Nightingale 1990). Others are produced by lecturers in higher education, usually those who organize management courses for headteachers (e.g. Day *et al.* 1985; Paisey and Paisey 1987; Bell 1988; Hill 1989).

Across these texts three issues can be identified. First, the writers tend to accept uncritically management and organizational theories developed in other settings. Few raise to prominence issues of transfer and relevance when adopting these theories (Southworth 1987: 61–4). Nor has any examination of the underlying values of these theories been undertaken. Second, they take a reasonably consistent view of a head-teacher's work. All devote space to school organization, children, staff, governors, parents, leadership, curriculum, management of change. While the writers attach different emphases to these aspects of a head's work, cumulatively the texts provide a uniform view of a headteacher's responsibilities. Third, all the texts locate the head at the centre of the school. For example, Day *et al.* (1985: 7) state that the 'head is regarded by all groups as the focal point of school life'. The pre-eminence of the head-teacher in his/her school is strongly emphasized.

As a counterbalance to the importance of the headteacher several writers argue for the involvement of other staff and counsel the devolution of leadership to others (e.g. Dean 1987: 1; Bell 1988: 45; Hellawell 1991: 336). Such calls for staff participation in the management of the school create for heads a dilemma between participation and control (Ball 1987: 157–60). While, on the one hand, heads are being urged to involve staff, on the other, they are being told that they remain in control and are responsible for all that occurs in the school. Southworth (1987), Menter *et al.* (1995) and Webb and Vulliamy (1996) draw attention to this dilemma with reference to primary school heads, but little empirical work has been undertaken to investigate how individual heads actually resolve the issue in 'their' respective schools.

The overall impression to be gained from these prescriptive texts is that heads are *the* single most influential person in the school. It is clear that staff consultation, dele-gation and participation in decision-making are to be regarded by heads as:

> concessions rather than professional necessities and Renshaw's assertion (1974, p. 9) that most primary schools remain 'static, hierarchical and paternalistic' with little real collective involvement in decision-making and with staff at the mercy of heads' 'spontaneous and intuitive' whims probably still holds for many schools, if not so extensively as in the early 1970s.
>
> (Alexander 1984: 163)

The significance of these texts is in the way that they conceive a particular and con-sistent role model for heads. It should not escape attention, either, that this role model is derived from a group of predominantly male authors.

Descriptions

Descriptions of primary headteachers' work can be divided into five groups. First, there are those which list the duties and responsibilities of heads (e.g. Harling 1981; Whitaker 1983). In recent years these lists have been superseded by the *School Teachers' Pay and Conditions Document* (DES 1989), which sets out the conditions of employment of headteachers.

Second, there are other 'official' descriptions of what heads do which need to be taken into account. For example, HMI's (Wales) report on leadership in primary schools (DES (Welsh Office) 1985) acknowledges that within schools it is heads who have the highest authority to make decisions and that their effectiveness as leaders is a crucial influence upon the life and work of schools. The work of heads is described as being composed of two sets of factors: external and internal. External factors include working with the school's governors and responding to LEA guidance on the curriculum and administration. Internal factors were seen as the most influential in shaping heads' perceptions of role. Nevertheless, HMI recognized that heads retained considerable autonomy in determining curricular matters, pedagogic issues and general school policies (p. 2).

The internal factors which influenced heads' perceptions of their role include 'the need to administer and maintain the school organisation, the need for clearly defined policies, the need to evaluate the curriculum and standards of work and the need to build a team of competent teachers' (p. 3).

HMI noted that the leadership of the head was a key factor in the design and implementation of the curriculum (p. 8). Indeed, their constant reference to heads' responsibilities and obligations signals HMI's belief that heads are the linchpins of 'their' schools. There is a tendency in many of the descriptive accounts to disregard the ethics of leadership. Functions and tasks are presented as if value-free, and so too the management of people. This creates an oversimplified and wholly instrumental view of leadership.

The third group consists of investigations which have studied actual headteacher behaviour. Several studies have been conducted into how headteachers spend their time. Clerkin (1985) analysed the time diaries of three primary heads, supported by evidence from 40 heads who completed a questionnaire. His analysis shows that heads' most time-consuming activities were various kinds of face-to-face communications with staff and pupils and general administrative duties (p. 292). More significantly, his analysis

> indicates that headteacher activity is more often about tackling a high intensity of tasks with frequent interruptions rather than a systematic ordering of curricular or organizational programmes based upon agreed policies or clearly understood management structures . . . this can sometimes lead to situations where the majority of a head's energy is devoted to 'keeping the school ticking over' in the short run with only limited opportunity to consider important longer term issues.
>
> (p. 298)

Harvey (1986) investigated 32 heads' intended and actual use of time. Extra teaching to cover for absent colleagues and unanticipated or unexpectedly prolonged visits accounted for differences between the two. Harvey concluded that heads needed to develop coping strategies to deal with the unexpected (p. 66).

Another, fourth, strand of this subgroup of enquiries are 'Mintzberg-type' studies (Coulson 1988: 5), so called because they are derived from Mintzberg's (1973) observational study of managerial work in commercial settings. Davies (1987) used this approach (open-ended observation, diary methods) to study four primary heads. He found that each head was at the centre of the school's information network and was in a unique position to have knowledge about what went on in the school (p. 45). However, the heads' days were also characterized by brevity, variety and fragmentation, with nearly one-quarter of all activities undertaken being interrupted (p. 44). Much the same picture emerges from an investigation into headship in the 1990s. Southworth (1995b) interviewed ten heads who reported that their work was unpredictable and required them to be reactive to situations and responsive to the needs of parents, pupils, staff and governors (pp. 16–17).

Coulson (1986) has provided an interpretative account of an undisclosed number of heads' managerial work, based largely upon participant observation. However, the precise details of his methodology are not reported. What emerges is a form of category analysis, since he too relies upon Mintzberg's classification, albeit modified to incorporate Hughes's (1976) distinction between chief executive and leading professional roles in headship. Coulson argues that there is a close identification between heads and their schools and, as a result, the actions and attitudes of headteachers are expected by teachers to exemplify to a high degree the personal and organizational values which are expected of other members of staff, an observation supported by other studies (Nias et al. 1989, 1992). Moreover:

> It has been suggested that the head as Figurehead and Spokesman represents and symbolises the school. This symbolic aspect of leadership is also important for the head in his capacity as Leading Professional for, in Sergiovanni's (1984) words, 'The symbolic leader assumes the role of "chief" and by emphasising selective attention (the modelling of important goals and behaviours) signals to others what is of importance and value.'
>
> (Coulson 1986: 78)

Here Coulson moves our understanding of headship onto a rather different plane. While the work of heads can be described as hectic and fragmented, Coulson suggests that the significance of heads' work lies in the meaning of their actions to themselves and their staff groups.

The same point was made by Nias, Southworth and Yeomans (1989) in their ethnographic study of five primary schools' cultures. The researchers describe the headteachers' part in developing and sustaining their schools' cultures. Heads were shown to be such important figures in 'their' schools that they are described as the owners of them (p. 99) because of their close association with the school and the way in which they established a sense of mission for it (p. 98). These notions of ownership and mission led the researchers to claim that the heads were the founders of their schools' cultures. In that capacity the heads exemplified and promoted a set of educational, social and moral beliefs which, in three of the schools, became the foundational values shared by all or the great majority of the staff. While these heads behaved in ways similar to those depicted in the time study reports and in Coulson's (1980, 1986) work, the research also showed that each head worked steadily towards establishing and maintaining a set of shared beliefs among the staff. In other words, the significance of the heads' work lay not so much in their behaviour as in the meaning of their behaviour.

A similar picture of headship emerges from Nias, Southworth and Campbell's (1992) study of whole-school curriculum development in five primary schools. The heads of these schools provided a vision for the staff and school. Moreover,

They all worked hard in a variety of ways to secure their staff's allegiance to their particular visions and to ensure that the educational beliefs and values on which these rested were put into practice in classrooms. Sometimes the heads relied upon their authority and were direct in their efforts to establish a common set of educational beliefs among their teachers. At other times they were indirect, relying upon influence rather than authority.

(Nias *et al.* 1992: 148–9)

These heads were 'powerful figures who exercised a controlling influence upon the school and its development' (p. 247).

Reflecting on the findings of these two school-based projects (Nias *et al.* 1989, 1992), Southworth (1993) suggests that heads are motivated to work hard because their leadership is the pursuit of their individual visions. Primary headship can be the promotion of the head's educational values and beliefs (pp. 23–4).

This idea is evident in Acker's ethnographic study of a primary head. Acker (1988) conducted her enquiry within a larger project producing an insightful picture of a (female) headteacher's work in an urban primary school. It too supports the picture of the head's work as varied, fragmented and people-centred (pp. 5–6). Yet Acker goes on to say that this was a cause of some dissatisfaction to the head, who often experienced a discrepancy between what she wanted to do and the situation which circumstances forced her into (p. 7). Acker shows that the events the head dealt with or was caught up in had emotional, dynamic and dramatic qualities (p. 7). Also,

Although Mrs Clarke, the head, was clearly the dominant figure in staff meetings, she was sometimes jokingly disparaging about her own tendencies to forget things . . . the use of humour served to soften the edge of the 'formidable concentration of power' (Alexander, 1984, p. 161) vested in the primary headteacher . . . Fragmentation and constant changes in the head's work were counteracted . . . through the stability provided by the school's ethos. The head, the 'educational supercook' (Burgess, 1983) or less respectfully 'the school's resident and sole philosopher' (Alexander, 1984, p. 180), has a key role in shaping the values of the school.

(Acker 1988: 31–2)

Acker, in line with Nias *et al.* (1989), argues that headship is deeply concerned with values.

Southworth (1995a) has produced a case study of a single primary headteacher at work in his school. Based upon close observation over a school year Southworth developed an ethnographic portrait of the head, 'Ron Lacey', which showed that

He worked long hours being deeply committed to the school he led. Much of his work, during and after the school day, was devoted to dealing with people. Although he handled documents and wrote letters and reports, most of his work was oral; talk was the work. Ron dealt with a wide range of topics and issues, but he was most strongly interested in teachers and children, teaching and learning. He monitored what was happening in the teaching areas of the school, offered advice and support to teacher colleagues, reflected on what he saw or heard about and evaluated the work taking place in the school. He saw himself as a developer of the staff, the curriculum and the school as an organization.

Ron led through a blend of influence and authority. He was involved in the micropolitics of the institution. He knew, by a variety of means, what was happening in the school and he was at the centre of an information web. He was aware of the interpersonal dramas in the school and sensitive to their implications for the running of the school. Staff accepted his leadership, respecting his experience and knowledge. No one challenged his authority. Indeed, Ron was the predominant and controlling figure in the school. He regarded headship as individualistic and personal. He promoted his professional and personal beliefs and wanted to see them enacted throughout the school.

(Southworth 1995a: 214)

The portrait of Ron Lacey provides empirical evidence to confirm the general picture reviewed in this section.

These studies (Coulson 1986; Acker 1988; Nias et al. 1989; Nias et al. 1992; Southworth 1995a) begin to build a reasonably consistent picture of primary headship. They show that heads are active and energetic individuals, managing an unpredictable flow of work. They also present heads as powerful figures in their schools, striving to install and spread among the staff a set of commonly held educational beliefs.

The fifth group of texts focus upon the changing nature of headship. Educational reforms triggered by the 1988 Education Act (e.g. LMS, opting out, open enrolment, the introduction of the National Curriculum) have impacted on school leadership, as a number of studies have demonstrated. Nightingale (1990: 77–85), for example, notes the tension between primary head as teacher and head as manager (see also Boydell 1990; Hellawell 1991). Edwards (1989) notes the widening role of the primary head. Mortimore and Mortimore (1991) present six heads' views on headship in England and Wales and note that these headteachers had been living through the transition from the old order to the new and did not know whether to welcome or regret the changes (p. 128). The heads referred to 'the aftermath of the recent legislative hurricane' (p. 15) and the effects of LMS (pp. 29 and 46).

Alexander, Rose and Woodhead (1992) also draw attention to the changing nature of headship. There are four points to highlight from their discussion paper. First, they noted that there 'are two broad approaches to primary headship', the head as administrator and the head as educational leader (p. 46). Second, they suggest that the advent of LMS was creating the view that primary heads must be administrators. Third, they reject 'absolutely' (p. 46) this view. Fourth, they argue that primary heads should take a lead in ensuring the quality of curricular provision by maintaining an overview of the school, judging its strengths and weaknesses, monitoring the teaching and learning and providing a 'vision of what their schools should become' (p. 47). Two further points can be made about Alexander et al.'s thinking. First, in rejecting so strongly the possible impact of LMS upon the head's role, they signal a deep concern about the potential effect of the reforms. Their shrill note betrays both their anxiety about the direction of headship and the fact that there are forces at work which could reshape the work of heads. Second, in arguing for educational leadership they continue to regard heads as the single most important figure in their schools.

Webb's (1994) research suggests that headship has altered in some ways, but not in others. In the 1990s there is a greater administrative and managerial load to bear because of LMS (p. 38). Elsewhere Webb and Vulliamy (1995) note how deputy heads described their heads as becoming increasingly preoccupied with the school's budget, administration and teacher appraisal (p. 55). Heads have also had to come to terms with competing in the market-place for pupils because of open enrolment and dealing with the burgeoning responsibilities of school governors. Yet in other ways, heads continue to work much as they did. Webb's survey of 50 schools and the implementation of the National Curriculum at Key Stage 2 shows that the heads worked in ways similar to those described by Nias *et al.* (1989, 1992). All the heads held visions of what they wanted their schools to become, maintained an overview of the curriculum and informally evaluated initiatives. While heads in the 1990s have different tasks to do, underneath their day-to-day chores they continue to hold a strong and controlling interest in their schools.

This interpretation is supported by Menter *et al.*'s (1995) research into headship in the 1990s. While the authors perceive some signs of a shift in the self-concept of the primary head, 'from that of educational-leader/paternalist/community-servant to that of a manager/salesperson of an educational commodity' (p. 302), they describe headship as a blend of 'old' and 'new' approaches. There have been significant changes in the working practices of heads but it is:

> too simple to refer to 'the new primary head' . . . the centrality of the head's role in the management of the school is as clear as ever. Legally, the governing bodies of schools bear a greater increased responsibility. The perception of the heads themselves, who after all are themselves legally more accountable than before to their governing bodies, is that there is no doubt who carries the bulk of the day-to-day responsibility. It is indeed heads who are still carrying the can.
>
> (Menter *et al.* 1995: 311)

Both Webb and Menter *et al.* show that although primary headship has changed in some respects, it also continues to be the same in terms of the distribution of responsibilities and power relations.

This conclusion is also consistent with the findings of another study investigating primary headship in the 1990s (Southworth 1995a). Interviews with ten experienced heads showed that the work had become more complex and demanding than it was. The work of heads appears to have intensified, resulting in them working longer hours than formerly, especially in terms of the number of evenings spent back in school. Yet the work was also seen as rewarding, with several enjoying the variety and challenge of the role. All recognized that they were influential in their schools – indeed, that was a major attraction to the role – and understood that they had a central contribution to make to the schools' development (p. 44).

As in other studies (Nias *et al.* 1989, 1992; Webb 1994; Webb and Vulliamy 1995), while the involvement of other staff in the schools' leadership was apparent (e.g. deputies, co-ordinators) the pivotal importance of the head implies that the part these colleagues play in the school is contingent upon the heads' assumptions about the roles of senior staff (Southworth, 1995b: 44). There are signs that deputies are sometimes seen as assistant heads (Webb and Vulliamy 1996) and that in a number of primary schools senior management teams have been established (Menter *et al.* 1995: 306), but the formal responsibilities and informal spheres of influence of deputies are ultimately controlled by headteachers (Webb and Vulliamy 1995: 58).

Together, these descriptions deepen our understanding of headship. The observational studies have begun to get beneath the surface appearance of school leadership and explore meanings and the way values and vision influence the role. However, although there are now one or two detailed, close-up studies of headteachers, more are needed. As Blase (1987: 194) says, we need more data on the processes of school leadership, the 'little stuff of everyday life'.

Headteachers and effective schools

In recent years there have been a growing number of attempts to analyse and describe 'effective' schools (e.g. Purkey and Smith 1983; Reynolds 1985; Reid et al. 1987). One characteristic commonly associated with effective schools is the quality of leadership provided by the head. This characteristic has been noted in North American studies and in reports in this country (e.g. Rutter et al. 1979; Mortimore et al. 1988). Moreover, it is a finding which HMI reinforce in their reports (DES 1977, 1990). For example, 'The leadership qualities of headteachers and the manner in which they fulfil their management responsibilities are key factors in determining the effectiveness of their school' (Scottish Education Department 1990: 16).

It is not surprising then that the term 'effectiveness' appears in the title of many publications. Indeed, there is a taken-for-granted quality about both the notion of effectiveness and the idea that heads are key determinants of it in schools. The DES report on school management training, for example, includes the following statement:

> No two definitions of the effective school are just the same. None the less, the list which follows clearly reflects both the inspection evidence reported by HMI and in other research work. Effective schools may be seen to have the following characteristics:
>
> - good leadership offering breadth of vision and the ability to motivate others;
> - appropriate delegation with the involvement in policy-making by staff other than the head;
> - clearly established staffing structures.
>
> (School Management Task Force (DES) 1990: 5)

Two points need to be made at this juncture, one general, the other specific. The first and general one concerns the concept of leadership. While numerous reports, commentaries and studies stress that leadership is a key factor in making particular schools 'effective', few provide a definition of the concept of leadership. The absence of a definition is worrying since the term is inherently hazy, slippery and complex (Bennis 1959, cited in Open University 1988: 15). Leadership may be a term with much currency, but little meaning.

If leadership is difficult to define in a generic sense, in terms of schools it appears to mean the part played by the headteacher in exerting influence upon the school as an organization (Nias et al. 1989: 95–7) and upon professional matters such as curriculum management (Hughes 1985: 278–85). However, a weakness with this view is the way it restricts leadership to headship.

Second, few school effectiveness studies have investigated effective primary headteachers. One reason for this is the dearth of studies in Britain which have focused upon effective primary schools. Only one study (Mortimore et al. 1988) has been undertaken into effective primary schools. This study, in line with other research into effectiveness, was concerned to examine the effects schools have on the pupils who attend them. Such effects are largely determined by measuring the educational gains pupils make. As such, 'the results of studies of school effectiveness are dependent, to a large extent, on the choice of measures of educational outcomes' (p. 4). Moreover, there tends to be an assumption that when a school is measurably effective, by association its head must be an effective leader. Despite these conceptual and empirical difficulties, and the limited amount of work into primary schools, the findings of effective schools research are given serious attention. For example, Coulson (1986) has attempted to describe the characteristics of an effective primary head. Bolam *et al.* (1993) have conducted a survey into heads' and teachers' views of effective school management, and Southworth (1990, 1995b) has examined the effective schools literature and provided a synopsis of the characteristics associated with effective heads. Additionally, the National Commission on Education (1996) has examined effective schools in disadvantaged areas and commented on four successful primary heads, while Sammons *et al.* (1995) and OFSTED (1995) have further reinforced the prevailing view about effective schools and headteachers. These studies and reports will be reviewed in turn.

Mortimore *et al.* (1988) studied 50 schools in London and, from a detailed examination of 2000 children over five years, identified 12 key factors which contributed to school effectiveness (p. 250). The first two characteristics are: (1) purposeful leadership of the staff by the headteacher and (2) the involvement of the deputy head.

[. . .]

The research team set out what they regarded as the main implications of their study for headteachers:

> In our view, heads need to have a very clear view of their leadership role. They need to be able to divide the decisions they are required to make into two groups: those which it is quite properly their responsibility to take and for which any attempt at delegation to a staff decision would be seen as a dereliction of duty and those which, equally properly, belong to the staff as a whole. In some cases it will be perfectly clear to which group a certain decision belongs: in others, it will be extremely difficult to decide. Mistakes will be made and the consequences – as when the staff discover that a decision affecting their way of working has been taken with no opportunity for them to voice an opinion on the matter, or where there is a conflict of interests between individual teachers on the staff – will have to be suffered. However, if the head is perceptive and sensitive she or he will soon learn to distinguish which decisions are which.
>
> (Mortimore *et al.* 1988: 281)

Mortimore and his associates provide some valuable ideas about the work of heads. However, although based upon some observational data (as well as much quantitative data), there is a noticeable absence of illustration. Also, the data concerning heads are rather piecemeal. There is no attempt to synthesize the data or to provide a picture of an 'effective' head. The study provides data on aspects of headship, but not a portrait of a head, or heads, at work.

Coulson's (1986) set of seven characteristics associated with successful heads is a personal view based upon his study of how a number of heads conducted their work. Successful heads are:

- *goal oriented* – they have a vision of how they would like to see their schools develop. They give a sense of direction to the school; they operationalize their goals through a long-term strategy and at the level of their day-to-day actions;
- *personally secure* – they do not feel unduly threatened; there is some measure of disengagement from traditionally strong ego identification between head and school;
- *tolerant of ambiguity* – they can cope with frequent change and uncertainty;
- *proactive* – they have an entrepreneurial attitude, they are not always reactive;
- *sensitive to the dynamics of power inside their schools* – they seek out sources of power and support through informal networking, and are sensitive to informal codes of professional practice which govern teacher and head and teacher relations;
- *analytical* – they solve problems and understand the meaning of individual problems for whole school;
- *in charge of the job* – they avoid being harried and swamped by demands; they are able to devote time and energy to activities which develop and sustain their individual visions.

(adapted from Coulson 1986: 85–6)

These seven characteristics could provide the basis for further discussion and analysis. Unfortunately neither has been attempted. Coulson's characteristics have not been amplified or tested. They are simply a list of ideas generated from his knowledge of the literature, especially in the USA (see bibliography, Coulson 1986) and a category analysis of English primary headteachers.

Southworth (1990) synthesized the literature concerned with effective leaders and primary heads including Coulson and Mortimore *et al.*'s work, noting several gaps in the literature (p. 12). Southworth produces a list of 16 features which form an initial outline of what an effective primary headteacher appears to look like. The list summarizes thinking in the 1980s and shows that there is a 'noticeable lack of in-depth, refined or longitudinal studies' (p. 15). He argues that there is a need to investigate how heads convey their values to others and deal with differences between themselves and other members of staff. He also notes the need to consider the effects of school size upon the work of heads.

Bolam *et al.* (1993) conducted a study into effective school management. Using union and professional association journals Bolam and his associates invited staff in schools to volunteer to participate. Those schools which signalled an interest were surveyed by questionnaire. Twelve schools were also selected to be visited in order 'to illuminate, deepen and extend the quantitative findings' (p. 3) concerning heads' and teachers' views of effective school management. Part of the project's report focuses on leadership and management (pp. 23–46) and Bolam and his colleagues set out the heads' views of themselves and the teachers' perceptions about school leadership.

Although all 12 heads of the visited schools 'espoused an essentially democratic approach to leadership' and none was autocratic 'in the traditional sense of management by dictat' (p. 25), five of the heads were 'influential, even dominant figures in their schools' (p. 26). All were 'very clear about the school they wished theirs to be' and 'they were determined to do all in their power to try to ensure that [their] objectives were widely endorsed by their staff and realised' (pp. 26–7). Bolam *et al.* set out, in the light of their findings, summarizing lists of the personal and managerial qualities which the teachers they interviewed and surveyed associated with effective school leaders (pp. 30–1). Later, in discussing their findings Bolam *et al.* comment:

'Having examined teachers' comments, the power of the traditional image of the head-teacher, as someone strong, dynamic and in charge comes across forcefully' (p. 43).

In other words, effective heads are expected to be assertive, trenchant and potent figures. There is a tacit assumption that effective heads provide the vision for the school and shape the direction of the school. As Bolam *et al.* acknowledged, 'there could be no doubting whose voice ultimately counted the most' (p. 26).

As part of his enquiry into headship in the 1990s, Southworth (1995a) focused on the heads' views about effective school leaders. Their views were broadly 'in line with Bolam's work (pp. 22–3) and endorsed contemporary thinking about heads and effective schools. Reflecting on his findings, Southworth suggests that lists of the characteristics of effectiveness do not provide a very clear view as to which characteristics matter most. The challenge of searching for the secrets of successful leadership is that 'no one can predict which of the characteristics matters most because so much depends on the specific circumstances of the school in which the head is working' (p. 39). Lists only offer an initial outline of effectiveness and show that we are at an early stage in understanding effective headteacher behaviours. Indeed, we need to consider the possibility that

> We may never know all there is to know about effectiveness. School leadership may be just too complex, too organic, too unpredictable and too contingent upon so many variables that we can never be sure of very much. There may just be 'too many moving parts' (Huberman 1992) for us ever to develop a clear and definitive understanding.
>
> (Southworth 1995a: 40)

Nevertheless, studies continue to search for what appears to make some heads especially successful. The NCE (National Commission on Education 1996) report focuses on four primary schools which are 'succeeding against the odds'. In a summarizing chapter there is an attempt to identify the lessons in success. The review of the work of the heads covers the four primary heads, as well as the heads of six secondary and one special school. The features of their management and leadership which benefited the schools were: judgement, omnipresence, personal style, shared leadership, team building, and developing the team (pp. 335–46). The NCE report not only draws attention to the importance of the headteacher as a professional leader, but also sustains this theme in line with many other studies.

Likewise, OFSTED (1995) believes that it is headteachers 'who are responsible for the quality of teaching in their schools and that heads ought to see their role as, above all else, one of monitoring and raising standards' (p. 33). The attributes of effective primary heads are summarized as:

> A vision of the curriculum and a real personal sense of appropriate standards; the strength of personality and the interpersonal tact needed to engage with teachers in raising standards; the administrative drive to plan programmes of improvement and see that they were carried through.
>
> (p. 33)

OFSTED and the NCE report are broadly similar with Sammons *et al.*'s (1995) summary of effective schools research which suggests that one of the factors associated with effective schools includes professional leadership which, in turn, is firm and purposeful, involves others and is participative and in which the head is the leading professional (pp. 9–10).

These latter studies continue the pattern of listing attributes and qualities. However, they do not develop them and so provide only a superficial sketch of effective leaders.

Issues arising from the literature

In this section I will discuss the main issues arising from the foregoing review of the literature. There are six issues to highlight.

First, the main theme to emerge from the texts is the power of the head. Primary heads are seen to be very powerful figures inside the schools they lead. They are perceived to be possessive about 'their' schools (Coulson 1980; Nias et al. 1989); are regarded as holding a 'formidable concentration of power' (Alexander 1984: 161); exercise control over the form and direction of development in their schools (Campbell 1985: 109); dominate the schools they lead (Southworth 1995b); and are believed to be one factor, admittedly among a number of others, which determines the effectiveness of the school. By contrast, there is a marked lack of attention paid to other staff who hold senior positions in the school's hierarchy. The sheer amount of attention devoted to heads in school management texts signals the central importance of headteachers.

While 'the according of massive responsibility and power to the primary head is a constant in all recent writing on primary schools' (Alexander 1984: 161), and continues to be so, those who draw attention to it (e.g. Coulson 1976; Alexander 1984; Campbell 1985) frequently fail to provide a definition of power. In other words, although the concept has been raised and discussed, the failure to define terms means the discussion lacks analytical rigour and depth.

The second issue concerns the lack of attention devoted to differences in school size and their possible effects upon the work of heads. Although primary schools range in size from below 50 pupils on roll to schools with over 600 pupils, discussions about headteachers generally fail to take differences in school size into account. In particular, there is a failure to attend to the nature of headship in small schools where the headteacher is responsible, for the major portion of the working week, for a registration class of pupils. No major studies appear to have been conducted into headship in small schools. The tendency generally to speak about primary headship infers a sense of uniformity which is not matched by the variations in school size. Nor has uniformity been demonstrated since no comparative studies have been conducted into the effects, if any, of school size upon the work of headteachers.

The third issue centres upon the lack of any substantive account of what it feels like to be a headteacher. The felt-experience of headship, while a topic of interest in the USA (e.g. Blumberg and Greenfield 1986), has not been paralleled in this country although glimpses of this aspect of the work can be detected in Sedgwick (1989). There is a lack of knowledge concerning what it feels like to be a headteacher. It seems inadequate to note that heads have considerable power without developing this theme further by enquiring into the felt-experience of headship. Southworth (1995a) attempted to explore this issue in his case study of a headteacher at work, but other than raising the issue and seeing headship as an identity, was unable to delve very deeply into the area. How do heads emotionally respond to being held accountable for the whole institution and exercising power over others? Until these and other related questions are examined the affective dimension of headship will remain unexplored. Indeed, until such matters are addressed we might be 'taking the actors out of the play' (Huberman 1988: 120).

Fourth, the lack of attention to other school leaders is a significant gap in our knowledge and understanding of leadership in primary schools. For some time the view has been held that what deputies and other leaders in a school do is contingent upon what their heads will let them do (Whitaker 1983: 87; Reay and Dennison 1990: 45). Yet such dependency has not been explored from the deputies and co-ordinators' perspectives. Nor have the micropolitics of a head's dominance and its effect upon the deputy and other leaders been examined, although it has been noted (Southworth 1995a: 139–41, 144–6). Moreover, despite some useful work (see Purvis and Dennison 1993; Webb and Vulliamy 1995), the impact of recent changes upon the work of school leaders has yet to be developed in depth. The idea of heads and deputies working in partnership (Southworth 1994a), the renaming of some deputies as 'assistant heads' (Southworth 1994b: 5) and the increase of senior management teams in primary schools (Webb 1994: 47) are largely unexplored developments. So too is the deputy heads' curriculum leadership (Morrison 1995). Indeed, curriculum leadership may be in a transitional phase during the mid-1990s. OFSTED is promoting increased levels of classroom monitoring, yet there are no examples of what this looks like in practice. Neither have the views of coordinators about monitoring been investigated. Also, the very job title of coordinators may be changing since OFSTED (1994) has begun to call them 'subject managers'. This may mark a significant shift of emphasis, signalling more widely distributed management. It might also imply that while management tasks are to be delegated to colleagues, leadership remains in the control of headteachers. Clearly, much remains to be learned about shared leadership and power relations in primary schools.

Fifth, there is a paucity of detailed observational studies. There is only one, close-up study of a headteacher at work (Southworth 1995a). Few ethnographic studies into headship have been undertaken. Insufficient attention has been paid to developing a moving picture of the fluidities of leadership and managerial work in its different guises, or which might indicate the diversity and variation in managerial jobs (Hales 1986: 93). When this criticism is added to the lack of survey data then it has to be acknowledged that the research base for understanding primary headship, let alone leadership, is neither abundant nor ample. In particular, the empirical foundations of our knowledge about leadership are incomplete. At best, our knowledge of primary school leadership is partial.

The sixth issue concerns theory. There are two points I wish to make. First, a large number of the reports and studies adopt ideas from other investigations and settings, yet the authors do not address the issue of the transferability of these insights. Also, there is a tendency for particular concepts to be applied in an uncritical manner. For example, leadership style is treated as unproblematical. Moreover, whichever theoretical concepts are adopted by writers interested in headship, the tendency is for the concepts to be applied to heads rather than the reverse. The concepts (e.g. typologies of styles) have not been tested for their relevance to or validity for primary headteachers. Furthermore, there is little or no attempt to develop 'grounded theories' (Glaser and

Strauss 1967: 3) about headship, and this compounds the unidirectional nature of theorizing about headship.

Second, much of the literature concerned with primary school leadership is dominated by a particular form of rationality. Bartlett (1991), for example, argues that school management is dominated by a form of rationality which is characterized by:

> a complex division of labour, stable authority channels, power centralised at the apex of an hierarchical system, one-directional communication, impersonal relationships, standardisation and an assumed value neutrality. These features affect the dominant rationality of organisations in Western culture. This rationality may be described as bureaucratic.
>
> (p. 25)

A bureaucratic rationality treats educational issues and dilemmas as problems that can be resolved through the application of 'precise standards and sophisticated engineering' (p. 28). Bureaucratic rationality is principally concerned with efficiency and effectiveness in managing the organization: 'Every bureaucratic organization embodies some explicit definition of costs and benefits from which the criteria of effectiveness are derived. Bureaucratic rationality is the rationality of matching means to ends economically and efficiently' (MacIntyre 1985: 25).

Foster (1989) calls this form of rationality bureaucratic-managerial and argues that it produces a particular model of leadership which

> normally describes the way business and other managers and scholars of management talk about the concept of leadership. This model contains a number of assumptions. Among them is the assumption that leadership is a function of organizational position; the 'leader' is the person of superior rank in an organization. This assumption is almost universally held among management writers and forms the basis for the various models of leadership which have been developed in the last thirty years. A related assumption is that leadership is goal-centred and that the goals are driven by organizational needs.
>
> (p. 43)

The pre-eminence of a bureaucratic rationality means that formal models of management (Bush 1986: 22–47) have mostly been applied to both primary schools as organizations and the work of primary heads. Consequently conceptions of primary headship and leadership have tended to draw on role theory, and there has been an absence of alternative studies and commentaries. For example, Bush (1986: 48–108) has suggested that there are four other models of management theorizing (democratic, political, subjective and ambiguous). As an antidote to the single, unchallenged model of rational leadership it is necessary that some studies into primary leadership apply and explore some of the concepts and assumptions within the alternative models.

Southworth's (1995b) study was, in part, a response to these criticisms. Applying a symbolic interactionist perspective, as against a bureaucratic rationale, he developed a grounded theory, namely, that primary heads dominate not simply because of their tacit acceptance of power relations in schools, but because dominance was part of their professional identity. For some, headship is neither a matter of style nor role, but of *occupational identity*. This interpretation suggests that for some, leadership is not a matter of adopting an objectivized role, but is a deeply internalized sense of occupational self. Yet this hypothesis, although explained and defended, needs to be tested and developed. In particular, life histories and personal accounts are needed to update our knowledge and deepen our understanding of leadership.

Overall, this review shows that our knowledge of primary headship is partial and largely confined within a single set of theoretical assumptions. The literature shows there is a need for further work which addresses the deficiencies in our awareness of headship in particular and primary school leadership in general.

References

Acker, S. (1988) Managing the drama: the headteacher's work in an urban primary school. Paper presented at the Conference on Histories and Ethnographies of Teachers at Work, Oxford, University of Bristol mimeo.

Alexander, R. (1984) *Primary Teaching*. London: Holt, Rinehart and Winston.

Alexander, R., Rose, J. and Woodhead, C. (1992) *Curriculum Organisation and Classroom Practice: a Discussion Paper*. London: DES.

Ball, S. (1987) *The Micropolitics of the School*. London: Methuen.

Bartlett, T. (1991) Rationality and the management of curriculum change, *Educational Management and Administration*, 19(1): 20–9.

Bell, L. (1988) *Management Skills in Primary School*. London: Routledge.

Blase, J. (1987) Dimensions of ineffective school leadership: the teachers' perspective, *Journal of Educational Administration*, 24: 193–213.

Blumberg, A. and Greenfield, W. (1986) *The Effective Principal: Perspectives on School Leadership* (2nd edn). Newton, MA: Allyn and Bacon.

Bolam, R., McMahon, A., Pocklington, K. and Weindling, D. (1993) *Effective Management in Schools: a Report from the Department of Education via the School Management Task Force Professional Working Party*. London: HMSO.

Boydell, D. (1990) '. . . The Gerbil on the Wheel': conversations with primary headteachers about the implications of ERA, *Education 3–13*, 18(2): 20–4.

Burdin, J. L. (ed.) (1989) *School Leadership: a Contemporary Reader*. Newbury Park, CA: Sage.

Bush, T. (1986) *Theories of Educational Management*. London: Harper and Row.

Campbell, J. (1985) *Developing the Primary School Curriculum*. London: Holt, Rinehart and Winston.

Chapman, J. D. (1984) *A Descriptive Profile of Australian School Principals*. Canberra: Commonwealth Schools Commission.

Clerkin, C. (1985) What do primary school heads actually do all day? *School Organization*, 5(4): 287–300.

Coulson, A. A. (1980) The role of the primary head, in T. Bush *et al.* (eds) *Approaches to School Management*. London: Harper and Row, pp. 274–92.

Coulson, A. A. (1986) *The Managerial Work of Primary School Headteachers*, Sheffield Papers in Education Management, no. 48. Sheffield Polytechnic.

Coulson, A. A. (1988) Primary school headship: a review of research. Paper presented at BEMAS Conference, Cardiff, April 1988; reprinted in R. Saran and V. Trafford (eds) (1990) *Research in Education Management and Policy: Retrospect and Prospect*. London: Falmer Press, pp. 101–7.

Craig-Wilson, L. (1978) *School Leadership Today*. Boston, MA: Allyn and Bacon.

Davies, L. (1987) The role of the primary school head, *Educational Management and Administration*, 15(1): 43–9.

Day, C., Johnston, D. and Whitaker, P. (1985) *Managing Primary Schools: a Professional Development Approach*. London: Harper and Row.

Dean, J. (1987) *Managing the Primary School*. London: Croom Helm.

De Bevoise, W. (1984) Synthesis of research on the principal as instructional leader, *Educational Leadership*, 41(5): 14–20.

DES (1977) *Ten Good Schools: a Secondary School Enquiry by HMI*. London: HMSO.

DES (Welsh Office) (1985) *Leadership in Primary Schools*, HMI (Wales) occasional paper. Cardiff: DES/Welsh Office.

DES (1989) *School Teachers' Pay and Conditions Document*. London: HMSO.

DES (1990) *The Teaching and Learning of Reading in Primary Schools: a Report by HMI*. London: DES.

Edwards, G. (1989) Primary headship – a widening role, *Management in Education*, 3(4): 30–2.

Foster, W. (1989) Towards a critical practice of leadership, in W. J. Smyth (ed.) *Educating Teachers: Changing the Nature of Pedagogical Knowledge*. Lewes: Falmer Press.

Glaser, B. and Strauss, A. (1968) *The Discovery of Grounded Theory*. London: Weidenfeld and Nicolson.

Greenfield, W. (ed.) (1987) *Instructional Leadership: Concepts, Issues and Controversies*. Newton, MA: Allyn and Bacon, pp. 56–73.

Hales, C. P. (1986) What do managers do? A critical review, *Journal of Management Studies*, 23(1): 88–115.

Hall, V., Mackay, H. and Morgan, C. (1986) *Headteachers at Work*. Milton Keynes: Open University Press.

Halpin, A. (1966) *Theory and Research in Administration*. New York: Macmillan.

Harling, P. (1981) School decision-making and the primary headteacher, *Education 3–13*, 8(2): 44–8.

Harvey, C. W. (1986) How primary heads spend their time, *Educational Management and Administration*, 14: 60–8.

Hellawell, D. (1991) The changing role of the head in the primary school in England, *School Organization*, 11(3): 321–37.

Hill, T. (1989) *Managing the Primary School*. London: Fulton.

Holtom, V. (1988) 'Primary school headteachers' conceptions of their professional responsibility in England and France: change and the implications', unpublished M.Phil. thesis. University of Bristol.

Huberman, M. (1988) Teacher careers and school improvement, *Journal of Curriculum Studies*, 20(2): 119–32.

Huberman, M. (1992) Critical Introduction, in M. Fullan (ed.) *Successful School Improvement*. Buckingham: Open University Press.

Hughes, M. (1976) The professional-as-administrator: the case of the secondary school head, in R. S. Peters (ed.) *The Role of the Head*. London: Routledge and Kegan Paul, pp. 50–62.

Hughes, M. (1985) Leadership in professionally staffed organisations, in M. Hughes *et al.* (eds) *Managing Education: the System and the Institution*. London: Holt, Rinehart and Winston, pp. 262–90.

Johnston, J. (1986) Gender differences in teachers' preferences for primary school leadership, *Educational Management and Administration*, 14: 219–26.

Kent, G. (1989) *The Modern Primary School Headteacher*. London: Kogan Page.

Kmetz, J. T. and Willower, D. J. (1982) Elementary school principals' work behaviour, *Educational Administration Quarterly*, 19(4): 62–78.

Lloyd, K. (1985) Management and leadership in the primary school, in M. Hughes *et al.* (eds) *Managing Education: the System and the Institution*. London: Holt, Rinehart and Winston, pp. 291–307.

MacIntyre, A. (1985) *After Virtue* (2nd edn). London: Duckworth.

Menter, I., with Muschamp, Y., Nichols, P., Pollard, A. and Ozga, J. (1995) Still carrying the can: primary school headship in the 1990's, *School Organization*, 15(3): 301–12.

Mintzberg, H. (1973) *The Nature of Managerial Work*. New York: Harper and Row.

Morgan, C., Hall, V. and Mackay, M. (1983) *The Selection of Secondary School Headteachers*. Milton Keynes: Open University Press.

Morrison, K. (1995) The deputy headteacher as the leader of the curriculum in primary schools, *School Organization*, 15(1): 65–76.

Mortimore, P. and Mortimore, J. (1991) *The Primary Head: Roles, Responsibilities and Reflections*. London: Paul Chapman.

Mortimore, P. *et al.* (1988) *School Matters: the Junior Years*. London: Open Books.

National Commission on Education (1996) *Success Against the Odds: Effective Schools in Disadvantaged Areas*. London: Routledge.

Nias, J. (1989) *Primary Teachers Talking: A Study of Teaching as Work*. London: Routledge.

Nias, J., Southworth, G. and Yeomans, R. (1989) *Staff Relationships in the Primary School*. London: Cassell.

Nias, J., Southworth, G. and Campbell, P. (1992) *Whole School Curriculum Development in Primary Schools*. Lewes: Falmer Press.

Nightingale, D. (1990) *Local Management of Schools at Work in Primary Schools*. London: Falmer Press.

OFSTED (1994) *Primary Matters*. London: OFSTED.

OFSTED (1995) *Teaching Quality: the Primary Debate*. London: OFSTED.

Open University (1988) *Managing Schools*, E323, Block 2: Leadership and decision-making in schools. Milton Keynes: Open University Press.

Paisey, A. and Paisey, A. (1987) *Effective Management in Primary Schools*. Blackwell: Oxford.

Purkey, S. and Smith, M. (1983) Effective schools: a review, *The Elementary School Journal*, 83(4): 426–52.

Purvis, J. R. and Dennison, W. F. (1993) Primary school deputy headship – has ERA and LMS changed the job? *Education 3–13*, 21(2): 15–21.

Reay, E. and Dennison, W. F. (1990) Deputy headship in primary schools – is it a real job? *Education 3–13*, 18(1): 41–6.

Reid, K., Hopkins, D. and Holly, P. (1987) *Towards the Effective School*. Oxford: Blackwell.

Reynolds, D. (1985) School Effectiveness Research: a review of the literature, *School Organization and Management Abstracts*, 1(1): 5–14.

Rutter, M., Maughan, B., Mortimore, P. and Ousten, J. (1979) *Fifteen Thousand Hours: Secondary Schools and their Effects on Children*. London: Open Books.

Sammons, P., Hillman, J. and Mortimore, P. (1995) *Key Characteristics of Effective Schools: Review of School Effectiveness Research*. London: OFSTED.

School Management Task Force (DES) (1990) *Developing School Management*. London: HMSO.

Scottish Education Department (1990) *Effective Primary Schools: a Report by HM Inspectors of Schools*. Edinburgh: HMSO.

Sedgwick, F. (1989) *Here Comes the Assembly Man: a Year in the Life of a School*. London: Falmer Press.

Sergiovanni, T. and Corbally, J. (eds) (1984) *Leadership and Organizational Culture*. Chicago: University of Illinois Press.

Sheive, L. T. and Schoenheit, M. B. (eds) (1987) *Leadership: Examining the Elusive*. Alexandria, VA: Association for Supervision and Curriculum Development.

Southworth, G. W. (1987) Primary school headteachers and collegiality, in G. W. Southworth (ed.) *Readings in Primary School Management*. Lewes: Falmer Press, pp. 61–75.

Southworth, G. W. (1990) Leadership, headship and effective primary schools, *School Organization*, 10(1): 3–16.

Southworth, G. W. (1993) School leadership and school development: reflections from research, *School Organization*, 12(2).

Southworth, G. W. (1994a) Headteachers and deputy heads: partners and cultural leaders, in G. W. Southworth (ed.) *Readings in Primary School Development*. London: Falmer Press, pp. 29–47.

Southworth, G. W. (1994b) Two heads are better than one, *Managing Schools Today*, Nov./Dec.: 3–8.

Southworth, G. W. (1995a) *Looking into Primary Headship: a Research Based Interpretation*. London: Falmer Press.

Southworth, G. W. (1995b) *Talking Heads: Voices of Experience; an Investigation into Primary Headship in the 1990s*. Cambridge: University of Cambridge Institute of Education.

Viall, P. (1984) The purposing of high-performing systems, in T. Sergiovanni and J. Corbally (eds) *Leadership and Organizational Culture*. Chicago: University of Illinois Press, pp. 85–104.

Webb, R. (1994) *The Changing Nature of Teachers' Roles and Responsibilities in Primary Schools*, Report commissioned by the Association of Teachers and Lecturers. London: ATL.

Webb, R. and Vulliamy, G. (1995) The changing role of the primary school deputy head-teacher, *School Organization*, 15(1): 53–64.

Webb, R. and Vulliamy, G. (1996) A deluge of directives: conflict between collegiality and managerialism in the post-ERA primary school, *British Educational Research Journal*, 22(4).

Weindling, D. and Earley, P. (1987) *Secondary Headship: the First Years*. Windsor: NFER-Nelson.

Whitaker, P. (1983) *The Primary Head*. London: Heinemann.

Winkley, D. (1983) An analytical view of primary school leadership, *School Organization*, 3(1): 15–26.

Wolcott, H. (1973) *The Man in the Principal's Office: an Ethnography*. Prospect Heights, IL: Waveland Press.

Yukl, G. (1975) Towards a behavioural theory of leadership, in V. Houghton *et al. The Management of Organizations and Individuals*. London: Ward Lock.

4 | Critical leadership studies

GERALD GRACE

Critical leadership studies (CLS) consists of a corpus of writings generated by writers in the UK, the USA, Canada, Australia, New Zealand and elsewhere, who have reacted in various ways against what they have seen as an emergent hierarchical, 'strong leadership' and market-dominated culture of educational leadership in their respective countries. CLS does not represent a coordinated oppositional movement but rather a series of critical responses to developments in a number of countries. However, it can be claimed that its intellectual coherence is to be found in a number of unifying themes which set out its alternative agenda for study.

An important impetus to CLS was given in 1986 with the publication of Thomas Greenfield's paper 'The decline and fall of science in educational administration'. In a wide-ranging critique of the field of educational administration, Greenfield argued that most existing studies were ahistorical, narrowly technical, mechanistic and unnecessarily boring. The study of educational administration and the study of educational leadership had become the prisoners of a 'neutered science' (Greenfield 1993: 141).

Following Hodgkinson (1978: 272), Greenfield endorsed the view that 'the central questions of administration are not scientific at all. They are philosophical', and he pointed out that the devaluation of administrative studies had impoverished understanding: 'with the elimination of values, consideration of the conduct of organizations is reduced to technicalities' (Greenfield 1993: 146).

In setting out an agenda for future enquiry, Greenfield called for new perspectives which would use interpretive and qualitative methods of enquiry; which would focus upon power, conflicts, values and moral dilemmas in educational leadership and which would examine the changing role of language and discourse in constructing new administrative 'realities'.

The need to develop a more humane study in the face of the existing limitations of the field has been powerfully elaborated in Greenfield's most recent writings:

The exclusion of values from administrative science, the exclusion of both the human and the humane, the exclusion of passion and conviction . . . does leave a residue for study – and one that is perhaps scientifically manageable. The most obvious consequence of this exclusion leaves a field that is regrettably and unnecessarily bland and boring. The difficult and divisive questions, the questions of purpose and morality, the questions arising from the necessary imposition of one person's will upon another, the questions that challenge the linking of ends and means – all these matters are set aside in a search for a pallid consensus and an illusory effectiveness. The great issues of the day in education are similarly set aside.

(Greenfield and Ribbins 1993: 164–5)

For Greenfield the critical study of educational leadership must engage with such issues and such questions.

This agenda for a new approach to the study of educational leadership has been endorsed and developed by Smyth (1989) and by Bates (1992). Smyth (1989: 4) argues against contemporary trends towards strong leadership and 'salvationist and hegemonic views of leadership' and for a study and understanding of leadership which is informed by critical theory.[1] Such critical theory will focus attention upon notions of the empowerment of all school participants; the educative potential of leadership; and the conditions necessary for the creation and sustaining of community in educational institutions.

Bates (1992) has made a powerful case that educational leadership can only be understood in the context of its wider cultural setting. In other words, there is a crucial school leadership–culture relation which defines what it is to be a leader and which goes beyond the scope of education management studies. The understanding of this leadership–culture relation requires insights from history, philosophy, religion, political economy and cultural analysis. Leadership, in this sense, is a more complex and comprehensive concept than that of management and its proper understanding requires a wider range of scholarship.

Bates points out that educational leadership often has to be exercised against a background of 'culture battles' in society. In contemporary conditions these battles involve

the battle between lifeworld and system;[2] the dangers of a commodification of culture and the emergence of repressive regimes of power and truth. These are battles that affect both individual and collective futures. Schools are centrally concerned with such futures and those who would exercise leadership in such times need not only an understanding of such issues but also of ways in which they can be articulated through the message systems of the school.

(Bates 1992: 19)

For Bates, therefore, the essential point about educational leadership is that it 'involves the making and articulating of choices, the location of oneself within the cultural struggles of the times as much in the cultural battles of the school as in the wider society' (p. 20).

In these ways, CLS has been constituted as a new framework for the understanding of educational leadership. It is a framework which not only attempts to move attention from educational management to educational leadership, but which also articulates new and emancipatory notions of what such leadership could be.

Transformation and ethical leadership

In calling for new thinking about educational leadership and resistance to its commodification in management culture, Foster (1989) has set out a radical agenda for educators. For Foster, 'leadership is at its heart a critical practice', and this involves educational leaders in the necessary practice of reflective and critical thinking about the culture and organization of particular institutions and about the ways in which this culture may need to change.

There are, however, important differences between the celebration of a culture of critical reflectiveness in the literature and the practice of critical reflectiveness in contemporary conditions of schooling. Various impediments to leadership as critical practice exist. Indeed, a powerful argument can be made that the contemporary conditions of schooling in many societies involve an *intensification* of work for headteachers, teachers, pupils and governors, so that the spaces and opportunities for critical reflection upon practice have been seriously curtailed.

Closely related to Foster's concept of leadership as critical practice is his notion of leadership as transformative. From this perspective, the leader works with others to obtain transformations of undesirable features of schooling culture and practice. These features might be the existence of racism and sexism in educational practice; the existence of prejudice against particular religious or regional groups; or against those with a range of disabilities and disadvantages. The leadership project is to attempt a transformation of culture and social relations in a particular institution, not as an act of individual, charismatic leadership but as a shared enterprise of the teachers, the pupils and the community. Transformative leadership involves considerable social skills of advocacy, intergroup relations, team building and inspiration without domination.

For the English schooling system, these ideas are radical and challenging. English schooling culture is familiar with the idea of transformative leadership but, in general, related to an individual and charismatic 'headmaster'. Transformation has been the outcome of individual, hierarchical and patriarchal forms of school leadership for the greater part of English educational history. The idea that transformative leadership could be exercised by a community of leaders rather than by a formal and hierarchical leader would itself require a significant transformation of existing consciousness among teachers, parents and pupils. This is not to say that such change could not occur but to observe that it would involve a profound reorientation of existing expectations and concepts, and that it would directly challenge the emergent strong leadership culture of the 1980s and 1990s in English political life. If transformative leadership of this kind is to be a credible alternative to traditional concepts of transformative leadership, then educational and professional development programmes would be necessary for its realization among headteachers and aspirant headteachers. In short, new forms of academic and professional education would have to resource new forms of transformative leadership in the schools.[3]

Drawing upon the work of Fay (1987), Foster argues that existing educational leaders have a responsibility to use education as a means of empowerment for all:

This educative aspect of leadership is intended to have citizens and participants begin to question aspects of their previous narratives, to grow and develop because of this questioning, and to begin to consider alternative ways of ordering their lives. The educative aspect, in other words, attempts to raise followers' consciousness about their own social conditions and in so doing to allow them, as well as the 'leader', to consider the possibility of other ways of ordering their social history.

(Foster 1989: 54)

From this perspective a responsibility of educational leadership is to ensure that all members of the institution have access to powerful information; have spaces and opportunities to debate policy and practice; and are freed as much as possible from the communication impediments of hierarchy, formality and status consciousness. The educative leader attempts to establish the conditions for dialogue, participation and respect for persons and their ideas. If present schooling arrangements limit, in various ways, dialogue, participation and respect for persons, then there are serious ethical issues to be addressed in a framework which goes beyond management culture. It does not seem inappropriate, in this context, that the leadership of an educational institution should be defined as primarily 'educative' in this whole institutional sense rather than primarily managerial or executive.

It seems also appropriate that ethical considerations should be a prime responsibility for educational leaders. Foster's view is that

Leadership in general must maintain an ethical focus which is oriented towards democratic values within a community. This has to do with the meaning of ethics historically – as a search for the good life of a community . . . Ethics here refers to a more comprehensive construct than just individual behaviour; rather it implicates us and how we as a moral community live our communal lives.

(p. 55)

This emphasis upon the ethical commitments and responsibilities of educational leadership is one that is familiar to English schooling culture. Notions of the good life and of education as one of the means for attaining this in an ethical sense are strong in the historical discourse of English schooling both in the state and private sectors. Notions of moral community and of the particular responsibilities of head-teachers for generating such community in schooling similarly have a long history in English cultural life. What is much less established in the English tradition is that such ethical considerations should be shaped by democratic values.

It is an important part of the agenda of critical leadership studies that democratic values should not only permeate schooling but should transform the nature of leadership itself.

Schooling and organizational democracy

English schooling culture in the twentieth century has always had, at its heart, a major paradox and contradiction. Formally designated as the cultural agency for 'making democracy work' and involved, at specific periods, with explicit pedagogical projects to enhance education for citizenship, its own practice has remained largely undemocratic. Among a complex of reasons for this lack of democratic practice in school life, the influence of the hierarchical 'headmaster tradition' has been significant. While this tradition may have modified over time into more consultative forms, the fact remains that most headteachers are the operative school leaders and that few examples exist of serious organizational democracy involving major decision making by headteachers in association with teachers, pupils and other school staff. This lack of democratic culture and practice in English school life, it can be claimed, is itself a mediated form of the historical hidden curriculum of English political and social culture. Despite an early achievement of formal political democracy in England, social and cultural forms have remained pervaded by aristocratic and hierarchical values, in particular the notion that there is a leadership class. The hidden curriculum of English culture teaches its citizens that this leadership class *will* emerge as the natural leader of society by reasons of its confidence and its relevant cultural capital and that democratic processes will not seriously affect this outcome.[4] In a similar way, English headteachers have also historically constituted a leadership class in schooling and the idea that schools could be run 'properly' by forms of organizational democracy has always seemed far-fetched and improbable.

It was to challenge such aristocratic assumptions that Pat White of the London Institute of Education made two crucial contributions to the literature of critical leadership studies. In her 1982 paper, 'Democratic perspectives on the training of headteachers', White argued that headteachers should be given training opportunities to reflect upon their role in relation to the enhancement of democratic values and democratic practice in schools. For White, if the political ideal of participatory democracy in English society was ever to move beyond the level of rhetoric, then a prior educational practice must lay the foundations for its active realization. This would involve a new culture and ethos in English schools to be generated by a new form of democratic educational leadership:

> In an institution run on democratic principles there should be increased opportunities for individuals to exercise 'genuine leadership'. In saying that I am assuming that by such leaders people have in mind dynamic individuals who are able either to describe ends, or strategies for achieving ends, in such a way that other people are inspired to think that they might be possible to achieve. Clearly the organization of the school on democratic lines will present ample opportunities for such 'inspirational' leadership without tying it to a person or an office.
>
> (White 1982: 75)

This notion of organizational democracy should, in White's view, extend beyond simply the involvement of teachers and other adults in educational decision-making, to include the pupils:

> The democratic head will also be keen that pupils should take a more active role within the school, both in the management of their own and others' learning and in the organization and running of the school itself . . . because for pupils such participation will be a part of their earliest formal political education.
>
> (p. 77)

These ideas were developed in greater detail by White's subsequent text *Beyond Domination* (1983) which elaborated arguments for participatory democracy in a range of social institutions. Making the interesting observation that among the few writers making serious cases for participatory democracy, women were prominent, White (p. 5) asked:

> Is it that women are drawn to explore theories which plan for the control of power so that everyone can flourish and live autonomous, morally responsible lives, because, whatever their country or social class they are likely to have experienced domination in many forms?

The question of gender relations and consequences for power relations and for *thinking* about power relations is an important constituent of critical leadership studies, and it will be examined in a later section of this chapter. For the present, it can be noted that Pat White's 'unashamedly radical' thesis of 1983 went beyond conceptions of the democratic headteacher to consider future scenarios where even the role would not exist:

> It might be expected that a good part of this chapter would be an elaboration of the role of the headteacher in such a [democratic] society, but this is not so. The reason is simple. There would not be headteachers, as we know them, and therefore special heads' training programmes would not be required. In a participatory democracy there would be training for the whole staff in school organization and the role of the 'head' would be radically different . . . for instance there may be administrative chairpersons with a limited term of office.
>
> (p. 118)

The proposition that the role of the headteacher, as historically constituted in English schooling would, in the conditions of real participatory democracy, give way to elected, administrative chairpersons is as radical an antithesis to English headship traditions as can be imagined. Between Edward Thring's robust articulation of the headmaster tradition, namely 'I am supreme here and will brook no opposition' and Pat White's advocacy for the elected chairperson of the future, an immense cultural divide exists. It is a divide between a schooling culture marked by hierarchy and patriarchy and one which aspires to be democratic and participative. The domination of English schools by their headteachers has a long history. The forms in which that domination is expressed may have changed over time and may appear now in modern management and chief executive modes. Despite surface change, however, power relations can be remarkably constant and, as White (1982: 75) puts it, 'authoritarianism need not have an ugly face and yet it is authoritarianism for all that.'

Any project which attempts to transform the authoritarian legacy of English school headship has to recognize that it is dealing with a strong historical formation that will not easily yield to notions of real participatory democracy (as opposed to rhetorical endorsement). If such a project is to be successful it has, above all, to refute pervasive notions of both the technical necessity of hierarchical leadership and the impracticability of ideas of organizational democracy in schools.

It is precisely these objections to organizational democracy in schools which have been addressed by Rizvi (1989). Rizvi examines the arguments that hierarchical leadership is inevitable in complex organizations in the context of Michel's (1958) much quoted 'iron law of oligarchy'. He also critically analyses the case that the existence of hierarchical leadership and control is necessary for the technical efficiency of an institution.

Rizvi's counterthesis, which constitutes his 'defence of organizational democracy' consists of two major arguments. The first is that

> The iron law of oligarchy or indeed the 'inner logic' of bureaucratic organizations need not be regarded as inescapable. It is only under certain structural conditions that bureaucracy or oligarchy presents itself as natural and necessary – there is no reason to suppose that under different conditions, human relationships might not be ordered differently.
>
> (Rizvi 1989: 222)

Rizvi's second argument is that the idea that hierarchical decision making is more efficient is, in general, untrue:

> Many recent organizational thinkers, such as Fischer and Siriaani (1984) and Crouch and Heller (1983) have gathered a great deal of empirical evidence to suggest that participation is a necessary condition for bringing about greater 'efficiency' . . . Participation induces, they claim, enterprise, initiative, imagination and the confidence to experiment.
>
> (p. 216)

For schooling, this argument implies that the realization of a school's mission statement is more likely to be achieved where a headteacher uses high levels of participation rather than hierarchical enactment.

Rizvi recognizes that the introduction of more developed forms of organizational democracy in schools will be a slow and locally variant process depending upon existing historical and cultural experience: 'each situation has to be examined in the context of its own unique historical and social features. Changes can only come about when the individuals who belong to a particular organization can see the point in changing' (p. 227). In coming to such a decision (or not) headteachers, teachers and community members will be influenced by local and national conditions and trends in the wider society. However, Rizvi makes the important point that much more use should be made of comparative studies in education which demonstrate the strengths and weaknesses of organizational democracy in schools in different national and cultural settings.[5]

An important literature is emerging within CLS which suggests that many of the 'inevitabilities' of leadership theory and practice are an outcome of masculine and patriarchal assumptions rather than of some immutable features of these phenomena. In other words, a growing and significant feminist critique of educational leadership exists which challenges the conventional masculine wisdom about the nature of leadership.

The feminist critique

The feminist critique of patriarchal education management studies and culture was given impetus by the work of Charol Shakeshaft, Chairperson of the Department of Administration and Policy Studies at Hofstra University, New York. In an influential text first published in 1987 and revised and updated in 1989, Shakeshaft argued that administrative and management studies in education had, in effect, been gender blind. What had claimed to be a comprehensive field of study was in fact only a study of male educational leadership. Shakeshaft offered her text, *Women in Educational Administration*, as a contribution to the critical extension of this limited field:

> This is not a book on how to make it in administration, nor is it a book instructing women to be more like men. If anything, it is a book that asks us to question the assumptions of the so-called 'self-help' tracts that have first analysed how men manage and then urged women to do the same. I am saying something quite different in this book. The effective woman does not copy the effective man, nor does she find that what works for him, necessarily works for her.
>
> (Shakeshaft 1989: 12)

In calling for more research into the differences between the ways that women and men manage schools, an essential part of the thesis of *Women in Educational Administration* is that there are already indications that a 'female culture' of educational leadership and management exists with distinctive characteristics. These characteristics include greater interpersonal and care sensitivities; a strong and central focus upon the quality of teaching and learning and of relationships with children and students; and a more democratic and participatory style of decision making, with different conceptions of relations with the wider community, of the use of power and of the nature of educational leadership.

While recognizing that notions of male culture and female culture applied to educational leadership do not refer to entirely distinct categories (i.e. cultural overlap does exist), Shakeshaft nevertheless contends that women approach the leadership and management task in education with different sets of priorities, values and modes of working. Her proposition is that 'this female world exists in schools and is reflected in the ways women work in school (p. 196). If this is the case, then women headteachers in England might be expected to encounter sharper professional dilemmas than their male colleagues, as English school culture moves towards a line management, business executive and market commodity style of operation. Women headteachers in primary schools might, in particular, feel a growing disjuncture between their interpersonal/pupil relationships and their increasing preoccupation with management and financial control issues more sharply than male headteachers.

While Charol Shakeshaft has characterized the distinctive aspects of a female culture of education management, Jill Blackmore (1989) has concentrated upon a feminist critique of educational leadership. Blackmore's critique of the field is more radical and more fundamental than that of Shakeshaft, because she calls for a paradigm change in theory and in discourse and not simply for a change in the focus of research:

> Feminist theory does not ask merely to include women as objects in the patriarchal discourse, in which sameness is emphasised rather than difference. It rapidly becomes evident that it is impossible to incorporate or 'add on' a feminist perspective. Rather, a feminist critique ultimately leads to the need to reformulate the methodologies, criteria of validity and merit . . . Feminists demand not just equality, but that they become the subjects and objects of an alternative, autonomous discourse which chooses its own measures and criteria.
>
> (Blackmore 1989: 120)

For Blackmore, a feminist reconstruction of the concept of an educational leader is necessary. Such leadership would involve a move away from notions of power and control over others towards a leadership defined as the ability to act with others. Leadership would involve being at the centre of a group rather than at a hierarchical distance from it. A feminist discourse and practice in educational institutions would, from this viewpoint, encourage caring and reciprocal relations to be at the heart of organizational culture. In recognizing the qualities required for educational leadership, community activities and child rearing experience should have equal status with male experience in the formal and public sphere of education. Educational leadership reconstituted in these ways would, Blackmore argues, hold out the possibility that schools might become, for the first time, fully human communities for the education of young people. However, it is recognized that the construction of this alternative culture for schooling and leadership faces major external cultural and political impediments, as

> This would require going against the renewed push towards more masculinist notions of leadership embedded in corporate managerialism, the impetus for current restructuring of secondary and tertiary education, which equates efficiency and effectiveness with organisational rationality and hierarchy.
>
> (p. 124)

While Blackmore's specific references are to educational developments in Australia, they apply with equal force to changes in educational policy and practice in England. If there is a feminist project in English schooling to reconstitute the nature of educational leadership, then it faces not only the accumulated weight of a historical, patriarchal tradition but also the potency of new forms of 'masculine' corporate management.

Ozga (1993: 2) argues that:

> Education management, like management elsewhere, is largely done by men and is therefore defined by men. Such a definition may be very restricted: at best it may be inappropriate for women; at worst it is hostile to the fostering of management qualities which may represent more ethical and also more effective ways of managing people – and managing people is what educational management is primarily about.

For Ozga a crucial part of the feminist project for reconstructing the nature of educational management and leadership involves the collection of accounts from women with such responsibilities who are able to demonstrate that different cultural styles exist which are based upon different sets of values.

Adler, Laney and Packer (1993) have pointed out that women in educational management are not a homogeneous group and that analytical distinctions have to be made between 'women in management' and 'feminists in management'. From this perspective, a defining quality of feminism is a resistance to hierarchy and authoritarianism and a search for shared decision making. The possibility for realizing feminist principles in current educational arrangements is recognized as a difficult and contradictory project:

> We see a contradiction between being a feminist and being a manager in education today, although not between being a feminist and working with a feminist

management style. There is an inherent contradiction between maintaining feminist principles and holding a powerful position in a linear hierarchy. A manager,
by definition, is in a high position on the linear scale. Feminism is wary of
pyramidal and linear models and looks to alternatives to hierarchies, to providing multi-dimensional ways of working.

(Adler *et al.* 1993: 135)

Nevertheless, for all the difficulties which beset the feminist project for the reconsti-
tution of leadership and management in English education, Adler *et al.* argue that current trends in management outside of the schooling system are moving in the direction
of principles of feminist management rather than of hierarchical and confrontational
patriarchal styles.

Educational leadership as a moral art

In *The Philosophy of Leadership* (1983), Hodgkinson raises the interesting suggestion
that educational leaders have responsibilities which go beyond financial audit, teaching quality audit and learning outcomes audit, to include value audit:

> For the leader in the praxis situation there is an obligation, a philosophical obli-
> gation, to conduct where necessary a value audit. This is an analysis of the value
> aspects of the problem he [*sic*] is facing . . . It is the careful reflection upon such
> questions . . . prior to administrative action, which is the hallmark and warrant
> of leadership responsibility.

(Hodgkinson 1983: 207)

It is necessary therefore for educational leaders to demonstrate some understanding
of moral complexity and some capacity for making explicit the relations between
values and proposed actions in educational institutions.

The model for educational leadership is that of practical idealism, i.e. a capacity to
interrelate technical competence and moral complexity. Failure to achieve such a relationship leads, in Hodgkinson's view, to formal educational leaders becoming simply
careerists, politicians or technicians. Hodgkinson is well aware that contemporary
developments in education policy and practice in a number of societies give legitima-
tion to leadership concepts other than that of practical idealism. When institutional
survival is in the balance, an awareness of moral complexity may not appear as the
first requirement for leadership.

While recognizing the force of these contextual arguments, Hodgkinson (1991)
nevertheless argues that, properly understood, educational leadership has to be seen
as a moral art:

> It is not too much to say that, properly conceived, education can be considered
> as the long sought after 'moral equivalent for war'. Certainly the conduct of its
> business and the leadership of its organization should be more than mere prag-
> matism, positivism, philistinism and careerism.

(Hodgkinson 1991: 164–5)

Sergiovanni (1992) has also argued for the importance of moral leadership in
education, making a case that the moral school will be also the effective school. For

Sergiovanni the desired goal for publicly provided education in America is the creation of the 'virtuous school' characterized by 'a covenant of shared values' and by an ethos of caring and respect for persons. Leadership in such a school would be a demonstration of stewardship and of a manifest serving of the common good – 'in the virtuous school, the leader would be seen as a servant' (p. 115). The religious discourse and imagery of Sergiovanni's thesis is very clear, and in particular his construct of the leader as servant is one that is central to the culture of religious schooling, at least in its formal rhetoric.

As part of the literature of critical leadership studies, Hodgkinson challenges education management studies to recognize the centrality of philosophical and moral issues in education. Sergiovanni challenges its rational and secular discourse with a discourse derived from a much longer religious tradition.

Educational leadership as a 'vocation to serve' is not a concept or a discourse routinely found in textbooks of education management studies. Neither is it found in the rational and secular discourse of critical leadership studies. However, it is alive in the discourse of many religious cultures, Christian, Jewish, Islamic and multi-faith. Religious-educational cultures of many traditions carry messages about leadership which stand in a critical relation to those currently dominant or rising to dominance in secular culture. These traditions give pre-eminence to the spiritual and moral responsibilities of leadership, to notions of vocation in education and to ideas of commitment relatively independent of reward or status. The extent to which these ideas are realized in practice by the leaders of religious schools is an empirical question of great interest and relevance for the various faith communities and others. However, the very existence of a religious culture of leadership, when applied to education, provides a sharp antithesis to contemporary constructs of the principal or the headteacher as chief executive of a schooling corporation.

Notes

1 Brian Fay (1975: 103) argues that in its educative role, critical social theory tries to enlighten social participants so that 'coming to see themselves and their social situation in a new way, they themselves can decide to alter the conditions which they find repressive'. One of the aspirations of critical theory is to raise the consciousness of social participants while respecting the intellectual autonomy of those participants, i.e. to avoid programmed 'solutions'.

2 'Lifeworld' refers to culture, values, interests and commitments; 'system' 'to those activities within society that are organized through the medium of money and power (markets and bureaucracies)' (Bates 1992: 9).

3 Similar points have been made by White (1982, 1983) and by Al-Khalifa (1989).

4 Green (1991) argues that this aristocratic and leadership culture is sustained by a separate system of public (i.e. private) schooling in England: 'The public schools are the most notorious of Britain's old institutional anachronisms and the most out of place in a modern, supposedly democratic society. They are probably the feature of our education which most baffles foreign observers. Even the name is incomprehensible to most people, apparently saying the exact opposite of what it actually means.

In England, a uniquely prestigious and influential private sector exists whose main purpose is to provide an intensive education for the children of the upper middle class which gives far better access to positions of influence, power and affluence than do other schools' (pp. 14–15).

5 Comparative studies of organizational democracy in schooling are, as yet, a relatively undeveloped field of enquiry.

References

Adler, S., Laney, J. and Packer, M. (1993) *Managing Women: Feminism and Power in Educational Management*. Buckingham: Open University Press.

Al-Khalifa, E. (1989) Management by halves: women teachers and school management, in H. De Lyon and F. Migniuolo (eds) *Women Teachers: Issues and Experiences*. Milton Keynes: Open University Press.

Bates, R. (1992) Leadership and school culture. Paper presented at the University of Seville, December 1992. Faculty of Education, Deakin University, Australia.

Blackmore, J. (1989) Educational leadership: a feminist critique and reconstruction, in J. Smyth (ed.) *Critical Perspectives on Educational Leadership*. London: Falmer Press.

Crouch, C. and Heller, F. (eds) (1983) *International Yearbook of Organizational Democracy*. New York: John Wiley.

Fay, B. (1975) *Social Theory and Political Practice*. London: Allen and Unwin.

Fay, B. (1987) *Critical Social Science*. Cambridge: Polity Press.

Fischer, F. and Siriaani, C. (1984) *Critical Studies in Organization and Bureaucracy*. Philadelphia, PA: Temple University Press.

Foster, W. (1989) Towards a critical practice of leadership, in J. Smyth (ed.) *Critical Perspectives on Educational Leadership*. London: Falmer Press.

Green, A. (1991) The peculiarities of English education, in Education Group II (ed.) *Education Limited: Schooling and Training and the New Right since 1979*. London: Unwin Hyman.

Greenfield, T. (1993) The decline and fall of science in educational administration, in T. Greenfield and P. Ribbins, *Greenfield on Educational Administration: Towards a Humane Science*. London: Routledge. Originally published in 1986.

Greenfield, T. and Ribbins, P. (eds) (1993) *Greenfield on Educational Administration: Towards a Humane Science*. London: Routledge.

Hodgkinson, C. (1978) The failure of organisation and administrative theory, *McGill Journal of Education*, 13(3): 271–8.

Hodgkinson, C. (1983) *The Philosophy of Leadership*. Oxford: Basil Blackwell.

Hodgkinson, C. (1991) *Educational Leadership: the Moral Art*. Albany, NY: State University of New York Press.

Michel, R. (1958) *Political Parties*. Chicago: Free Press.

Ozga, J. (ed.) (1993) *Women in Educational Management*. Buckingham: Open University Press.

Rizvi, F. (1989) In defence of organizational democracy, in J. Smyth (ed.) *Critical Perspectives on Educational Leadership*. London: Falmer Press.

Sergiovanni, T. (1992) *Moral Leadership: Getting to the Heart of School Improvement*. San Francisco, CA: Jossey-Bass.

Shakeshaft, C. (1989) *Women in Educational Administration*. Newbury Park, CA: Corwin Press.

Smyth, J. (ed.) (1989) *Critical Perspectives on Educational Leadership*. London: Falmer Press.

White, P. (1982) Democratic perspectives on the training of headteachers, *Oxford Review of Education*, 8(1): 69–82.

White, P. (1983) *Beyond Domination: an Essay in the Political Philosophy of Education*. London: Routledge and Kegan Paul.

5 | Women in educational management*

VALERIE HALL

Introduction

Compared to the United States, research on women in educational management in Britain is still in its infancy. Ask Shakeshaft's (1989) question, 'Does this research or theory include or explain the experiences of women?' of educational administration in Britain and the answer is a resounding no. The sterility of the field is well illustrated in Hough's (1986) review of a leading professional journal (*Educational Management and Administration*). He found it to be as androcentric as its counterparts in the United States had been found to be. He defines androcentrism as viewing the world and shaping reality through a male lens. According to this view the experiences of men and women educators are assumed to be the same. As a result research on males is deemed appropriate for generalising to the female experience. Of the 140 articles analysed by Hough, only five or six indicated strong gender awareness and thoroughly explored gender related issues. Eighty-eight per cent had male authors, 10 per cent female and 2 per cent joint. Although he detected a trend towards more articles showing improved awareness of gender issues, the subsequent five years' issues show 70 per cent still to have male authors only and relatively few address gender issues.

The absence of women authors reflects, no doubt, the relative absence of women from academic life or their more humble positions in the research hierarchy. Lyon and West (1992) show their under-representation in polytechnics and universities and their concentration in the lower ranks of both hierarchies. While questioning the definition of productivity being used to judge academic output, the authors acknowledge the effects of a multitude of factors combining to create the glass ceiling through which it is so hard for women to penetrate and which, potentially, limits their publication rate. [. . .]

* This material has been edited and originally appeared as 'Women in educational management: a review of research in Britain'.

The failure to include gender issues in discussions of educational management extends well beyond the journal pages. Analyses of school leadership in Britain from 1986 on fail to integrate gender as a relevant concept. When it is considered (e.g. Hall *et al.* 1986; Torrington and Weightman 1987; Weindling and Earley 1987) it is an aside rather than a significant contribution to a conceptualisation of school leadership. [. . .]

The association of one set of qualities with 'masculine' or 'feminine' remains unquestioned and is treated as unproblematic. Even Jones (1987), writing as a successful senior woman educator, gives no more than a passing reference to gender as a factor in leadership of tomorrow's schools. In most cases a plea for additional research is made, but gender continues to be treated as a separate issue rather than a powerful tool for restructuring conceptualisations of school life and leadership.

[. . .]

The focus of this chapter is on research published since 1980. Most of it relates to women in school management, with only a few references to women in further and higher education. Studies fall mainly into two categories. The first re-examines the concept of career (including selection, promotion and training) to take account of women's experiences. What, for example, are the psychological and institutional factors that deter women from assuming positions of school leadership? The second looks for evidence of a typical female style of management and raises questions about the equation of management with men. Are there sex differences in the performance of leadership? Do women bring something different to the role of leader compared to men?

Overall the research is mainly descriptive and based on small samples. Described in terms of Schmuck's (1987) developmental model to trace thinking about gender as a relevant concept in educational administration, it is very much at stage four, that is women are seen as oppressed by institutional processes which treat them differently. The 'New Scholarship' which constitutes Schmuck's fifth stage (in which gender is a primary area of concentration) is only just emerging from the wings. As a result much of the research that has been done in Britain is compensatory and looks at women who have achieved roles primarily held by men. Exceptions are work by Evetts (1990), Powney and Weiner (1991), Acker (1992), all of whom reject the notion of men as the norm. [. . .]

Together with Shakeshaft, Schmuck has set the agenda for research into gender and educational administration in both the United States and Britain. Both review a range of theories purporting to explain the under-representation of women in senior educational posts. Shakeshaft (1989) holds firmly to the view that the most satisfactory model is the one which sees male dominance leading to conditions that keep women from advancing into positions of power and prestige. But, as she points out, the same data can be explained in a variety of ways. Ball (1987) and Byrne White (1987) demonstrate this with their different theoretical perspectives on evidence of women's under-representation in management posts in schools in Britain. In spite of attempting to incorporate a gender dimension into his analysis of the micropolitics of schools, Ball's discussion is restricted to a reiteration of the organisational constraints argument (Schmuck 1986) and the identification of group affiliation as a collective response to something (unequal promotion opportunities) that is not otherwise defined as a valid concern. His profiles of 'women who make it' are drawn mainly from the United States or outside education. Byrne Whyte attempts a four part typology of women's attitudes to promotion, influenced first by organisational and work culture structures that accept or reject women and second, by the character of women's relationships with their male partner. Having explored the 'moral superiority' view (that women prefer to avoid competition, value co-operative social and working relationships and find hierarchical structures antipathetical), she concludes that women's under-representation at senior levels is a consequence of their position in the workforce which leads to the perception that they are not suited to leadership roles. This in turn is combined with variations in their personal relationships which influence the degree of support available to them in furthering their careers. She is critical of the tendency of most explanations to assume women to be a homogeneous group, thereby failing to do justice to 'the variety of human relationships and responses among members of the same sex to personal and professional demands' (p. 181). Acker's (1980) feminist analysis of women in academic life points to the tendency to identify just one specifically sociological variable (family) relating to women academics to explain their under-representation at senior levels of the academic hierarchy. In her view it combines with a deficit model of women which operates to make it impossible for them to be acceptable or even visible within the androcentric culture of academia.

Outside education, Marshall's (1984) research on women managers as travellers in a male world has contributed significantly to extending the theoretical boundaries. Having considered and rejected a purely 'reformist' viewpoint (in which women are encouraged to aspire to a management world defined in male terms) and a purely 'radical' perspective (all men are oppressors) she develops a third theoretical position that culls from both. This is based on the principles of 'agency' and 'communion' as strategies for dealing with uncertainty. She distinguishes these two orientations in terms of their aims and characteristics. Agentic principles relate to control and independence with an emphasis on achieving change and mastery through 'doing'. Communion approaches, in contrast, value union and interdependence, adaptiveness and 'being'. Application of these principles to management leads her to redefine it in terms of the integration of the two, neither the exclusive property of either men or women. While many of her findings about women's exclusion from the masculine world of management echo the school research, the question remains whether the organisational cultures which are the focus of her study (retail and publishing) are similar enough to education to make comparisons feasible and useful.

Women teachers' careers

Setting the agenda

If women were promoted in proportion to their numbers in the teaching workforce and assuming they are no less capable than men, they would hold at least 60 per cent of senior posts in schools and colleges, instead of the minority position they hold now. Only in LEAs has there been a notable increase in the number of women senior managers. In 1985 there were no women chief education officers. In 1990 there were 12 out of 116 and more being appointed. While this might reflect equal opportunities policies coming to fruition (in a way that has not been evident in other areas of education) it may equally reflect the envisaged demise of LEAs, making them a less attractive career proposition for men. If this is the case, the concomitant lowering of status means that it is more likely that women will be considered for senior posts and the risk of appointing one more easily taken. There is an interesting parallel in elementary schools in the United States where, Fullan (1991) notes but does not seek to explain, the fact that fewer men are entering or heading such schools at a time when they are seen increasingly as undesirable workplaces.

As well as being under-represented at senior level, women's promotion position has deteriorated over the past 20 years. During the 1980s explanations of their differential position proliferated, with an increasing focus on how their experience of career differed from that of men. This interest paralleled the shift of research focus into teachers' careers from large scale surveys such as Hilsum and Start's (1974) to life history accounts such as Sikes *et al.* (1985). Both strands were androcentric in that they failed to question the concept of career in the light of women's experiences although both also referred to differences in promotion opportunities. Sikes *et al.*'s life history approach opened up the way for questioning definitions of career which assumes 'a succession of related jobs, arranged in a hierarchy of prestige through which persons move in an ordered, predictable sequence' (p. 127). They postulated for both men and women an alternative version of career which is subjective, takes a whole life view and is concerned with a teacher's on-going development and identity.

Acker (1989), in contrast, makes gender the central theme of her book on teachers' careers. She sees her task to map the variations in promotions, subjects taught, administrative responsibilities and daily experience. In this way she aims to rectify a situation in which 'many possible questions about teachers' careers and experiences have not yet been answered or even asked, because the dominant model has limited the scope of our collective imagination' (p. 18). One example demonstrates well how the focus of attention has shifted. Hilsum and Start's 1974 study found a strikingly low promotion orientation among women teachers, based on their evidence that only 16 per cent of women teachers interviewed wanted headships compared to 50 per cent of men. Apart from their very small interview sample (only 69 women and 71 men) they fail to question why this might be so. In 1980, a National Union of Teachers' study of promotion and the woman teacher analysed 2,829 returns from women teachers and concluded that 'Female teachers, both married and single, show a high degree of career orientation and would welcome the challenge and opportunity of promotion' (p. 34). In common with Davidson (1985) they scotched a whole range of myths about women teachers which previous research had failed to challenge.

In the United States, Shakeshaft (1989) took the debate about women teachers' motivation still further by questioning explanations of women managers' behaviour based on male paradigms of leadership and effectiveness. In her view, given the constraints on women's careers, their 'promotion orientation' is bound to emerge as lower if it is interpreted within this paradigm. The concepts need to be redefined if they are accurately to reflect women's experiences. Martini *et al.* (1984) carried out a comparative study of men and women teachers in ILEA to provide an explanation of their different application rates and attitudes to promotion. The authors concluded that women teachers have a different rather than lower orientation to promotion. Women weigh more carefully the benefits of their present job against what promotion might bring and are more discriminating in their applications (p. 8).

Grant (1989) set out to celebrate the success of women who had achieved deputy headship in comprehensive schools. Her interviews with 38 women deputy heads in one LEA led her to question the concept of aspiration levels as a static and objective measure of career intentions, as based on male experiences (p. 41). Her proposal for an alternative model of 'career' contrasts with the continuing use of an androcentric model in Spencer *et al*.'s (1987) report of interviews with six women in senior positions in further and higher education. They view their respondents' careers from a perspective which highlights the masculine environment of further and higher education and how women adapt in order to succeed.

The focus has shifted from measuring women's career performance alongside men's in teaching to interpreting women teachers' careers within a new paradigm that has women rather than men as its starting point. This shift is best exemplified in the work of Evetts (1990), whose analysis of women in primary teaching supports an alternative model of career. Her interviews with 25 primary headteachers focus on how individuals have constructed and developed their careers and what having a career means to the individuals involved. She describes primary women teachers' careers as characterised by strategic compromises to negotiate the constraints and make use of the occupational advantages of teaching. She uses the concepts of 'local primary teaching labour markets' and 'occupational culture' as relevant to explanations of women's promotion prospects in primary schools. The concepts are relatively unexplored in research using a gender perspective at secondary school level apart from a small scale study by Cunnison (1985) that identifies the male dominated culture of the secondary school as an obstacle to women's promotion. In Evetts' view, the combination of the characteristics of the occupational culture of teaching and processes that encourage and discourage teachers from seeking promotion combine with individual teachers' subjective attempts to construct their careers.

The new research agenda for women's promotion experiences in teaching is effectively summarised and extended in Al-Khalifa's (1989) assertion of a convergence of masculinity and management roles. In common with Shakeshaft she discerns an association between theories of organisational leadership and masculinity which deter women from identifying with the role of manager. Alternative models of career need to be accompanied by a reconceptualisation of management to include women's experience and interpretation (p. 92). At this stage of limited research the proposition remains unsupported by empirical evidence.

Research that has been carried out into women teachers' career and promotion patterns falls into two strands. On the one hand are small and large scale surveys, either exclusively questionnaire or combining interviews and questionnaires (NUT 1980; ILEA 1984; AMMA 1985; Davidson 1985: Hunter 1987; Earley and Weindling 1988; AUT 1989; Weightman 1989; Jones 1990). Both the Earley and Weindling and Weightman accounts are based on larger surveys of school managers (Weindling and Earley (1987 and Torrington and Weightman 1987) in which women as managers was not taken as a specific focus for study. Conclusions about their different career paths and experiences are extrapolated rather than integrated with the main substance of the report. The same is true of Morgan *et al*.'s (1983) study of the selection of secondary heads which includes a section on the experiences of women applying for headship. Evetts' (1991) follow-up study also includes women rather than making them the exclusive focus. All the others have women teachers as their central focus but are mainly descriptive and atheoretical, aiming to paint a picture of where women are in teaching compared to men.

The other strand of research uses structured and semi-structured interviews, including the collection of life history accounts, with small samples of women teachers (Williams 1981; Spencer *et al.* 1987; Grant 1989; Evetts 1991; Powney and Weiner

1991). The interview method allows in-depth exploration of women teachers' own perceptions of their promotion experiences, choices and strategies within the constraints imposed by the historical, social and occupational structures that shape their lives. Ozga (1992) presents a range of interesting accounts by women who are senior managers in education but they are accounts only, not based on research nor analysed and interpreted. Powney and Weiner's study includes men and women since their interest is in the strategies used and obstacles faced by women and black managers in educational institutions.

All these studies share a concern to depict and offer explanations for women's position in education management. Explanations of women's under-representation are mainly in terms of organisational constraints, demonstrated particularly in the barriers to promotion constituted by current arrangements for selection, re-entry and management development. A fourth barrier emerges in some of these studies as an important component of explanations of women in education management; the conceptualisation of management as masculine and schools, particularly secondary schools, as representing masculine cultures.

In contrast, the studies based on interview data attempt to extend the theoretical boundaries by questioning traditional concepts of career, motivation and labour markets. What is not apparent in the research literature are the previously popular 'deficiency' explanations of women's under-representation. These are summarised in Davidson's (1985) 'unfriendly myths about women teachers': they contribute less than men, want promotion less, are less well qualified, have less experience, are less committed to the job, are less respected as teachers by pupils. All the studies cited above provide evidence that refutes one or more of these myths and points to alternative explanations of women's position in educational management.

The empirical studies challenge the 'unfriendly myths' mainly by identifying the organisational barriers to promotion. They show that getting selected constitutes a primary obstacle, if only because women's different conceptions of career are not yet understood by the majority of selectors who judge them in typically androcentric ways. Both Evetts (1991) and Grant (1989) show the importance of career encouragement and sponsorship, not always available to women in systems dominated by male preferment. Those women candidates for promotion who felt they were compared unfavourably in interviews to male norms (Grant 1989: 46) would find their fears confirmed in Morgan et al.'s (1983) POST Project on selection for secondary headship. At a time when LEAs had a main responsibility for selecting heads, the POST Project showed the process skewed by the predominance of men among education officers. Although the 1988 *Education Act* has shifted that power to governors, there is now an even greater concern that, in the absence of explicit criteria, lay selectors may rely still more heavily on 'unfriendly myths' to guide their choice. For example, Mortimore and Mortimore (1991) conclude from the accounts of eight secondary heads that 'The traditional image of a white, middle class headmaster is still widely held, despite the increasing numbers of highly effective headteachers who are women or who are members of black or ethnic minority communities' (p. 167). Hunter's (1987) sample reported questions about childcare, marriage plans and family planning still being asked in spite of complaints procedures.

Morgan et al. (1983) found that although women applied in smaller numbers (which in no way reflected their proportion of the whole teaching force) they proportionately stood the same chance of succeeding as male applicants. Men, however, were more likely to get headships of girls' schools than women of boys' schools. POST found that to be considered seriously alongside men, women candidates had to be tough (but not too tough) and overcome a whole range of stereotypes in selectors' minds of women in positions of authority. Evetts' (1991) interviews with ten men and ten women headteachers found that gender differences in the achievement of headship posts continued to be very large in spite of the claimed objectives of both LEAs and teacher unions in the equal opportunities policies. She attributes changes in the process of selection to changing perceptions of the headship role. Although the selection processes currently reflect some of POST's recommendations regarding more systematic and 'fair' selection, the changes in the headship role may result in even less women applying or in being successful when measured against a model of headship that reflects Marshall's 'agentic' principles (competitive, efficient, task-centred) rather than 'communion'.

Martini *et al.* (1984) looked particularly at possible sex discrimination in teaching appointments at all levels. They found that more women thought they might be discriminated against in selection than reported experiencing it, and commented on the difficulties of actually establishing whether negative discrimination has occurred. A related methodological issue is noted by Spencer *et al.* (1987) when interviewing women who had been successful in further and higher education. The fact that none of their respondents reported having experienced discrimination led them to the rather surprising conclusion that 'successful women are unlikely to have encountered discrimination'. This ignores the subtle ways (particularly since equal opportunities legislation) in which it continues to operate and the negative consequences on application rates of women's perceptions that it might occur. [. . .] She gives as an example those 'successful' women in her sample who valued classroom competency more than professional activities outside school in the early stages of their careers, a choice not necessarily also valued by promoters. Her findings lead her to advocate clear identification of promotion criteria and regular career reviews to support women's promotion prospects. Similarly Morgan *et al.* (1983) concluded that 'differential treatment of women is one of the strongest arguments for validated selection exercises' (p. 77).

The growing popularity of assessment centres for educational managers reflects a move in the direction of the POST recommendations but these involve mainly senior managers. Research suggests that much of the discrimination occurs at the earlier stages of a teacher's career, in job placement, the provision of opportunities for management development and in the distribution of scale posts.

Inequities in job placement are most likely to occur at the point of women's re-entry into teaching, where this has constituted a break in their career. Here researchers differ in their conclusions. Both Trown and Needham (1980) and Grant (1989) conclude that re-entry problems constitute in women's eyes a considerable barrier to advancement. The operation of an age-related career structure and limited childcare arrangements mean that the potential benefits of legitimate maternity leave are undermined. While recognising the problem, the experiences of Evetts' (1990) career history headteachers lead her to question the appropriateness of describing women teachers as having broken or interrupted careers. She found that stopping work to have a family was part of many women teachers' career strategies, adding positively to their personal and professional development.

The increasing emphasis of institutional staff development programmes on meeting whole school rather than individual teacher career needs could have negative repercussions for women who are less likely to be in posts defined as 'management'. A number of studies point to inequities in the allocation of points that disadvantage women in seeking promotion. Where Hilsum and Start (1974) attributed differential distribution to the lower application rate of women at all levels, more recent explanations are located in gender influences on the status given to subjects. Spencer *et al.* (1987) describe further and higher education as labour markets internally segregated by gender. As a result promotion goes mainly to those in 'men's' subjects, whereas male entrants into female areas have meteoric rises.

Weightman (1989) describes the MOSS study of 24 secondary schools which found not only that fewer women than men were in posts of responsibility but also that women had to do more for less by having a dual role or accepting a lower grading of similar work. As a result of their high profile and straightforward jobs men were clearly seen as managers doing management work. In contrast the complex, cross-school jobs typically performed by women obscured rather than highlighted their management responsibilities. Martini *et al.* (1985) and Hunter (1987) also found that men tended to have higher grades than women for posts of the same description.

[. . .]

Women's approaches to management

Research as opposed to informed opinion on how women behave as managers in education lags behind that in the United States. There, research on women as school leaders is being linked to studies of school effectiveness and the claim made that 'as a group women are more likely to evidence behaviour associated with effective leadership' (Fullan 1991). The links remain hypothetical, not proven. A similar baseline for linking women's management styles to effective schools is missing in Britain. A recent study of the perceived characteristics of effectively managed schools (Bolam *et al.* 1993) used a sample of both men and women heads but deliberately obscured gender distinctions by altering the gender of teachers referred to on a random basis. This makes it impossible to associate with men or women the leadership styles identified as effective.

A useful starting point for reviewing the debate is Al-Khalifa and Migniuolo's (1990) discussion of the identification of management in schools with masculinity. [. . .] Management is seen as technicist, requiring rational problem solving techniques, strong task direction and detachment. The same perspective emerges in Lyon and West's (1992) review of research on women academics and the variability of the extent to which they are willing to engage in and compete within the androcentric culture of the university. They comment on women academics' apparent unwillingness to conform to the meritocratic ethos of university life. They interpret this as a resistance to 'a discourse of rationality' that characterises the 'hegemonic male culture of academia'. In both these instances, women's attitudes to promotion and becoming managers are seen as shaped by the association they make between management and masculinity. Though the research evidence supporting the validity of the association is lacking, Marshall's study also shows it to be a powerful influence on women's career strategies and how they behave as managers.

Decisions about selecting and developing women for management posts can also be seen to be influenced by judgements about the extent to which they are seen as capable of meeting a masculine conception of its demands. Even if, as was suggested earlier, women managers in schools are less likely to be placed in sex stereotyped roles, the association of management and masculinity continues. For example, Wallace and Hall's (1993) study of senior management teams in secondary schools shows that the decision to bring a woman on to the team was in most cases associated with a recognition of the need to have someone specifically responsible for staff development, an area of school management with a heavy emphasis on interpersonal skills. This was combined with a concern on all the teams about the under-representation of women in their membership. Stereotypical definitions of leadership in terms of masculine traits and behaviours are common, particularly in a climate of educational reform that stresses competition rather than collaboration. In this respect the arrival of management can be seen as having transformed the predominantly female world of school teaching (Miller 1992) into the more masculine one of school management. Evetts' (1990) postscript to her study of women primary teachers questions the potential effects of the 'new managerialism' on the qualities sought in primary heads of the future:

> The new managerialism seems to give prominence to qualities such as efficiency, accountability, ambition, striving and competition. At the same time qualities such as caring, nurturing, loyalty and co-operation are difficult to measure and hence difficult to reward. Yet these are the qualities that have made primary teaching and promotion in primary teaching attractive to many women.
>
> (p. 183)

Evetts' conclusions arise out of her life history research interviews. Al-Khalifa's are the result of wide experience of working with women teachers with management responsibilities. Neither would claim that their assumptions about what women bring to their performance as managers are based on observation of how they actually behave. There is no firm research base to support empirically the association of one set of qualities (such as detachment, task directiveness and rationality) with men or women. For example, the tension between the competencies required by heads and principals to support collaboration and those needed if their schools are to compete successfully may be as acute for men as they are for women. Al-Khalifa's association of masculinity and management is also questionable in the light of the experience of firms in the non-educational sector of the kinds of strategies they judge as most likely to lead to effectiveness. The concept of the 'androgynous manager' arises from the recognition of the need to manage both task and people and to combine instrumental and expressive behaviours. Sargent (1983) makes a case for the androgynous manager based on qualities which should be available to everyone, regardless of gender. The problem is in the association of one set of behaviours with men and the other with women as a result of different socialisation.

Life history research confirms that women's different life experiences will influence their performance as managers. However, as Jayne (1989) points out, there is no documentation of how women headteachers lead schools which might support or refute the hypothesis that their different life experience in a patriarchal society might lead to a different enactment of headship. The possibly false equation of management with masculinity may be a factor in discouraging women from applying for management posts. However, once they have achieved management roles, they are managing.

Then, management can be defined in terms of how they are doing it, not according to a pre-determined model which they may or may not fit.

Marshall's (1984) research into women managers outside education led her to the conclusion that 'Women bring their femaleness with its connotations and status in society with them when they enter organizations' (p. 4). Her sample of 36 women managers in publishing and retail businesses was consistent in describing a core style that builds upon the qualities and advantages they have as a result of being women. At the same time they acknowledged their style as demonstrating both personal preference and a response to sex role stereotypes as well as the need at times to take responsibility for the disturbance their presence caused in predominantly masculine working environments.

Both Al-Khalifa in education and Marshall outside it conclude that the result of the identification of masculinity with management is a reluctance on the part of many women to move into the management role. They need confidence to apply and, if they are successful, to develop and use a style that may be continuously challenged as a result of sex stereotyping and unease about women in the leadership role, particularly if they have taken over from a man. Although Weindling and Earley's (1987) study looked at the early years of headship, it did not use the opportunity to discover whether women's experiences were influenced by whether they followed a man or woman head. They found no differences in the amount of professional support received by men and women in the early years of headship, but did not comment on how, for example, women secondary heads experienced their minority situation in heads' groups or working with governors with stereotyped expectations of headship behaviour.

David (1989) documents in detail her initial difficulties on moving to a head of department role in a polytechnic setting accustomed to men's style of leadership. Rejecting the 'business as usual' approach as sexist, she sought a personal style that allowed her to manage on her own terms and not within a white male paradigm. Similarly Powney and Weiner (1991) found personal self-confidence one of the keys to their sample of women and black managers in education becoming and remaining managers on their own terms.

What, then, are the qualities and skills associated with women managers in schools? What evidence is available to support the claim that women behave differently from men as managers in educational settings? Most of the studies use a comparative focus, that is they look at differences between men and women rather than what characterises women specifically. The problem with comparative studies is that they can encourage androcentric views by continuing to use a male concept definition of leadership. In contrast, studies (for example Evetts 1990 and Acker 1992) which start from the female world of administration, have as their focus how women perform, not how they are different from men – they assume the differences between women to be as important as the differences between women and men.

The debate about management styles in education has shifted significantly, to bring into question the appropriate qualities for school leadership and the extent to which they challenge traditionally 'masculine' approaches (for example, Gray 1987; Acker 1992). Some comparative studies and discussions of how men and women perform in school management hint at differences but the empirical base is thin (Cunnison 1985; Johnston 1986; Jayne 1989; Weightman 1989; Jones 1990; Powney and Weiner 1991). They are all based on questionnaires or interviews, not observation.

Apart from Acker's (1992) ethnographic study of one primary school, the first observational study of women in school management with a specific focus on gender is the one currently being conducted by the National Development Centre for School Management and Policy at the University of Bristol. This study combines in-depth interviews with focused observation over 18 months of a small sample of women primary and secondary heads. It aims to test the tentative claims about women as school managers that have emerged from studies in the last ten years.

[. . .]

Senior women in further and higher education reported problems of coping with a mainly male peer group and its expectations of them to be 'one of the boys' (Spencer *et al.* 1987). The characteristics needed to be successful were stereotyped as masculine. As a result, the women felt that the more they conformed to the 'masculine' stereotype and were also perceived by their male peers to be successful, they were also seen as 'unfeminine' and 'unnatural' women.

These interpretations of women's situation in educational institutions support a view of the dominance of a masculine ethos in shaping work opportunities. Studies of primary schools are less likely to show women teachers as marginalised (e.g. Nias 1989). They also tend to take gender for granted rather than something to be questioned.

Marshall (1984) acknowledges the power of the stereotype of appropriate behaviour for women to allow less self determination and less personal rights than stereotypes of masculinity. Like Cunnison, she also shows how those who choose not to break the stereotype (and risk the disapprobation of male peers) still achieve what they want through other means; for example, in the different use of power. Rather than using power agentically (i.e. assuming it to be competitive, controlling, owned by the individual and expressed through doing) she describes women managers' 'communion' approach which uses power co-operatively, based on joint ownership, directed towards influence and expressed in the individual's quality of being.

Women managers' preference for what Marshall calls 'communion' as a guiding principle for managing others in education is reflected in Gray (1987), Jayne (1989), Jones (1990), Powney and Weiner (1991) and Acker (1992). It is a matter of concern that so many of these mainly exploratory and small scale studies are quoted so widely as fact. Gray's (1987) proposals about distinctions between masculine and feminine styles are a good example. They are not research based but draw on his experiences of training programmes for education managers. He starts with the hypothesis that primary schools are predominantly feminine organisations and secondary schools masculine. The criteria for making this distinction are not given. The hypothesis is challengeable by those teachers in both sectors who are uncomfortable with the notion that their main purpose is to nurture (primary) or control (secondary). According to Gray, the gender-based association of characteristics creates problems for men at primary level, particularly headteachers who may not have the appropriate nurturing characteristics, and women at secondary level the required controlling abilities. Unusually for a discussion of gender considerations in educational management he mainly addresses the problems for men, particularly in primary school management, in recognising and using the 'female' side of their nature. In his view many heads are ineffective at management because they fear the feminine qualities this calls on (p. 302). Presumably he is here assuming headteachers to be men.

If, as a recent study has shown (Bolam *et al.* 1993), effective school leadership relates to leadership styles that are democratic, collegial, open, consultative and team

oriented (Bolam *et al.* 1993), and these styles are more evident in women's management styles, the implications for selection and management development are considerable. Jayne's (1989) argument is similar to Gray's, based on her experiences of
working with men and women managers in primary schools. Her starting point is
that there are differences in their approaches to management. The differences are not
innate (as Gray appears to claim) but the outcome of different socialisation patterns
and life experiences. For example, she has observed differences in how new heads
brought change into schools: 'men tell, women only use coercion as a last resort'
(p. 111). She argues that women's different use of power is the outcome of the fact
that they have less power in society and are therefore less likely to abuse it when
they have it. Her conclusion is that training courses need to pay more attention to
'traditional female qualities' and target not just women but those with whom they
work, to eliminate different expectations of men and women as leaders.

   [. . .]

Jones' (1990) study of men and women teachers' attitudes to promotion found
some differences in their expectations of themselves and others as leaders. Based on
what they said rather than what they did, both men and women favoured a democratic model of management which they saw both men and women heads as capable
of providing. However, while men saw themselves as more innovative than women
in introducing change, women did not see their male colleagues in this way. Women
preferred to use staff expertise in bringing about change, men drew on adviser support
and expertise. Interestingly, given Ball's point about men's relatively negative attitudes
to the exploration of gender issues, Jones had a 100 per cent response from women
teachers in her sample, and only 66 per cent from men, many of whom thought the
study sexist (p. 12).

   Powney and Weiner (1991) describe the strategies used by the women and black
managers they interviewed to fight back against the obstacles they faced once in
senior positions. The problems included: invisibility (being treated as though they
were juniors); visibility (being stereotyped); tokenism (assumed to be there for political
reasons only); hostility, harassment, patronage and exploitation. A number commented on their isolation, a sense of people waiting to see them fall. The authors question
the implications of this sense of isolation when set against the expressed preference of
most for a democratic style of leadership (p. 25). They suggest that potential conflict
between the two positions (of being isolated and encouraging participation) might
explain the group of six white women whose style is described as 'self doubting',
that is they advocate one management style but use another. Black women managers
in their sample were least likely to use participative approaches to management. The
study thus provides a useful basis for considering differences in women's management
styles as well as similarities. The descriptions of style are based solely, however, on the
interviewee's own comments and are not checked against others' perceptions of how
they behave or observation of their practice.

   Taken together, the studies described barely begin to scratch the surface of a
gender-influenced description of school leadership styles. Exponents of the debate
about differences in style distinguish their positions in terms of the extent to which
they are essentialists (women are 'naturally' different from men) or believe that how
women behave as managers is determined by how they are seen and treated, as well
as their personal characteristics. It was suggested earlier that the debate needs to be
set in the context of the concept of 'androgynous manager' a term which derives

from the work of Sandra Bem (1977). As a psychological term, 'androgyny' suggests that it is possible for people to exhibit both masculine and feminine qualities and that such qualities are present in both men and women. Sex role stereotyping has tended to polarise the qualities, so that 'masculine' characteristics are associated only with men and feminine with women. At their extremes both sets of characteristics become negative. Advocates of androgynous approaches to management argue for an integration of the characteristics so that management behaviours incorporate both masculine and feminine behaviours. According to this model, managers in schools, whether men or women, would be able to draw on both male and female qualities as the situation required. If empirical research based on observation was able to show that this is what effective leaders do, then contingency theories of leadership would need to be modified to take account of the new data. At the moment, the assumption is that effective leaders use contingency styles (Hoyle 1986), drawing from their repertoire of management skills and knowledge to fit the situation. What the theory has not so far addressed is whether men and women draw on different repertoires or repertoires that are limited by perceptions of gender-appropriate behaviour.

Conclusions

There is relatively little to date in research about women managers in education that can be used to challenge theories of educational management or lead to their reconceptualisation to include both women and men. Although definitions of career that do not work for women have been questioned, there is still only a limited quantitative research base in Britain about the career routes of both men and women teachers. The picture is even more sparse in further and higher education. Research by Hall *et al.* (1986) and Weindling and Earley (1987) provided portraits mainly of men administrators in education.

Other research is needed that challenges traditional stereotypes of what constitutes appropriate management behaviour and process. The association of management and masculinity has not been established as a fact yet it is treated as such, with negative consequences for women in education. Observation studies of managers at work in non-educational settings (Mintzberg 1973; Stewart 1982) make no distinction between men and women in the job and are based primarily on men. Hypotheses about women's style of management and its congruence with effective education management strategies, if proven, may well lead to a reversal of Professor Higgins' plea, so that selectors and developers in education will cry 'why can't a man be more like a woman'. Then both theory and prescriptions for action will truly have been transformed by the inclusion of gender as a relevant concept for understanding educational management.

References

Acker, S. (1980) Women: the other academics. *British Journal of the Sociology of Education*, 1(1): 81–91.
Acker, S. (1992) Gender, collegiality and teachers' workplace culture in Britain: in search of the women's culture. Paper presented at AERA, San Francisco, April.

Acker, S. (ed.) (1989) *Teachers, Gender and Careers*. Lewes: Falmer Press.

Al-Khalifa, E. (1989) An evaluation of the Open University's Managing Schools Course (E325). Milton Keynes: School of Education, Open University.

Al-Khalifa, E. and Migniuolo, F. (1990) Messages for management: the experiences of women's training, paper given at the Conference on Equal Advances in Education Management, Vienna 3–6 December.

AMMA (1985) *Women Teachers' Career Prospects – 1985: an AMMA Research Study*. London: AMMA.

AIT (Scotland) (1989) *The Situation of Women Members in Scottish Universities: a Questionnaire Study*. Edinburgh: Association of University Teachers.

Ball, S. (1987) *The Micropolitics of the School*. London: Methuen.

Bem, S. (1977) *Psychological Androgyny*. New Haven, CT: West Publishing Company.

Bolam, R., McMahon, A., Pocklington, K. and Weindling, D. (1993) *Effective Management in Schools*. London: HMSO.

Byrne Whyte, J. (1987) Under-representation of women in management posts in education: a critique of two theoretical explanatory accounts, in L. Unterkircher and I. Wagner (eds) *Die Andre halfte der Gesellschaft Verlag des Osterreichischen Gewerkschaftsbunden*.

Cunnison, S. (1985) Making it in a man's world: women teachers in a senior high school, occasional paper no. 1, University of Hull.

David, M. (1989) Prima donna inter pares? Women in academic management, in S. Acker (ed.) (1989) *op. cit.*

Davidson, H. (1985) Unfriendly myths about women teachers, in J. Whyte *et al.* (eds) *Girl Friendly Schooling*. London: Methuen.

Earley, P. and Weindling, D. (1988) Heading for the top: the career paths of secondary school heads, *Educational Management and Administration*, 16(1): 27–35.

Evetts, J. (1990) *Women in Primary Teaching: Career Contexts and Strategies*. London: Unwin Hyman.

Evetts, J. (1991) The experience of secondary headship selection: continuity and change, *Educational Studies*, 17(3): 285–94.

Fullan, M. (1991) *The New Meaning of Educational Change*. London: Cassell.

Grant, R. (1989) Women teachers' career pathways: towards an alternative model of career, in S. Acker (ed.) (1989) *op. cit.*

Gray, H. L. (1987) Gender considerations in school management, *School Organisation*, 17(3): 297–302.

Hall, V., Mackay, H. and Morgan, C. (1986) *Headteachers at Work*. Milton Keynes: Open University Press.

Hilsum, S. and Start, K. B. (1974) *Promotion and Careers in Teaching*. Slough: NFER.

Hough, J. (1986) Gender bias in educational management and administration, *Educational Management and Administration*, 16: 69–74.

Hoyle, E. (1986) *The Politics of School Management*. Sevenoaks: Hodder and Stoughton.

Hunter, J. (1987) *Women's Careers in Secondary and Primary Teaching: the Birmingham Study*. London: ILEA.

Inner London Education Authority (1984) *Womens' Careers in Teaching: a Survey of Teachers' Views*. London: ILEA.

Jayne, E. (1989) Women as leaders of schools: the role of training, *Educational Management and Administration*, 17(3): 109–14.

Johnston, J. (1986) Gender differences in teachers' preferences for primary school leadership, *Educational Management and Administration*, 14: 219–26.

Jones, A. (1987) *Leadership for Tomorrow's Schools*. Oxford: Basil Blackwell.

Jones, K. (1990) The attitudes of men and women primary school teachers to promotion, *Educational Management and Administration*, 18(3): July.

Lyon, K. and West, J. (1992) The trouble with equal opportunities: the case of women academics. Paper presented to the Conference on Social Order in Post Classical Sociology, to mark the retirement of Professor Michael Banton, University of Bristol, 8–10 September.

Marshall, J. (1984) *Women Managers: Travellers in a Male World*. Chichester: John Wiley and Sons.

Martini, R. *et al.* (1984) *Women's Careers in Teaching: Survey of Teachers' Views*. London: ILEA.

Miller, J. (1992) More has meant women: the feminization of schooling. London: Institute of Education, University of London.

Mintzberg, H. (1973) *The Nature of Managerial Work*. New York: Harper and Row.

Morgan, C. Hall, V. and Mackay, H. (1983) *The Selection of Secondary Headteachers*. Milton Keynes: Open University Press.

Mortimore, P. and Mortimore, J. (eds) (1991) *The Secondary Head: Roles, Responsibilities and Reflections*. London: Paul Chapman.

National Union of Teachers (1980) *Promotion and the Woman Teachers*. London: NUT.

Nias, J. (1989) *Primary Teachers Talking: a Study of Teaching as Work*. London: Routledge.

Ozga, J. (ed.) (1992) *Women in Educational Management*. Buckingham: Open University Press.

Powney, J. and Weiner, G. (1991) *Outside of the Norm: Equity and Management in Educational Institutions*. London: South Bank Polytechnic/Department of Education.

Sargent, A. (1983) *The Androgynous Manager: Blending Male and Female Management Styles for Today's Organization*. New York: American Management Association.

Schmuck, P. (1986) School management and administration: an analysis by gender, in E. Hoyle and A. McMahon (eds) *World Yearbook: the Management of Schools*. London: Kogan Page.

Schmuck, P. (1987) Gender: a relevant concept for educational leadership. Paper prepared for the National Graduate Research Seminar in Educational Administration, University Council for Educational Administration, Washington DC, 24 April.

Shakeshaft, C. (1989) *Women in Educational Administration* (2nd edn). Newbury Park, CA: Sage Publications.

Shakeshaft, C. (1989) *Women in Educational Administration* (updated edition). Newbury Park, CA: Sorwin Press.

Sikes, P., Measor, L. and Woods, P. (1985) *Teacher Careers: Crises and Continuities*. Lewes: Falmer Press.

Spencer, A., Finlayson, N. and Crabb, S. (1987) Women in further and higher education, *Coombe Lodge Report*, 20(3).

Stewart, R. (1982) *Choices for the Manager: a Guide to Managerial Work and Behaviour*. Maidenhead: McGraw-Hill.

Torrington, D. and Weightman, J. (1987) *The Reality of School Management*. Oxford: Blackwell.

Trown, E. and Needham, G. (1980) *Reduction in Part-time Teaching: Implications for Schools and Women Teachers*. Manchester: Equal Opportunities Commission.

Wallace, M. and Hall, V. (1993) *Senior Management Teams in Action*. London: Paul Chapman.

Weightman, J. (1989) Women in management, *Educational Management and Administration*, 17(3): Summer.

Weindling, D. and Earley, P. (1987) *Secondary Headship: the First Years*. Slough: NFER-Nelson.

Williams, H. (1981) The role of the deputy head. Is it changing? A study with particular reference to women in management in large comprehensive schools during the last five years, *CORE*, 5(1): March.

6 | Motivation in education*

COLIN RICHES

Work motivation and its relevance to management

The understanding of motivation and managing motivation

A study of work motivation has two basic strands: first, why people behave in the way they do in the workplace, and secondly, how they can be helped to engage in work behaviours which are beneficial to the organization – and themselves. If the experience of work has a negative effect on individuals they cannot give of their best in that sphere of their lives. If we are to make some relevant application of theoretical knowledge about motivation in educational management we need to understand something about the relationship between theories of motivation and theories of managing motivation. This will be an important consideration in this chapter.

Motivating people to get results through them is central to the purposes of management: 'Apart from developing the skill to work well . . . we need to look for ways of developing the will to work well' (Evenden and Anderson 1992). Motivation and its management is a core element of human resource management (HRM) just as the whole of the latter is the backbone of all effective management:

> Of all the resources at the disposal of a person or organization it is only people who can grow and develop and be motivated to achieve certain desired ends. The attaining of targets for the organization is in their hands and it is the way people are managed . . . which is at the heart of HRM . . . and optimum management.
>
> (Riches and Morgan 1989: 1)

An expanding interest in motivation has arisen because of an increasing emphasis on HRM. Katz and Kahn (1978) have argued that organizations need people who are:

---

* This material has been edited and was originally published as 'Motivation'.

(a) attracted to staying in an organization as well as initially joining it
(b) perform their tasks in a dependable manner
(c) go beyond this to engage in some type of creative, spontaneous and innovative behaviour. In a nutshell, effective organizations have to get to grips with how people are stimulated to participate and be productive at work.

Two factors in particular have contributed to an interest in motivation and its management:

1 A new environment of competition in western societies (and schools and colleges are no exception), in which organizational 'slack' is less tolerated and performance is paramount, forces attention on obtaining full benefit in particular from the human resources which are available. Thus attention is drawn to how management can best motivate employees to achieve the goals of the organization;
2 The increasing sophistication of technology in industry, and to a lesser extent in education, has heightened awareness that machines may be necessary for increasing efficiency and effectiveness in organizations but people and their motivation are seen more than ever as irreplaceable in key areas of operation. Thus personnel development programmes have come to the fore to help to provide a continuing reservoir of well-trained and highly motivated people. We can see this demonstrated increasingly in education as elsewhere, although the education service, with its concepts of 'professionalism' and teacher 'autonomy', has hitherto paid limited attention to motivation and personal development.

Defining motivation

One of the difficulties surrounding the study of motivation is that there is no overarching or single theoretical model which explains motivation. The etymological root of the term 'motivation' is the Latin word *movere*, meaning 'to move'. However such a definition is inadequate here. A preliminary definition of motivation is that it refers to individual differences with regard to the priorities, attitudes and aspects of life style that people seek to fulfil in work, i.e. those things which drive them on and make them feel good about doing so.

Different definitions emphasize to varying degrees a number of facets which constitute motivation. They are:

• the goals which people have which direct their behaviour towards something, e.g. power, status, friends, money
• the mental processes or energetic forces by which individuals (a) pursue/are driven towards particular goals, including decisions about what to aim for and how to go about it and (b) maintain or sustain such behaviour
• the social processes through which some individuals, e.g. managers, seek to retain or change the behaviour of others.

A comprehensive definition which incorporates all these aspects has been given by Johannson and Page (1990: 196):

Processes or factors that cause people to act or behave in certain ways. To motivate is to induce someone to take action. The process of motivation consists of:

- identification or appreciation of an unsatisfied need.
- the establishment of a goal which will satisfy the need
- determination of the action required to satisfy the need.

Clearly the concept is multi-faceted in that it incorporates what gets people activated (arousal) and the force exerted by an individual to engage in desired behaviour (direction or choice of behaviour).

A basic general model of motivation has the following building blocks:

(a) needs or expectations
(b) behaviour
(c) goals
(d) some form of feedback.

For example, an expectation that more effort in doing a job will lead to promotion or the need to be socially acceptable in the organization will usually result in a state of disequilibrium within individuals which they will try to reduce (behaviour) by working towards a goal, and information will be fed back to the individual concerning the impact of such behaviour (Dunnette and Kirchner 1965, quoted in Steers and Porter 1991). However, what actually happens is never so simple or straightforward. First, motives behind actions can never be seen; they are always inferred, when in fact motives may be multiple, disguised, and expressed in different ways according to the person and the culture in which the action takes place. Secondly, motives change and may be in conflict with one another. Thirdly, selection of motives and their intensity will vary between individuals. Finally, when certain prime motives for action are reduced, e.g. through thirst being satisfied, then other motives may become primary ones (see Herzberg *et al.* 1959; and below).

Some concepts related to motivation

Stress

Up to this point we have written of motivation in somewhat neutral terms and as if it was sanitized from negative manifestations. What happens to our basic model if a person's drive is blocked before reaching its desired goal? There are two possible sets of outcomes: constructive behaviour or frustration. Potential frustration may be reduced by managers addressing the problem in a positive way and employing various strategies according to the issue to reduce that frustration, e.g. effective recruitment, selection and training, careful job design and work organization, equitable handling of people, effective communications and a participative style of management. If the problem is not foreseen then actual frustration may well take place, and stress, in the negative sense of distress (for some stress may well be a beneficial driving force) is most likely to occur.

Job satisfaction

The relationship between motivation to work and job satisfaction is not at all clear. One view is that the motivation required for a person to achieve a high level of performance is satisfaction with the job but, although the level of job satisfaction may well affect the strength of motivation, this is not always so. Locke and Latham

(1990) claim that the motivation to work (exert effort) and satisfaction are relatively independent outcomes. Job satisfaction is not the same as motivation in that it is more an attitudinal state being associated with a personal feeling of achievement, either quantitative or qualitative. All that can be said with certainty is that motivation is a process which may lead to job satisfaction. Neither does job satisfaction necessarily lead to improved work performance. Vroom (1964), after examining 20 studies, found a low correlation (0.14) between job satisfaction and job performance. Luthans (1989) has concluded that 'Although most people assume a positive relationship, the preponderance of research evidence indicates that there is no strong linkage between satisfaction and productivity.'

Morale

'Morale' usually relates to the way people think about their work, and, while the term is sometimes applied to individuals (see for example, D. Evans 1992), it usually refers to group feelings, thoughts, actions, etc., whereas motivation is applied to individuals. Thus Kempner (1971: 260) defines morale as 'The extent to which the members of a group identify with the aims and activities of the group. In examining the state of morale in schools, Lawley (1985) suggests that there are three basic ways of identifying low morale:

- the psychological and physiological state of teachers
- the existence of injustice
- the undermining of status, or threats to personal equilibrium or personal insults.

Some factors affecting motivation

As we have seen, the variables affecting motivation are very numerous. Text books which deal with the subject have innumerable categorizations of those influences, and diagrams to indicate the way they impact on motivation. The most comprehensive scheme is provided by Betts (1993: 145) and is set out in Figure 6.1.

The categories are largely self-explanatory. Betts (p. 146) claims that 'override' factors

> upset the effect of all the previous factors, often regardless of their combined strength to motivate. Override comes into play on the spot: it has an immediate, powerful and dominating effect on motivation by altering behaviour because of some mental incapability, physical incapability or sudden change in the situation surrounding the individual.

The categories listed are not discrete; they interact with one another in complex ways. However, the mapping is helpful in raising awareness of the multiplicity of factors which go to make up motivation.

Needs

Betts includes 'needs' as one aspect of 'internal human pressures'. Needs may be classified as physiological (for food, drink, protection, work) or psychological (for security, belongingness, esteem), and the potency of each will vary between individuals.

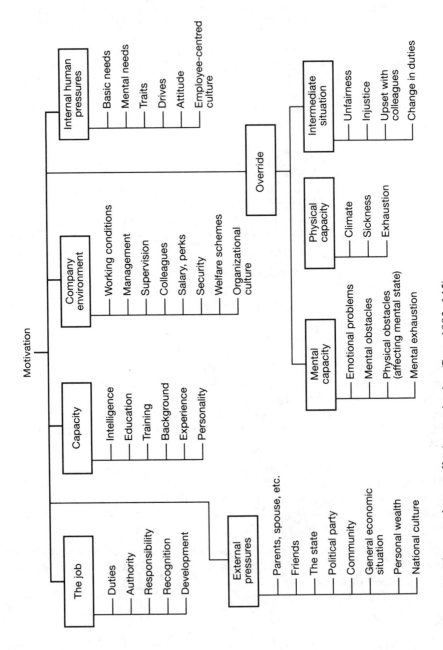

Figure 6.1 The main factors affecting motivation (Betts 1993: 145)

Drives are sometimes divided into basic or primary drives which are not learned and are derived from physiological needs such as thirst, sex, sleep; general drives that are not learned but are more psychological in character, like competence, curiosity, seeking affection and being active; and finally secondary drives which are learned and tend to take over from primary and general drives if the opportunity occurs. Examples of secondary drives are:

- *aggressiveness:* the drive to be powerful which expresses itself in hostility, awkwardness and being quarrelsome, which extremely, is expressed in violence and can be very close to the desire to escape
- *acquisitiveness:* the desire for protection and possession
- *self-assertion:* the drive to be important, often arising out of the need to be given credit for achievement
- *constructiveness:* the desire to be creative
- *gregariousness:* the urge to belong to a group and be accepted by it.

Needs and drives can, of course, come up against obstacles, which can be within one's own personality or external to it such as other people, the demands of society and culture and many other restrictions. Identifying obstacles to achieving goals and recognizing the way these are dealt with by individuals are highly significant for managers if they are to adopt strategies for dealing with them. However, as various theorists of motivation have pointed out, the processes and content of motivation make a linear understanding (need–drive–obstacle–solution–goal–achievement) less than satisfactory because so many variables intervene to complicate the picture.

Theories of motivation

Theories of motivation can be divided into content theories and process theories. The former concentrate on the specific things which motivate individuals at work. The latter attempt to identify and examine the dynamic relationships among the different variables which make up motivation. As the name suggests they are primarily concerned with the actual process of motivation; with how behaviour is initiated, directed and sustained.

Content theories of motivation

Maslow's hierarchy of needs

This is one of the most widely known theories of motivation and concentrates on a supposed needs hierarchy. Maslow (1943) suggests that human needs are arranged hierarchically and that needs which are low in the hierarchy must be largely satisfied before those which are higher in the hierarchy will motivate behaviour. These needs may be defined as:

- *physiological:* for sunlight, sex, food, water and similar inputs which are basic to human survival
- *safety-security:* for freedom from environmental threat, animals and people, for shelter, security, order, predictability and for a generally organized world

---

Self-actualization
Esteem and status or ego
Belonging or social
Safety or security
Physiological

Figure 6.2 Maslow's needs hierarchy
(Based on Gray and Starke 1988: 109)

- *belonging or social:* the need to associate with one's own kind, for relationships, affection, giving and receiving love, for feelings of belonging
- *esteem and status or ego:* for strength, achievement, adequacy, confidence, independence and for reputation, prestige and recognition
- *self-actualization:* the need to reach one's ultimate goals in life, to fulfil one's own destiny.

This hierarchy rests on two assumptions: that (a) unsatisfied needs motivate behaviour and (b) as a particular need becomes satisfied it becomes less of a motivator and the next in line takes on more importance. For most people the higher order needs will be less satisfied than the lower ones and differences in satisfaction will depend on cultures and individuals. This theory has not been confirmed by empirical work (see the review by Wahba and Bridwell 1976). While it may be useful to see the theory as operating over time at a general societal level, at the individual level it has serious drawbacks which include:

- there is a methodological issue: the theory was intended to predict changes in individuals' needs but most of the research has been cross-sectional, comparing the needs of different people at one point in time
- it is not easy for psychologists to define constructs such as self-actualization, let alone to test them
- it is difficult to see how the theory can predict behaviour by assessing the amount of satisfaction that one has to achieve at one level before passing on to the next
- people do not satisfy their needs, especially the higher order ones, through the work situation alone; they are satisfied through other areas of their lives as well
- the hierarchy 'may simply have reflected American middle-class values and the pursuit of the good life, and may not have hit on fundamental universal truths about human psychology' (Buchanan and Huczynski 1985: 54)
- individuals attach different values to the same need
- some outcomes at work satisfy more than one need
- even for people with the same hierarchical level the motivating factors may well be different
- the theory seems to ignore the notion of altruistic behaviour
- the theory does not acknowledge gender variables.

McGregor's 'X' and 'Y' theory

McGregor (1970), drawing on Maslow's hierarchy of needs model, states that there are two basic suppositions about human nature which will help determine the mode of management which is adopted to motivate people. Theory 'X' incorporates the following assumptions about human nature:

- people are usually lazy and work shy
- most must be coerced, controlled and threatened with punishment to achieve objectives
- the average person avoids responsibility and seeks direction, is unambitious and prefers security to anything else
- motivation (in Maslow's terms) occurs at the physiological and security levels only.

Theory 'Y' on the other hand, is based on the assumptions that:

- for most people work is natural
- people will be self-directed and controlled if they are committed to definite objectives
- commitment to objectives is because of rewards attached to achievement
- people usually want to accept responsibility
- motivation happens at the affiliation, esteem and self-actualization levels.

These contrasting theories of motivation are, of course, extremes and an over-simplification, but for McGregor theory 'Y' is the preferred way to motivate people because it is more likely to achieve the desired results.

Herzberg's two-factor theory

This theory, first proposed by Herzberg and his colleagues in 1959, was a major departure in thinking about work motivation. A study of 200 engineers and accountants concluded that satisfaction and dissatisfaction were conceptionally distinct factors caused by different phenomena in the work environment. The research found that feeling good was associated with a preponderance of factors dealing with the work itself and feeling bad with the work environment. Thus, one group of factors was found to cause job satisfaction and another job dissatisfaction. He called the former 'motivators' and the latter 'hygiene' factors, which when present caused dissatisfaction. Motivators generally relate to job content (the nature of the work itself) and hygienes to work context (the environment in which the work is performed). So Herzberg believes that job satisfaction and job dissatisfaction are different because the sources of each are different.

The theory has generated a good deal of criticism because the empirical evidence suggests that he has oversimplified reality. There are four major criticisms:

- the methodology causes the results: unless Herzberg's methodology is used it is difficult to support his theory
- the two factors are not distinct: empirical studies suggest that specific job content factors are sometimes listed by individuals as hygienes and job context factors, e.g. pay, as motivators. Female workers often list inter-personal relations as motivators while males see them as not so important
- human nature explains the findings: people tend to take credit for their own achievement (motivators) and blame others, e.g. the work organization, for their failures (hygienes)

- hygienes have been ignored under Herzberg's influence: his ideas may have led to an over-emphasis on higher level needs (particularly outside the sphere of professional workers) at the expense of basic needs.

The general conclusion is that empirical evidence does not support the two-factor theory although it does not clearly refute it. Maybe the construct of satisfaction/dissatisfaction is correct but hygienes and motivators will vary between individuals. Therefore, if managers knew which content or context factors operated as motivators or hygienes, in a given task for a given individual, this information could be used to effect individual performance.

Nias (1981) has applied Herzberg's theory to an educational context. Using a sample of 135 primary school teachers, she found that job satisfaction arose out of factors which were intrinsic to the job, but also identified 'negative satisfiers', which if removed would result in more job satisfaction, whereas the contextual dissatisfiers would not do so:

> The removal of the 'dissatisfier' does not provide a 'satisfier'. Thus teachers' views on leadership of their heads tend, by definition, to be expressed in negative terms. When they are satisfied with the management of their schools they do not mention it because good management is not, under normal circumstances, a 'satisfier' in its own right. Bad management is, by contrast, a 'dissatisfier'.
>
> (Nias 1980: 258)

Where there was purposeful leadership, and a close fit between the ideologies of teachers and the ideologies of the schools, then satisfaction was high. The most important single dissatisfier was the absence of a sense of purpose in the ethos of the school.

In more recent small-scale studies of primary school teachers, L. Evans (1992: 8) concluded that

> school-specific issues are generally more influential on teachers' . . . satisfaction levels than are centrally initiated policies and conditions of service . . . of the 18 teachers who participated in the research . . . six reported a strong desire (sometimes even a determination) to change schools due to dissatisfaction.

The evidence on job satisfaction for *heads* seems to suggest that achievement on task or in reaching specific standards of competence are significant (Vroom 1964; Locke 1965; Herzberg 1966). Conversely, loss of autonomy (e.g. trying to deal with problems over which they have no control) and powerlessness (e.g. the moving goalposts of government legislation) lead to job dissatisfaction. Steps which may be taken to reduce 'innovation shock' includes the development of teams to share the burdens, and careful preparation for headship.

Process theories of motivation

So far we have considered content theories only, which are concerned with identifying specific things which motivate the individual to work and the relative strengths of those needs, i.e. what motivates. Now we turn to process theories, which look at the dynamic relationships between motivational variables concerning the initiation, direction and sustaining of behaviour, i.e. the actual process of motivation. These approaches are represented by expectancy, equity and goal theories.

Expectancy theory

The basis of expectancy theory is that people are influenced by what they expect to be the impact of their actions. Expectancy theory is based on:

1 an individual's perceptions that she/he has about the results of alternative behaviours
2 individual perceptions, hence it helps to explain individual differences in motivation and behaviour, unlike Maslow's universal content theory
3 attempts to measure the strength of the individual's motivation
4 the assumption that human behaviour is to some extent rational, and individuals are conscious of their goals and motives, and therefore it is possible to predict behaviour.

The managerial implications of this complex but popular theory are that, because of its rational basis, it can be used to diagnose and resolve organizational problems. Neider (1980) has argued that managers need to realize that people work well only when they expect their efforts to produce good performance. Ideally, managers should:

• seek to give appropriate rewards for individual performance
• attempt to establish clear relationships between effort-performance and rewards as seen by the individual
• establish clear procedures for evaluating levels of performance (appraisal)
• give attention to intervening variables like abilities, traits, organizational procedures and support facilities, which might affect performance albeit, indirectly (Mullins 1993).

Equity theory

According to equity theory (Adams 1965), the motivation of individuals in organizations is influenced by the extent to which they feel they are being treated in a fair and equitable manner in comparison with the treatment received by others. Equity theory is based on staff inputs, what they believe will contribute to their job or organization, and their outcomes, what they perceive the organization provides in return. Because of the idea of trading inputs for outcomes, equity theory is often called exchange theory, which is closely related to micro-political behaviour. When both are in balance according to the perception of a given individual then there is equity, and in the case of imbalance, inequity. The theory assumes that on feeling inequity the individual is motivated to reduce it and this may result in a number of different behaviours:

• altering inputs, e.g. choosing to put more or less effort into the job
• altering outcomes, e.g. pay or working conditions, without changing inputs
• distorting inputs or outcomes rather than actually changing them so that a person may change her/his perceptions of what she/he is putting into the organization
• leaving the situation – asking for a transfer or quitting
• taking actions to change the inputs or outcomes (either actual or perceived) of others, e.g. saying to a colleague, 'You shouldn't work so hard, it's not worth it.'

- changing the person one is comparing oneself with to someone else, e.g. 'I may be worse off compared with X but I am getting a fair deal compared with Y.'

'Equity theory argues that perceived inequity creates feelings of discomfort and tension in a person and hence that a person experiencing such inequity will be motivated to restore equity via one of the previous methods' (Feldman and Arnold 1983: 118).

The theory seems to have usefulness in predicting staff behaviour and motivational levels. Its value in the sphere of education might increase as attempts are made to relate pay to performance (however defined), but paradoxically, in times of retrenchment, it has relevance as educational managers seek to assess the relationship between inputs and outcomes of staff when financial rewards are limited and satisfactions need to be engendered in different ways.

Goal theory

Locke (1968) argues that there are three cognitive processes which intervene between events which occur in the environment around a person, e.g. conditions of work, and that person's subsequent performance. They are the perception of that event by the person, his/her evaluation of it and the setting of goals and formulating of intentions. At this point a conscious decision is made about what to do. All types of incentive – direct and powerful, e.g. setting time limits on work to be done, and indirect and less influential, e.g. money, verbal praise, reproof and participation in decision-making – have an influence on behaviour via their effect on staff goals. However, what goals are set is important and there are a number of critical attributes or characteristics of goals to be considered. First, goal difficulty: the more difficult the goal set, the higher the level of performance brought about, provided it is not unrealistically high. Secondly, the more specific the goal set the greater is its impact on subsequent performance. Thirdly, for a goal to have a positive impact on a person's performance it must be accepted by that person, and thus participation in goal setting is very important. There is considerable potential in goal theory for influencing motivation and performance of members of organizations, provided managers are trained to develop the necessary skills in handling the goal-setting process sensitively and tactfully.

The high performance cycle

A recent model of work motivation (Locke and Latham 1990) provides both incorporation of many of the theories discussed above and a trenchant critique of what has gone before to give a guide through a maze of often conflicting theories. Their 'high performance cycle' has as its well attested basis the view that motivation to work (exert effort) and satisfaction are relatively independent outcomes. They have pieced together several theories into a coherent whole which 'explains' both the motivation to work and job satisfaction (see Figure 6.3).

The model takes the view that job satisfaction comes as the result of rewards measured against one's own appraisal of the job matched to one's value standards. The consequences of satisfaction or dissatisfaction appear to be many, depending on the individual choices which people make. Responses to dissatisfaction might be avoidance (most frequent), complaint, formal protest, illegal acts, passive-aggressive response, or even substance abuse (Henne and Locke 1985). Satisfaction is reinforced through

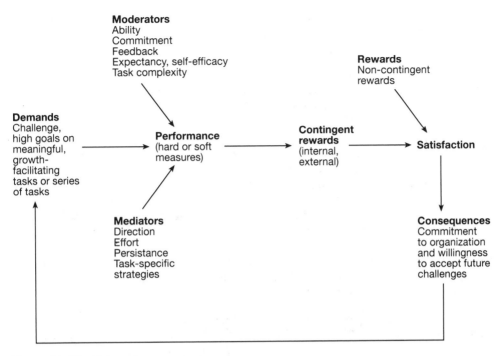

Figure 6.3 The high performance cycle
(Locke and Latham 1990: 4)

commitment to the goals and values of the organization and a desire to stay in the organization (Mowday *et al.* 1982). This brings us back again to the beginning of the 'circle' in the diagram. The 'high performance cycle' provides a coherent, advanced and enhanced explanation of the way individuals are motivated, perform and receive satisfaction in an organization.

Summary of approaches to motivation

Motivation is what drives individuals to work in the way they do to fulfil goals, needs or expectations. These are numerous, varied and changing. Content theories, which emphasize what motivates and the relative strengths of these motivators, and process theories, which stress the dynamic variables operating as motivation proceeds, have all evolved to try to explain the complex phenomenon of motivation. It has become apparent that there is not an all-embracing theory of work motivation and job satisfaction, but the model of Locke and Latham (1990) has been put forward as a useful integrating theory which has considerable explanatory power.
  [. . .]

The implications of theories of motivation for educational management

In this section we give a broad summary of some of the most significant implications that our theoretical knowledge has for the motivation of people by managers.

We start with the significance of the 'summarizing' cycle of Locke and Latham for management.

The broad implications of the 'high performance cycle' for management are as follows:

- Effective organizations should expect much from the people who work for them. Low expectations are certainly demotivating in the long run and will not help the school or college overall
- Managers must ensure that a sense of satisfaction is gained in return for effort
- Satisfaction will derive in part from personally meaningful work which members are capable of and in part from managers taking pains to reward performance. Managers need to ensure that they understand what influences each individual to be satisfied, or otherwise, in her/his employment
- Managers should encourage staff to set specific, challenging but realistic goals for high performance by them. Consultation and training are needed to ensure commitment to these goals
- Feedback on work performance helps staff to implement effective task strategies and to be motivated towards self-efficacy, and to reveal discrepancies between the goal set and present performance.

When thinking about managing motivation we always come back to the individual nature of the enterprise. The different needs of individuals usually demand different strategies to satisfy them. Kakabadse (1988) has suggested some potential strategies related to meeting the needs of staff in organizations including:

- results-focused appraisal, in which performance is measured against pre-determined goals, the achievement of which can lead to reward
- job enrichment or 'vertical job loading', where individuals can gain more responsibility, autonomy and control over the tasks they perform
- quality circles, where there is an emphasis on participative problem-solving and decision-making
- management training which can provide opportunities for evaluating skills, attitudes and on-the-job behaviour
- situational leadership where the appropriate style is fitted to the situation
- autonomous work groups where groups are given whole tasks and significant autonomy to decide how they should be completed
- staff benefits or rewards which are not tied to individual performance
- job design by accountabilities, in which jobs are clarified according to the different accountabilities of those who hold them.

One significant issue arising from motivation theory is the importance of valuing staff. Torrington and Weightman (1989) have linked this aspect to Maslow's esteem needs. They identified four types in the secondary schools they studied:

- *consideration:* that an interest should be taken in staff by their managers, e.g. the basic etiquettes of smiling, saying 'thank you', offering words of encouragement and praise, having a good working environment in the staffroom and elsewhere
- *feedback:* the need for tangible indications of success from colleagues, involving informal as well as formal assessment like evaluation and appraisal

- *delegation:* 'members of staff are valued when responsibility is delegated to them' (p. 49), and they are not just given a job to do
- *consultation and participation:* lack of consultation and participation in decision-making and in developing the culture of the school was a dissatisfier whereas the opposite engendered feelings of their opinions being valued because they counted for something.

The authors conclude that 'valuing of colleagues is something for *all* the adults in the organization to offer each other: it is not just for the mighty to confer on the lowly' (p. 52).

Conclusion

Certain management policies emerge from the evidence. As Guest (1984: 23) observes,

> on the one hand it may be possible to obtain high and productive motivation through judicious job selection and by using reactance principles (i.e. not seeing individuals as passive receivers and responders) to obtain high commitment to organizational goals, by using goal setting techniques, by careful job design to provide personal or group control over effort-performance-control links and by adopting facilitative leadership. On the other hand management may attempt to impose tight control using conventional control systems such as technology, authority structures and careful allocation of punishment and reward. The result will be a passive, compliant but possibly resentful workforce; the day-to-day work will be done but there will be little enthusiasm, initiative or commitment.

References

Adams, J. S. (1965) Inequality is social exchange, in L. Berkowitz (ed.) *Advances in Experimental Social Psychology*, 2. New York: Academic Press.

Betts, P. W. (1993) *Supervisory Management* (6th edn). London: Pitman.

Buchanan, D. A. and Huczynski, A. A. (1985) *Organizational Behaviour. An Introductory Text*. New York: Prentice Hall.

Evans, D. (1992) *Supervisory Management: Principles and Practice* (3rd edn). London: Cassell.

Evans, L. (1992) Teachers' morale and satisfaction: the importance of school specific factors. Paper presented at the 1992 Annual Conference of the British Educational Research Association.

Evenden, R. and Anderson, G. (1992) *Management Skills, Making the Most of People*. Wokingham: Addison-Wesley.

Feldman, D. C. and Arnold, H. J. (1983) *Managing Individual and Group Behavior in Organizations*. Auckland: McGraw-Hill.

Gray, J. L. and Starke, F. A. (1988) *Organizational Behavior, Concepts and Application* (4th edn). Colombus: Merrill.

Guest, D. (1984) What's new in motivation? *Personnel Motivation*, May: 21–3.

Henne, P. and Locke, E. A. (1985) Job dissatisfaction: what are the consequences? *International Journal of Applied Psychology*, 20: 221–40.

Hertzberg, F. (1996) *Motivation to Work*. New York: John Wiley.

Herzberg, F., Mausner, B. and Synderman, B. B. (1959) *The Motivation to Work*. New York: John Wiley.

Johannson, H. and Page, G. T. (1990) *International Dictionary of Management* (4th edn). London: Kogan Page.

Kakabadse, A. *et al.* (1988) *Working in Organizations*. London: Penguin.

Katz, D. and Kahn, R. (1978) *The Social Psychology of Organizations*. New York: John Wiley.

Kempner, T. (ed.) (1971) *A Handbook of Management*. London: Penguin.

Lawley, P. (1985) Tackling morale, *Education Administration and Management*, 13(3): 199–206.

Locke, E. A. (1965) The relationship of task success to task liking and satisfaction, *Journal of Applied Psychology*, 49: 379–85.

Locke, E. A. (1968) Towards a theory of task motivation and incentives, *Organizational Behaviour and Human Performance*, 3: 157–89.

Locke, E. A. and Latham, G. P. (1990) Work motivation: the high performance cycle, in U. Kleinbeck, H-H. Quast and H. Hacker (eds) *Work Motivation*. Brighton: Lawrence Erlbaum Associates.

Luthans, F. (1989) *Organizational Behaviour* (5th edn). New York: McGraw-Hill.

Maslow, A. (1943) A theory of work motivation, *Psychological Review*, 50(4): 370–96.

McGregor, G. (1970) *The Human Side of Enterprise*. Maidenhead: McGraw-Hill.

Mowday, R. T., Porter, L. W. and Steers, R. M. (1982) *Employee Organization Linkages*. London: Academic Press.

Mullins, L. J. (1993) *Management and Organizational Behaviour* (3rd edn). London: Pitman.

Neider, L. (1980) An experimental field investigation utilizing an expectancy theory view of participation, *Organizational Behaviour and Human Performance*, 26(3): 425–42.

Nias, J. (1980) Leadership styles and job satisfaction in primary schools, in T. Bush, R. Glatter, J. Goodey and C. Riches, *Approaches to School Management*. London: Harper and Row.

Nias, J. (1981) Teacher satisfaction and dissatisfaction: Herzberg's 'two-factor' hypothesis revisited, *British Journal of Sociology of Education*, 2(3): 235–46.

Riches, C. and Morgan, C. (1989) *Human Resource Management in Education*. Milton Keynes: Open University Press.

Steers, R. M. and Porter, L. W. (1991) *Motivation and Work Behaviour*. New York: McGraw-Hill.

Torrington, D. and Weightman, J. (1989) *The Reality of School Management*. Oxford: Blackwell.

Vroom, V. H. (1964) *Work and Motivation*. New York: John Wiley.

Whaba, M. A. and Bridwell, L. G. (1976) Maslow reconsidered: a review of research on the need hierarchy theory, *Organizational Behaviour and Human Performance*, 15: 212–40.

7 | Managing stress in educational organizations

MEGAN CRAWFORD

This chapter looks at the concept of stress and the ways it can be managed on both an individual and institutional level. Various models of stress will be examined, and the key issues of personality, coping strategies and relationships discussed. This chapter acts as a short introduction to the field, and as a stimulus for discussion. It aims to help reflection on the definition and concept of stress. Also, managing people requires skills both in self-management, and in managing others. In order to do this, the relationship of stress to the workplace – such an important aspect of overall stress management – will be closely examined. Although the word 'stress' often has negative connotations, it must be emphasized at the outset that some stress can be positive and beneficial, and is actually necessary to make us effective in the tasks we set ourselves. Learning to recognize stress in oneself, and its nature, is the first stage of effective management.

Towards a definition

Kyriacou and Sutcliffe (1978) defined stress in teaching as the experience by a teacher of unpleasant emotions such as tension, frustration, anxiety, anger, and depression resulting from aspects of the work teachers do. They emphasize the role of the teacher's perception of the circumstances, and the degree of control s/he feels. It can be argued that most stress comes from the way that the person thinks about it and appraises it. A survey for the Industrial Society (December 1995) suggested that it is a major problem in nine out of ten workplaces, leading to rising absenteeism and low morale. Trying to achieve some common understanding of stress is by no means an easy task. Teaching is but one of many occupations in which it is claimed that the job causes excessive stress. Disagreements over what stress is may arise because when people discuss stress they are not necessarily discussing the same thing. This variation in meaning means that the whole subject area can become quite confusing. Some people may even feel that the word 'stress' is used to describe difficulties from severe personality problems to moaning about employers. The amount of change in education may be seen as a factor in causing stress levels to rise dramatically over recent years and is often cited as a reason for teachers taking early retirement. *The Guardian* (Carvel and Macleod 1995) reported that recruitment to the profession is failing to keep pace with increasing stress-related early retirement. One might agree with Millstein and Farkus (1988: 232) that incidents of reported stress are 'merely a product of an articulate group being encouraged to grumble in public'. However, research carried out in the early 1980s before the recent upsurge in the incidence of stress disagrees with this view. Smilansky (1984: 85) argued that work stress has special meaning in relation to the teaching profession, in that only in teaching is an individual required to play so many roles such as 'supportive parent, disciplining taskmaster, stimulating actor and information resource person . . . the special affective characteristics of the profession exert pressure towards presenting an understanding, supportive and optimistic appearance.' Also, with the rapid changes in education, roles may have become more fluid and staff may suffer from the unreasonable expectations of others perhaps external to the organization. This loss of control may lead to stress.

Stress has its origins in 'fight or flight', a physical reaction occurring when humans were faced with a frightening situation. The hormones involved in making the body ready to fight for its existence in the wild are now being used to gear up for action in a different way. So people may not be able to attack those who are causing them stress, but some of the physical signs will be the same – raised blood pressure, sickness in the stomach, etc. If these 'attacks' continue then people collapse from stress-related illnesses. Even if there is a refusal to recognize the stress, eventually the body will begin to show unmistakable signs. There can be many visible responses when people are feeling stressed, e.g. anxiety, poor concentration and difficulty in decision making. Increased adrenaline can of course be beneficial as one strives to finish a task on time. The downside of this can be a pattern of frustration, anxiety and exhaustion; a downward spiral develops. Selye's classic framework (1956) for stress may be helpful in understanding how stress causes such problems to so many. He described a framework for examining the four basic variations of stress, which classifies the different types of stress:

1 hyperstress or too much stress
2 distress or bad stress
3 hypostress or understress
4 eustress or beneficial stress.

Too much stress leads to the symptoms detailed above; too little means that people don't perform at their best. Hebb (1972) emphasizes that too few demands make for boredom, and that the individual must somehow balance external demands to meet personal capacities and therefore achieve peak performance. In fact there is much less written about understress, but it can be just as serious a challenge for a manager to motivate those who are underused or in some way underachieving as to tackle the signs of bad stress. Physical responses to perceived threats vary widely from individual to individual. Many studies (e.g. Kyriacou and Sutcliffe 1978; Cook 1992; Dunham 1992) look at the factors that teachers identify as causing stress (stressors). Although all the writers emphasize that each must be placed within its own particular organizational context, several sources of stress emerge repeatedly. These include relationships with students and other staff, work overload, physical working conditions, and status issues. All these sources can produce symptoms of stress. These may manifest themselves in many different physical and mental signs, unique to the individual, although there are some general patterns. Selye (1976) has identified the most common physical and mental symptoms experienced by those who are stressed. The list includes such things as being unable to concentrate, fatigue, excessive eating/smoking, headaches, etc. Changes from an individual's normal behaviour pattern may also become apparent, as may swings of mood. Greenberg (1984) suggests that these symptoms should be taken as warning signs of a problem, as would be the case in any other illness. He and others (e.g. Dunham 1992) have suggested that an individual can reduce the pressure by developing personal coping strategies. When they are unable to do this, mental and physical stress reactions follow. Watts and Cooper (1992) suggest that we need to look at the overall balance between our stress levels and individual vulnerability, using a stress equation: 'Life stress + work stress + individual vulnerability = stress symptoms outcome' (p. 57). This is actually much harder than it sounds, especially if the workplace is one where there is no culture of admitting to difficulties and it is seen as a sign of weakness. At a personal level, it may be necessary to accept feelings and admit that it isn't always possible to cope. Individuals may be involved in an institution where they can only partially mitigate the effects of stress. However, understanding something about personality, and seeking to comprehend how others work may help to bring stress to acceptable levels.

Personality and stress management

The nature of one's personality will also determine how threats are assessed and the strategies chosen to moderate the perceived stress. In studying the cause of heart problems, Friedman and Rosenman (1974) identified two types of personalities. Type A were more likely to have heart problems and were identified as being ambitious, competitive, hypercritical, perfectionist workaholics who were often anxious and insecure underneath. They often took on two or more tasks at the same time. Type B on the other hand were mostly able to give themselves time to reflect, were generally more laidback, and yet were still able to respond to situations effectively. They did not view work as the most important part of their existence, and adopted a more balanced approach. Kelly (1988) found that headteachers scored higher than average type A scores. Another factor to be taken into account when discussing whether people can be more prone to stress is the concept of hardiness. People with a hardy personality have several important attributes. Watts and Cooper (1992) call these attributes commitment (belief in self), control (belief that one can influence events) and challenge (a positive attitude to change). Hardy personalities seem to perceive clearly where they are going in life, and know that they are in control and responsible for their behaviours. When new stressors arise these will be seen as opportunities rather than threats. Closely linked to the concept of a hardy personality is the idea of 'locus of control'. This is the extent to which individuals see things that are happening to them as in or out of their control. It has two aspects, internal and external. Those who have an internal locus of control use their internal resources to control their environment. Those whose locus of control is external view life in a much more passive way, with them playing no real part in how events turn out.

Some people, it would appear, can tolerate stressful situations more than others, although even the most hardy may succumb eventually. This will vary depending on the context, the length of time the stress has been present, and the way that person views its worth to them as an individual. Because the individual is so important in stress management, stress will affect different people doing the same task in the same setting in different ways. Even the possibility of analysing stress will be seen by some as threatening because of the degree of self-searching that it requires. However, understanding one's own personal sense of stress is a necessary part of the process that will enable coping mechanisms to develop.

Coping strategies: the individual and the organization

So far the discussion has focused on how stressors can trigger a positive or negative response from individuals. This awareness of potential stressors needs to be ongoing, and coping mechanisms have to be flexible enough to alter in the light of those stressors. Although individuals can learn to change their individual responses to create a new situation with a more acceptable level of stress, and some individuals may well be more vulnerable to stress, other factors play a significant part. It would be easy if individuals could assume that there is some sort of panacea for all stress, a point made by Dunham (1992). He recounts being asked to speak to a group of headteachers on stress management. The letter of invitation concluded with the words: 'One of my colleagues has suggested that you might like to send us a tape so that we could try out the cure'! However, several sorts of individual 'coping patterns' or 'coping mechanisms' can be identified. The first strategy of many people is to deny the reality of the stressful situation for as long as possible. In order to do this successfully, palliative measures may be necessary. Palliative measures are those short-term ones that give an immediate relief (e.g. smoking, drinking and overeating) but that need to be replaced by a more effective overall response. Hughes (1990) suggests *palliative* measures as one of four strategies than an individual might use to cope with stressors. Any individual can employ a combination of these at any one time. *Direct* measures may include political action of some kind: trying to modify job demands by changing the system or possibly changing the culture of the organization. *Indirect* measures are when one as an individual may change responses to demands by using peer support groups, counselling and other strategies. *Compensatory* measures are patterns such as developing outside interests, e.g. swimming, a more balanced lifestyle overall.

Hughes's direct mechanisms impinge directly on organizational culture. Although individuals can maintain a happy balance in their life by successful coping strategies, the organization where they work plays a vital sustaining part. Effective stress management that pervades the culture of the organization follows from managers adopting a specifically organizational focus. The direct strategy is particularly relevant to those involved in management as it focuses on what can be done to prevent or alleviate stress in the institution. Managers can build up the resources for tackling stress in their organization, and at the same time strengthen the personal and interpersonal resources of their staff. This may imply long-term cultural change.

Individuals' personal realities need to be looked at in the context of both the home and the workplace, as home will be where people spend the majority of their time. Biographical details may give some clue to what may tip the balance for them from coping to distress. Home can be a valuable support system or the opposite, and it can be very difficult to leave concerns about family matters at home. A change or significant life event in someone's personal life must be seen as potentially distressing. Managing events such as bereavement requires skill and the knowledge that it may be better for the staff member to have a longer time out in order to recover than perhaps seems necessary. Making individuals return to work before they have got over a major life event may cause more problems for the organization in the longer term.

Managers can also help to alleviate stress in periods of organizational uncertainty and change by presenting relevant information to keep staff informed. Communication channels within the organization need to be examined to make sure they are operating effectively so that those in other levels hear the correct information. Open discussion and the use of conflict management skills may also help to decrease stress levels. Knowing how to approach the stressed colleague is a skill in itself. We have already noted that denial may be present in many stressed individuals. An organizational culture that allows a channel for expressions of problems may help to prevent this problem becoming serious. The way leadership in the organization is perceived may also have an effect on the amount of workplace stress. This does not mean just one person in a leadership position, but the way leadership is performed throughout all levels. The emphasis in a workplace may be on developing the team as a resource in handling stress. Those who have formal leadership roles may become stressed themselves, as one person cannot truly remain in control all the time. Some staff may even find an organization where decision making is taken out of their hands less stressful!

Stressful working conditions can create a climate of frustration and tension, often due to a long-term build-up of stress. This may lead to severe stress or 'burnout'. This concept is a useful one for highlighting some of the strategies we have already discussed. In a state of burnout, a person finds their emotional resources exhausted, they may feel undervalued or worthless. It comes about as a response to severe stress, and too many demands. The only way for this individual to go is downward, and depression or other ill health may be the result. It could be argued that the nature of teaching makes burnout a possibility at all times. The threat to self-esteem of admitting that one can't cope is huge. Teachers and lecturers fear they may be seen as weak, and may have recourse to some of the palliatives described earlier, which exacerbate the situation even faster. Blaming an individual for something is of course an easy way to avoid tackling root problems in the organization, but burnout happens to all kinds of individuals when a situation arises that they cannot cope with by their usual coping strategies. They can become overloaded with too much change, too many demands on their time, and not enough time in which to do the core job effectively. If time is given to such a person by those in management positions to listen, support and help, then the vicious cycle of perceived worthlessness can be avoided, and also perhaps long-term sick leave. So we have the idea that valuing individuals within an organization may mitigate the effects of some of the forces that are feeding the feelings of stress and inadequacy.

Cook (1992) makes several positive suggestions for handling individual stress, some of which have applicability to the organization as well. She suggests that most individual strategies have to be introduced by those with power to implement change and support personal growth. Greenberg (1984) suggests that managing stress success-fully requires many of the strategies that a good teacher would use, such as reviewing, involving others, and planning what is attainable with the available resources, both in the long and short term. He suggests that the following questions should be looked at:

- In what aspects of my life do I need to reduce stress most?
- What stresses and strains should I reduce now, and which can wait?
- What techniques for reducing stress seem best suited to my lifestyle?
- How can my family help, if at all?
- How can I use my friends and colleagues for support?
- How much time should I give to stress-reduction activities every day?

(adapted from Greenberg 1984: 99–100)

Managers can help individuals set realistic goals, and they can make suggestions for doing the same thing differently. Many individuals have developed a habit which is particularly stress inducing, and it often needs someone else to point this out. The use of support from colleagues can be very effective. Having a 'review partner' to talk things over with can help put things in perspective. Another strategy might be a diary reflecting on what causes individual stress and ways of tackling it. Organizations and individuals can make time for 'emotional breathers' that allow staff to recharge their batteries. An example of this would be making sure that breaks are taken, as stressed people often overwork. It is important for those who manage to remember that some individuals will want to work things out on their own or with more inten-sive one-to-one support. The latter may mean referral to outside agencies. If none of these helps reduce work-related stress levels significantly, an individual may need to contemplate moving jobs. This shouldn't be seen as running away but rather as making a better choice. Of course, a new organizational setting may prove to have even more potential stressors! The institution can do much to reinforce stress manage-ment by creating the climate where individual needs are met.

It would be no help if, as well as the initial stress suffered, individuals begin to feel guilty or more stressed about their inability to become more self-knowledgeable! Stress-reduction training in the form of improved communication skills and relaxation training could be part of the answer. Some schools have introduced a 'workout' session after school on Friday, which they find very beneficial in relieving stress and releasing tension before the weekend. Assertiveness training has also been used as a means of promoting stress reduction on both a personal and institutional level. It has been found to be particularly effective for women as it helps build up self-esteem. This form of training assumes basic rights which need to be respected, and teaches the skills that are needed to achieve this.

Summary

Stress can catch the unprepared individual before he or she realizes the situation is get-ting serious. People who work in education are pressured in many ways, and some-times for long periods without tangible rewards. Only an individual can tailor a stress management plan to fit particular goals and aspirations, which can be altered as situations change. The relationship between personal coping strategies and the organizational context is a complex one, but it is clear that the way the organization is managed plays a part in the stress felt by staff. Systems can be put in place for regular surveys of the situation, and managers can focus on the positive rather than the negative effects of stress. The individual role in monitoring his/her own stress levels needs to be seen as only a part of the process. Those that manage individuals need to understand the causes and symptoms of stress, and the strategies that can be employed to the benefit of the organization, and the individual.

References

Carvel, J. and Macleod, D. (1995) Ministers face teachers shortage time bomb. *Guardian*, 12 December.

Cook, R. (1992) *The Prevention and Management of Stress*. Harlow: Longman.

Dunham, J. (1992) *Stress in Teaching*. London: Routledge.

Friedman, M. and Rosenman, R. (1974) *Type A Behaviour and Your Heart*. London: Wildwood House.

Greenberg, S. F. (1984) *Stress and the Teaching Profession*. Baltimore, MD: Paul Brookes.

Hebb, D. (1972) *Textbook of Psychology*. Philadelphia, PA: Saunders.

Hughes, J. (1990) Stress: scourge or stimulant? *Nursing Standard*. 5(4): 30–3.

Kelly, M. J. (1988) *The Manchester Survey of Occupational Stress in Headteachers and Principals in the UK*. Manchester Polytechnic.

Kyriacou, C. and Sutcliffe, J. (1978) Teacher stress: prevalence, sources and symptoms. *Educational Psychology*, 48: 159–67.

Millstein, M. and Farkus, J. (1988) The overstated case of educator stress. *Journal of Educational Administration*, 26(2) July: 232–49.

Selye, H. (1956) *The Stress of Life*. New York: McGraw Hill.

Selye, H. (1976) *Stress in Health and Disease*. Woburn, MA: Butterworth.

Smilansky, J. (1984) External and internal correlates of teachers' satisfaction and willingness to report stress. *Educational Psychology*, 54: 84–92.

Watts, M. and Cooper, S. (1992) *Relax: Dealing with Stress*. London: BBC.

8 | Managing conflict in organizations*

R. E. WALTON

Interpersonal conflict in organizations

Interpersonal conflict is defined broadly to include both (1) substantive disagreements such as differences over objectives, structures, policies, and practices, and (2) the more personal and emotional differences that arise between human beings.

The following are examples of conflicted relationships in organizational settings:

1 Two managers needed to work together but continued to cancel each other's ideas and blunt each other's initiatives.
2 Members of a divisional staff were engaged in a disruptive conflict, which resulted in ill-defined goals and poorly coordinated activities.
3 Two members of a team continually had disagreements that frustrated the development of the team's self-management capabilities.

In each case the conflict was continual, had become embedded in the relationships, and interfered with individual and joint performances.

Interpersonal relations in organizations are created by interdependencies involving physical work flows, technical services, information, or advice. One's actions may be controlled by the actions of another person just as one's performance may be evaluated by another. These and other interdependencies make conflict inevitable. Even if it were thought to be desirable, it would not be possible to create organizations free from interpersonal conflicts.

While conflict between organizational members is natural, indeed inevitable, direct approaches to dealing with this fact of organizational life are not. Several tendencies explain why.

---

* This material has been edited and was originally published as the Introduction in *Managing Conflict: Interpersonal Dialogue and Third-Party Roles*.

Inhibitions are a factor. To express anger, resentment, or envy toward another member of a work organization may be considered bad manners or immature. But if these feelings are not expressed directly, they usually will be indirectly, often in ways that create new conflict issues or incur other costs.

The immediate energy requirements also influence the way conflict is managed. It takes emotional energy to suppress the conflict totally, and it may take even more emotional energy to confront it. Therefore, conflicts often are played out in some indirect mode, which usually takes the least energy – in the short run. Indirect conflicts, however, have the longest life expectancy and have the most costs that cannot be attributed to the original conflict.

Another factor is risk. Important differences over policy and procedure may not surface because one or both of the principals fear that the conflict might create a residue of interpersonal antagonisms and hurt their careers. These risks are often real, but they can be minimized by understanding the ingredients for more effective dialogue and skill in supplying these ingredients.

The dialogue approach

The premise is not that interpersonal conflict in organizations is necessarily bad or destructive and that either those directly involved or third parties must inevitably try to eliminate or reduce conflict. Interpersonal differences, competition, rivalry, and other forms of conflict often have a positive value for the participants and the social system in which they occur. First, a moderate level of interpersonal conflict may increase motivation and energy. Second, conflict may promote innovation because it highlights diverse viewpoints. Third, people may develop increased understanding of their respective positions, because the conflict forces them to articulate their views and to bring forth all supporting arguments.

On the other hand, conflict can be debilitating for the participants, can rigidify the social system in which it occurs, and can lead to distortions of reality. Both the nature of the interdependence between the parties and the level of conflict will determine the nature of the consequences for the parties.

One can distinguish between resolution and control as different goals of conflict management. The principals themselves or a third party may attempt to gain resolution, so that the original differences or feelings of opposition no longer exist; or they may attempt merely to control conflict, so that the negative consequences of the conflict are decreased, even though the opposing preferences and antagonisms persist.

Conflict management may involve dialogue, but it need not. If the conflict between two managers is primarily a decisional conflict, about how to allocate resources between two projects, say, then it may be more appropriate for their supervisor to hear them out and make the allocation decision. If the underlying issue is already understood to result from contradictory role requirements, and if other interpersonal issues are already understood to be incidental to the conflict, then a structural change may be both appropriate to the task and helpful to the relationship. If there is a strong emotional component to the relationship and one or both of the parties can readily be transferred to another assignment, then terminating the relationship may be a good solution. Even if the conflict has a complex mix of substantive and emotional components and the relationship is one that would be costly to terminate, alternatives to dialogue must be considered. If by some means other than dialogue one or both of the principals gain the necessary insight into the dynamics of the conflict, then each may take unilateral steps to control the conflict, for example by avoiding the conditions that trigger conflict behavior.

Acknowledging these alternative solutions, let us turn to the dialogue option. *Dialogue* means that the parties directly engage each other and focus on the conflict between them, including aspects of their relationship itself. Dialogue can be instrumental to either resolution or control. The constructive outcomes of the three conflict examples introduced are illustrative.

1 At the suggestion of their common superior, the two managers who persisted in canceling and blunting each other's contributions entered into dialogue about their differences. Each regarded the other as a rival for the same opportunities for promotion. With the assistance of an internal organizational consultant who had been working with the unit on other matters, the two managers identified what each person was doing to transform their normal rivalry into a destructive conflict. They resolved to learn how to manage both trust in their task relations and feelings of rivalry in their striving for advancement. They were largely successful.

2 The divisional managers whose conflict led to poor coordination and confusion about goals were brought into dialogue to explore their differences and find some basis for accommodation. Both personal style and contradictory role definitions were contributing to the ongoing conflict. The outcome: although they did not significantly change their respective personal styles of relating, they did modify and integrate their respective role definitions, and they moderated their emotional conflict.

3 The conflicting workers were urged by other members of the team to address their differences, in this case with the help of the team's supervisor, who wanted to accelerate the team's development of self-management capabilities. The interpersonal conflict was traced back to an earlier incident in which each had misinterpreted the intentions of the other. Subsequent issues were symptoms and tactics resulting from the ensuing distrust. After a period of wariness, traces of this interpersonal conflict disappeared completely.

The basic objective of dialogue is to manage the conflict by resolution or better control, certainly to reduce its costs and, it is hoped, to improve the quality of the working relationship. A good working relationship has the following attributes:

- identification of and commitment to the largest set of common goals appropriate to the co-workers' respective roles
- mutually agreed roles
- mutual trust and respect
- shared norms and expectations
- respect for individual differences and tolerance for diversity of views.

Ideally the co-workers will be capable of effective and efficient communication and will find their relationship energizing rather than enervating. The importance of such attributes varies depending on task interdependence and context of the working relationship. However, they illustrate conditions that can result from better management of interpersonal conflict and can in turn enable better management of differences in the future.

When facilitated by a third party, the conflict management process described here can be educational or developmental for the participants, improving their skills for diagnosing conflict and resolving it through interpersonal dialogue.

The dialogue approach demonstrated here involved a third party, but the approach can work equally well for the conflict participants by themselves. It works well for two reasons. First, the diagnostic framework for analyzing the dynamics of inter-personal conflict offers to the participants themselves many of the same options for managing their conflicts it offers to would-be third parties. For example, it provides the participant the choice of entering into dialogue or taking other steps to control the conflict.

Second, the dialogue approach described here is based on a functional theory; it pre-scribes the functional requirements that must be met for a dialogue to be constructive, acknowledging that an array of techniques can be utilized to meet them. The require-ments include mutual reinforcement of motivation, balanced power in the situation, and an optimum level of tension. Thus, one or both of the parties themselves can attempt to assess the adequacy of these required ingredients. Preliminary assessment by a person considering a dialogue may establish that some of the specified conditions are already favorable and that the others can probably be implemented by the par-ticipants themselves. Many, but not all, of the possible mechanics by which these ingredients are provided can be implemented by the parties to the conflict.

Thus one or both of the principals themselves can make more informed judgments, not only whether to enter into a dialogue, but also whether a third party is required; and if so, whether a colleague or a professional consultant is needed, and if not, what they themselves need to do to increase the effectiveness of their encounter.

We turn now to trends that underscore the need to consider the general relevance of the dialogue concepts and methods in organizational settings.

Trends in organization and the management of differences

Several important trends have been underway recently, affecting the way we should think about the problem and the approach to it outlined here.

One of the most fundamental changes has been increased competition. One direct effect of the heightened competition is that there is less tolerance for overtly individual-oriented or department-oriented behavior and more insistence that actions must be good for the organization as a whole. For this reason alone certain forms of intergroup behavior that were commonly observed a decade earlier appear to be somewhat less common now.

Other indirect effects of heightened performance requirements on conflict and con-flict management are even more significant. We are witnessing a profound transforma-tion in the way organizations attempt to utilize human resources. The transformation includes the following features.

There is a trend toward flatter organization, with broader spans of control. Jobs or positions are more broadly defined, their requirements contingent upon changing task conditions. Team structures are used more, with the group rather than the individual defined as the accountable unit. There is more delegation of responsibilities for coordi-nating different functions to lower levels of the organization. And there is more use of project and matrix organizational forms, task forces, and participative problem-solving groups such as quality circles, as well as more forms of employee consultation.

These changes all affect conflicts to be managed because (1) they rely more on lateral coordination and less on hierarchical control, (2) they involve more *mutual* influence between persons at different hierarchical levels, (3) they deliberately design roles in which responsibility exceeds formal authority, (4) they expand the bases of influence beyond the more traditional concept of positional authority to include more dynamic factors like information and expertise, and (5) they involve inherently more ambiguity.

The net effect is to put a higher premium on interpersonal skills, including communication and conflict management. But that does not mean that the gap has increased between required and actual competencies. Fortunately, while the level of requirements for such competencies has been rising over the past decade, so too have the actual competencies. What is expected of managers and what is rewarded has changed. [. . .]

The increased consciousness of process is especially important for the dialogue approach because, combined with the generally increased organizational skills, this greater attention to process has brought about a redefinition of the role of organization development has a specialization in the corporate organization.

[. . .]

Therefore we emphasize even more than we did in the past the potential of team members, staff members, even organizational superiors to promote constructive dialogue between their colleagues who are experiencing persistent differences.

A further implication of these changes is that the types of assistance provided managers in conflict by colleagues often is more appropriately called 'facilitation' than 'third-party consultation'.

There is a trend for resolution of conflict to occur in more varied and less formal ways. In recent years the types of dialogue described here have often occurred naturally and been facilitated relatively implicitly in organizational settings. The basic functional requirements have not changed; nor have the types of behaviors that provide those requirements changed in any systematic way. What has changed is the skill of the participants in dialogue, which has become greater, as has their reliance on organizational colleagues to provide the third-party facilitation required.

[. . .]

Relation of dialogue to other approaches to conflict management

The appropriateness of different approaches to conflict management depends importantly on the nature of the conflict. Three basically different processes are involved in the interaction between conflicting parties. The first process is *bargaining* over fixed-sum issues, in which what one party gains another must lose. The second process is *problem solving* to resolve variable-sum issues, in which, because the principals' underlying interests are not mutually exclusive, it is possible for them to identify these underlying interests and invent win/win solutions. The third process is *relationship structuring*, a process by which parties redefine or reinforce their mutual perceptions and attitudes, the meaning of their roles and relationship, and the norms that govern their interaction in the other processes.

These several processes are interrelated. Most of a party's actions directly instrumental to any one of these processes have side effects for one of the other processes. For example, openness in the service of problem solving may create vulnerability in the bargaining process. Also an irrevocable commitment instrumental to bargaining can hurt an established relationship.

The product of the third process, the state of the relationship, is a major factor determining how efficient and effective the parties will be in compromising their inherent differences via bargaining, and in integrating their interests via problem solving. For example, the more mutual trust and respect, the more effective the substantively oriented processes, especially those involving a mixture of problem solving and bargaining.

How do the dialogue method and the third-party role relate to different combinations of these processes? Dialogue and, if necessary, third-party facilitation of the dialogue become appropriate when there is deemed to be a need to improve the quality of the future relationship or at least to improve the attitudes and understandings sufficiently to enable the parties to deal with acute issues or problems. However, when the salient processes are strictly bargaining or a combination of bargaining and problem solving, then mediation is the relevant third-party role. In some circumstances, of course, this distinction between the mediator and the third-party role becomes a matter of emphasis. Mediation may need to generate a change in relations in order to obtain a resolution of the dispute in question; and the dialogue approach to improving a relationship may require the resolution of some substantive dispute at the heart of the deteriorated relationship.

The basic premise underlying the emphasis on improving conflictful *relationships*, rather than resolving specific issues in conflicts, is that the quality of the relationship itself is a determinant of the performance of the parties to the relationship and their ability to handle future differences.

PART 2

Working in teams

9 | Staff teams and their management

LES BELL

[. . .] Teams need to be deliberately and carefully managed. Tasks within the team need to be shared and responsibilities distributed. This does not involve a 'hard' approach to management founded on directing, controlling, commanding and ordering. In a community of professional colleagues, involvement, co-operation, participation, delegation and effective two-way communication are the essence of management. It is important, however, that teamwork is based on good, professional working relationships which may not be the same as good social relationships. In short, this approach to management will need to be based on effective teamwork throughout the school.

What is teamwork?

The school staff team will have a number of characteristics. It will have a process for discussing its aims and it will seek to identify and achieve common objectives. Whatever its structure, the effectiveness of the group will be increased if there is recognition of the importance of agreed perceptions of the task and of a shared achievement of these common objectives. Thus, shared and agreed plans for the development of the school and for the part to be played in that process by identified individuals is important. Each staff team, whether it is the whole staff group working together or a smaller group of colleagues with a shared function, will have to develop working relationships which are consistent with the overall philosophy of the school. These relationships will need to be negotiated within the group. Once these are established, they will need to be managed. Building and managing staff teams is the prime responsibility of the headteacher and senior staff. It is also an important responsibility of any individual teacher who happens to be leading a group of colleagues at any particular time. This is especially true of those in middle management positions in schools, to whom much of the responsibility for team building and managing is normally delegated. Thus, although professional or subject expertise may be the basis of such leadership, the leadership function can only be carried out to its maximum effect if the staff team is consciously built and effectively managed.

In any discussion of team building and managing, an understanding of the nature of teamwork is crucial but seldom considered. It is generally assumed that everyone knows what teamwork is. Thus, when 'staff team' is mentioned teachers are expected to have a shared perception of what that means. Most staffroom discussions of this matter will reveal just how erroneous that assumption is. For example, the prevalent notion of professional or staff development among almost any group of teachers will focus on developing the skills, knowledge and experience of individuals; but the key to successful teamwork is to be found in the way in which groups of teachers work with each other. Teamwork, therefore, extends beyond 'years' or 'departments'. Teams may be cross-curricular or cross-phase, and long-term or short-term staff groupings. Team or group development, therefore, should be seen as no less important than individual development because teamwork means individuals working together to achieve more than they could alone. The success of the school staff team, then, depends not only on the individual skills of its members but on the way the teachers support and work with each other (see Table 9.1).

Teamwork has been described as playing from the same sheet of music. The implication of this statement is that teamwork can build upon the strengths of individuals and create confidence within the group which individuals on their own may lack. Thus teamwork, which is demanding and time consuming, can help to reduce stress and pressure through the mutual support which it can provide. Within most schools the individual teacher has hitherto been regarded as the focal point for change and innovation and the locus of expertise. It has been argued here that the team – the collection of co-operating colleagues – will increasingly be the focal point of professional activity within the school. Such activity, if it is well managed, may bring significant benefits to individuals, to groups and to the whole school, as Table 9.2 shows. Thus, the collegial approach to management in schools, while it may be developing through force of circumstance, may bring with it some important benefits to schools. For this to happen the nature of teamwork has to be thoroughly understood. Effective teamwork will not happen automatically by placing groups of individuals in a room together with a task to perform. It requires a set of management strategies. These must be employed by the team leader whether she is the headteacher working with the whole staff or one teacher using her expertise in a particular area of the school's

Table 9.1 Teamwork

What is teamwork? A group of people working together on the basis of:

- shared perceptions
- a common purpose
- agreed procedures
- commitment
- co-operation
- resolving disagreements openly by discussion.

This will not happen automatically. Teamwork has to be managed if it is to be effective.

Table 9.2   The benefits of teamwork in the school

- Agreeing aims
- Clarifying roles
- Sharing expertise and skills
- Maximising use of resources
- Motivating, supporting and encouraging members of the team
- Improving relationships within the staff group
- Encouraging decision-making
- Increasing participation
- Realising individual potential
- Improving communication
- Increasing knowledge and understanding
- Reducing stress and anxiety

work in conjunction with a group of colleagues with responsibility, say, for the same year group. Colleagues may be members of several teams at any one time. Some teams may be temporary with specific and limited tasks such as planning part of an in-service day or a school concert. Others may be permanent, with responsibility for a subject, pastoral duties or part of the functioning of the school such as industry links or TVEI.

These groups are functional teams. They have a task or series of tasks to complete. They will all consist of a number of individuals with their own skills, experience and responsibilities as well as their own levels of commitment, personal concerns, pressures and influences. They will be guided by a team leader who accepts overall responsibility for the development of the team, its aims, the standards which it sets and the results which it achieves. The leadership of any such team may not depend on factors such as position in the school, experience or seniority. Team leaders will tend to be those people with direct and relevant expertise. Therefore, the teacher accepting responsibility for leading the work of a particular team – in a subject department perhaps – may be a relatively junior colleague. In that team may be the headteacher or a deputy head as a team member and not a team leader. The leadership will be provided by the teacher with the expertise. It is therefore crucial that all members of staff in schools understand the processes involved in managing and leading teams.

Team work is a group of individuals working together towards some common purpose and, in so doing, achieving more than they could alone. The justification for the existence of a working team in any school would seem, therefore, to be self-evident. Few enjoy working in a situation in which they are isolated, alienated, criticised, over-controlled or where they feel frustrated and dissatisfied with their own performance as a teacher or colleague. Successful teamwork can only take place when the team has the facilities required to gather relevant information, to make sound, informed decisions and to implement those decisions. The absence of any of these factors can mean that the team cannot work effectively or that it will not work at all. Lack of individual commitment can have a similar effect and so can a variety of personal issues which are not brought out into the open within the team context. Individuals may have undisclosed aims which they intend to pursue within the working of the team. The effect of such factors can be considerable. It is the responsibility of the team leader to be able to identify such factors and bring them into the open as part of teamwork.

Colleagues will contribute to the team only that which they feel, as individuals, they wish to contribute. This may include their knowledge and skills, but it may also include their dislikes and jealousies, their uncertainties and perceived or real lack of ability or experience. None of these factors needs to present the team leader with insurmountable difficulties provided she is aware of their existence and has strategies with which to manage them. Lack of skill may be overcome with training. Dislikes need to be aired within the team in a sympathetic and controlled way. Jealousies have to be countered by building self-esteem rather than by diminishing the worth of another individual within the team. An effective team leader will recognise that there are a number of psychological processes operating within any team through which colleagues come to identify with the team. These processes can be seen as a useful counterbalance to those factors which may make effective teamwork difficult.

Interaction between the individual and the team may take place on the basis of one or more psychological contracts which the individual may make, consciously or unconsciously, between herself and the team. The interaction may be based on:

(a) *compliance*, that is, the avoidance of some form of punishment or to gain some form of reward such as acceptance by the team. To the extent that the individual wishes to gain the reward or avoid the punishment, she will comply with what the team is doing;

(b) *identification*, that is, the need to find support for some course of action which the individual may wish to pursue and which she regards as being compatible with the activities of the team. The interaction may be based on rationality: on the recognition that the individual does not have to like the advice for this form of contract to be effective;

(c) *internalisation*, that is, the belief that what the team is doing, or how it seeks to perform its functions, is worthy of support and participation.

This latter is the strongest form of contract and the one which is likely to generate the greatest commitment from the team members to the team itself. Nevertheless, the other forms of contract should not be dismissed or disparaged provided that the team leader can identify them, recognise them for what they are and be aware of the limitations which they imply, for it is with bricks such as these that successful working teams are built.

Team development

Good teamwork needs to be based on an understanding of the different reasons for and ways of participating in a staff team. Each individual will participate to a slightly different extent and for somewhat different reasons depending on the nature of the psychological contract she has made between herself and the team. The effective leader of a staff team has to be aware of these factors. They constrain the extent to which colleagues are prepared to be involved in the workings of the group, but they are not the only factors affecting involvement. The individual factors mentioned in the previous section are also relevant and so is the way in which teachers perceive the staff team itself. People are usually more willing to commit themselves to expending their time and energy on a staff team if they understand clearly what they are doing and why they are doing it. This means that the team leader has to understand

and communicate to colleagues the rationale which underpins the work of the staff team. In other words the existence within the school of a clear and agreed approach to education, as formulated in the school's statement of aims and approached through the development plan, is a crucial element in the effectiveness of the staff team.

It will be clear from the way in which the school is organised that the activities of any staff team are only one part of the total work of the school. Realistically, therefore, there are limits to the problems with which it can cope and the issues which it can address. It serves no useful purpose to have an exaggerated view about what is possible within the framework of the working team. For example, neither the team nor its leader can necessarily be held responsible for having the wrong people appointed to the staff. No amount of teamwork can fit a square peg into a round hole. The team can, however, attempt to develop training programmes for those members who may lack certain skills or information. These need not be as elaborate as a full-blown in-service course, but might simply be the provision of an opportunity for an experienced colleague to work with a less experienced one on a particular aspect of school life.

The team cannot necessarily address directly the problems created by a confused or inappropriate organisational structure in which, for example, a particular group is not functioning effectively or, conversely, is too powerful for the good of the whole school. The team can only try to ensure that it achieves as much as it can in the circumstances. Nor can the team deal with situations which are characterised by a lack of overall planning within the school, low morale in the school or in the wider education system, an inappropriate system of rewards and promotions or other similar problems. These are management problems which are not capable of solution within the staff team. They will be part of the context within which the team has to work and over which its members have little or no control. They do not make effective teamwork impossible but they may make it more difficult. What, then, is effective teamwork?

An effective team consists of a group of individuals working together in such a way that much of what they do depends upon and overlaps with the activities of others. This interaction must take place smoothly, efficiently and effectively so that the general provision of education within the school is maintained and improved. This is only achieved by a careful consideration of the five main elements of teamwork: the aims and objectives of the team; its procedures; its processes; the ways in which team members relate to those processes; and the ways in which the activities of the team are reviewed and monitored. All teams are concerned about the image which they have of themselves and which others may have of them; about the standards which are set and the results which are achieved; about the extent to which they can improve and develop both and therefore about the extent to which individual needs, as well as those of the team, are taken into account when activities are planned and responsibilities allocated.

All of these concerns crystallise around the nature of the tasks which the team is expected to undertake. In any staff team the members will, to a greater or lesser extent, be aware of what has to be done. Successful teamwork, however, is best achieved when the aims and objectives are clear and when all members subscribe to them. The distinction between aims and objectives in this context is a crucial one.

Aims, in the context of managing a team in any school, are best regarded as being derived from the overall philosophy of the school and are broadly strategic in nature.

An appropriate aim for a pastoral team may be to provide guidance for colleagues on developing their teaching in pastoral and social education (PSE). This also needs to be expressed in terms of objectives.

The objectives are statements about what needs to be done, by whom, with whom, by when, to what standard of proficiency and what should be done as a result. These are the tasks of the team. Each team member should understand exactly what is required of her, and should be informed about the scale and urgency of the task to be carried out. It should not be assumed that team members have this information. The leader of the team should accept the responsibility for providing that information, for checking that it has been assimilated and understood, and for ensuring that the appropriate actions are taken. This is not an intrusion on the professional autonomy of colleagues but, rather, an essential part of the process of effective team management. Nothing inhibits successful teamwork more than the perception, whether accurate or not, that a member of a team is failing in her responsibilities to colleagues or pupils. It is rare indeed for any teacher to believe that she is culpable in this respect. Staff teams will respond to a situation in which the nature of the task to be undertaken is discussed, agreed and fully understood, especially when outstanding disagreements about these matters are resolved before any action has to be taken.

Teams of teachers in schools will tend to operate in somewhat different ways according to their circumstances. The different mix of individuals who make up the teams and the nature of the larger organisation, which in this case will be the whole school, all affect the functioning of the team. It is important to recognise that teams cannot exist independently of each other, or of the school itself. Nor should they seek to do so. The team's preferred way of working should be clearly understood by all members. It might be that the team is organised on an open, fully participative basis. Alternatively, it might be firmly and directly controlled by the team leader. The preferred method of operating for many teams is somewhere between those extremes. It will be based on a policy of encouraging all team members to be involved in decision-making where appropriate, but within a clear and specific policy framework based on the school's overall philosophy, aims and objectives as identified in the development plan and negotiated with and agreed by the team members.

The extent to which it is appropriate to involve team members will depend on such factors as the nature of the immediate task. Does it require quick decisions and action? To what extent does it demand clear direction or arouse much emotion? When clear direction is required or when the issue is emotive, too much participation can be counterproductive. Who is affected by the issue or task? Where several team members are affected by the task it is essential to involve all of them in key decisions. Where several team members have knowledge, experience or even an interest in a particular task or issue then it may not be necessary to involve all of them. The appropriate method of operating, therefore, might be on the basis of a predetermined view about who should be involved or about who should take the decision to involve other team members. A team leader who has the trust and respect of the team will be able to carry out this function effectively and ensure that the team can adopt procedures for taking decisions and carrying out tasks. The team can then concentrate on the process of achieving results.

If the procedures adopted by the team dictate how the individuals in that team operate as a group then the processes it uses will influence how it sets about achieving its objectives, getting the results and attaining the standards which it has set itself. The process of task achievement should start by ensuring that all the members of the team fully understand the aims and the objectives. Once established, the objectives need to be divided into tasks, and resources allocated to those tasks. As part of the aim to improve PSE teaching, one objective may be to investigate resources. One task related to this objective will be to look at the use being made of textbooks and work sheets. To achieve this task it is necessary to decide how and by whom the monitoring will be done. Thus the team has moved from an aim, through the stage of identifying relevant objectives, to breaking objectives down into a series of tasks and onto task implementation. Identifying and carrying out those tasks are part of the process of teamwork. The team is already into the realm of planning. Planning is simply a matter of identifying what has to be done, by whom, with what resources and to what time scale. It involves allocating tasks so that everyone within the team knows who is responsible for what.

With those responsibilities should go the necessary authority to ensure that the task can be completed successfully. Resources, both human and material, must be analysed, known and allocated in order to meet the requirements of the various tasks in the most effective way possible. All too often tasks are allocated and resources deployed on the basis of tradition and common practice rather than on the basis of what is actually needed to complete the task in hand. Timing, similarly, is important. Time is always at a premium and it needs managing. One team member's deadline may be another's start time. If the deadline is not met then the next task may not be completed on time. If, for example, the review of existing equipment and the identification of existing textbooks and work sheets are not completed on time then it becomes very difficult for the colleague who has to monitor equipment use to carry out her responsibility. If this is not done, then it will not be possible for recommendations about the future purchase of equipment to be considered. It is worth ensuring, therefore, that the team member responsible for achieving this particular objective knows how this task fits into the overall programme. One member of the team may, as a routine function, ensure that the various schedules are met; a timekeeper, in fact, should be identified. Carrying out the plans, then, requires good communication but it also requires that team members should listen to each other, be supportive and allow ideas and suggestions to be generated and used where possible.

Once the task has been completed this process should still continue. Time should always be allocated so that the team can review what has been done. Team review is a valuable learning and team development activity. All of the team members should be involved in discussing such questions as:

- Did we complete the task successfully?
- What went well in our process and can be repeated next time?
- What went badly and held us back?

It is because these questions are important to present activities as well as for the future development of the team that all team members should be present at such discussions, even if their roles were only marginal to the enterprise being considered.

The tasks of any team may change over time, especially if the team is based on year grouping or on a subject that is in a state of change. The processes to be applied in any given situation may vary somewhat from that described but it is important to remember that the tasks of the team form only one dimension of teamwork. The membership of the team is of crucial significance because it transcends any single set of tasks and tends to persist over time. Commitment to, or membership of the team may vary according to the issue or the task. Colleagues will devote more energy to that which they think is important. They will also give their time if they believe that they can influence outcomes or that they have something of value to offer. Membership of the team should be regarded as a variable which may need to be taken into account, reconsidered, developed and cultivated. Team members may need encouraging, re-assuring and appreciating in order to establish and retain their membership in an active sense.

The effective team leader has to be aware of these recurring factors and, over a period of time, needs to ensure that the various members of her team feel themselves to be a valuable part of that team. This can be done simply and informally by obser-ving how far team members feel able to relax in the team meetings; how far they have private reservations about team decisions; how far they really accept and under-stand team objectives; how well the team operates as a group and to what extent influ-ence is shared by all team members or is concentrated in the hands of a very small number of colleagues. The effective team leader will be able to collect much of the information implied in these questions by observation, not by interrogation. In the same way the team leader will recognise the extent to which responsibility is really shared within the team and the degree to which differences within the team are sup-pressed and denied or are identified and worked through satisfactorily. However, the team can only be strengthened and developed by open discussion of such vital matters.

Team membership can be regarded as the single most significant variable in the development of a successful team. It has to be seen for what it is, a variable rather than a constant. It has to be kept under review if the team is to remain effective. Thus, for any staff team in any school four elements are essential for effective team development. Objectives need to be agreed, shared, clearly understood and subdivided into a number of tasks. Procedures for decision-making and planning should involve all team members. The resulting processes for carrying out tasks should be clear to all team members. These procedures should be reviewed frequently in terms of how far they are facilitating the achievement of team objectives at that time (see Table 9.3).

All individuals bring to the team certain strengths and needs. The combinations may vary but the categories remain the same. Maslow (1954) identified five factors which influence the extent to which colleagues are committed to a team and which help to determine the nature of that commitment. Colleagues might, for example, have basic needs related to survival and existence. Such people will obviously be motivated by the need to earn money and, to the extent that they feel their rewards are just, they can be expected to function reasonably well. When, for example, a significant number of people feel that their rewards are not just, or conditions being imposed are unaccept-

Table 9.3   Developing the staff team

Team development	
Objectives	The objectives of the team should be clearly understood by all members.
Procedure	All team members should be involved in making important decisions.
Process	All team members should be clear about what has to be done, by whom, by when, with what resources.
Review	The team should review its work regularly as part of a development process.

able, then motivation may depend directly on changes related to basic rewards. Closely related to this is the need for safety and security. This is an especially powerful need when closure, re-organisation or redundancy threaten. Higher order needs can only motivate after these lower order needs have been satisfied. If teachers feel that their jobs are under threat they will not be concerned with esteem, status or professional development.

The third, fourth and fifth categories constitute what Maslow termed the higher order needs. These are the need for an acceptable self-image. Team members can be helped to become valuable team members by helping them to become the people that they want to be. Few people want to exist in isolation and most value being a member of a group.

The fourth category is the need to do something useful or meaningful. Clearly this is related to self-image but it does point out to the team leader that effective team management depends on understanding what colleagues want as much as knowing what the team objectives are. Fifth is the need to grow and develop. This can be a firm basis on which to build team membership. This is particularly true when the team can also provide the opportunity for personal development and, in so doing, meet the need to grow and develop which is experienced by most people. This need is recognised in pupils and is often expressed in terms like fully stretching them or allowing them to reach their full potential. Teachers have a similar need. A good team leader will be aware of that and manage to provide opportunities for team members to grow as part of the team's activities.

Colleagues who have a need for achievement will like to take personal responsibility, will value succeeding through their own efforts and will welcome feedback on how they are performing. The need for affiliation leads colleagues to be concerned with developing and maintaining group relationships rather than with decision-making and task achievement. The need for power finds expression in a desire to achieve results by working through other people. This formulation shows that, apart from financial reward, it is possible to provide rewards in several different ways. Those directly related to achievement might include:

- giving more responsibility, a more interesting activity, freedom to plan and implement, or a change in working conditions such as office space in which to work;
- providing more opportunity to express a particular talent, the chance to develop or improve knowledge or skill, or the chance to exercise full control over some aspects of the team's activities.

Those related to affiliation will include:

- giving approval, co-operation, friendship;
- providing opportunities to work with, to help and to support colleagues within the team.

The need for power can be met by:

- giving opportunity for planning and implementing a long-term or medium-term project;
- involving in broader management of the team and/or the school;
- giving responsibility for part of the work of colleagues.

These possibilities all provide the team leader with opportunities to manage her team to obtain the best effect, both for the individual and the group, while also achieving team objectives.

The importance for effective team management of being clear about the nature of the task has been emphasised throughout this chapter. Setting clear and attainable objectives for the team, allocating responsibilities within it, identifying targets and establishing ways of measuring its progress towards meeting those targets are all part of the duties of the team manager. Planning to ensure that the group attains the success which its members would not otherwise achieve either as individuals or without the management skills of the team leader is, therefore, a crucial part of the role of the effective staff team manager. Central to this is the ability to identify, define and communicate the nature of the tasks of the team members. Equally important are the ability to explain why the team is performing the tasks which have been identified and the flexibility to redefine tasks and encourage the team to reallocate responsibilities and resources when this becomes necessary. A plan is only good as long as it is relevant and is taking the team where the team wishes to go. Management, in this context, includes the ability to recognise when things are going wrong as well as knowing when they are going right.

When things are going right the essential task of the team leader is to maintain the team and ensure that it continues to work together as a co-operative, supportive entity in its own right. With encouragement this will usually happen but, at times, things do go wrong. When this happens it is frequently explained away by the glib phrase 'conflicting personalities', implying that team members are so different and difficult that hostility is endemic and conflict is inevitable. This extreme form of social determinism appears to have very little validity in real situations since it is possible to improve most situations. It might be more useful to view any threat to team co-operation in terms of a conflict of expectations rather than of personalities. Whenever the behaviour of one person violates the expectations of another it can reasonably be anticipated that co-operation may be withdrawn and conflict result. People will then attempt to hurt or punish colleagues rather than help or support them. In such a situation the team leader has to recognise what is happening and maintain the integrity of the team. This will, more often than not, have to be done by helping team members to explore their own behaviour with the intention of highlighting where the conflict in expectation is located but without attempting to attribute blame. Such team maintenance activities are the third dimension of effective team management in the school.

The final dimension of effective team management is the recognition that the leadership role will be different as the nature of the team's activities change (Adair 1983). For example, as already argued, the team will need firm and clear management when it has to complete a specific task within a limited period of time. Alternatively, when the team is exploring ideas and issues the emphasis needs to be on encouraging all colleagues to contribute and drawing contributions together in order to build upon them. At a briefing session, for example, the leader's skills of exposition, checking understanding and the management of information are of prime importance. Persuasiveness, openness and patience combined with the perceptiveness to recognise the importance of what is not being said as well as what is being said are also essential when reviewing.

These four elements – the individuals, the task, the team and the leadership role – have to be balanced by the effective manager of the staff team. This requires an understanding of the individuals in the team, an awareness of what is going on in the group, the skills to act upon this knowledge, and the recognition that different actions might be appropriate in different circumstances. If members are strongly motivated to achieve results, if the team has shared standards and targets, if colleagues seek ways to improve their processes through co-operation, and if individuals gain in confidence and ability through belonging to the team and contributing to its success, then the team leader has gone a considerable way towards ensuring that the basic elements of effective team management are all receiving attention.

It is still necessary to build on this, however. The team leader may have a duty to assist colleagues in their own professional development as part of and as an extension to the work of the team. This is related to delegation, but it must also involve some consideration of the career aspirations of team members. Team leaders need to consider these aspirations and try to allocate at least some of the duties within the team to help equip those colleagues to further those aspirations. Team leaders have a responsibility to broaden and expand the experience of staff in order to prepare them for their next promotion. The delegation and organisation of work within the team ought to be structured with this in mind. Team leaders at every level should maximise opportunities to develop colleagues and to assist them in gaining valuable and necessary experience to fit them for promotion, whether this is within the school or elsewhere. Such professional staff development can only take place if team leaders set aside time to talk to colleagues about their own development. Some team leaders may wish to initiate regular – although possibly not frequent – and relatively formal discussions with colleagues, while others may prefer to leave colleagues to take the initiative. However such discussions come about, they need to be given the same detailed attention that would be given to interviewing pupils or parents.

As with all other aspects of managing the team, however, the professional development function has to be seen within the context of the school as a whole. Teams do not work in isolation. They need to communicate with each other and to act as part of the whole school. The team will not control all aspects of its work since much of what it has to do will be circumscribed by school policy. This, in turn, contributes to the school's development plan which establishes curriculum, staff development, resourcing and management priorities for one, two or three years. The development plan creates the framework within which staff teams in the school are managed and resourced.

References

Adair, J. (1983) *Effective Teambuilding*. London: Pan.
Maslow, A. (1954) *Motivation and Personality*. New York: Harper and Row.

10 | The dynamics of teams*

MIKE WALLACE AND VALERIE HALL

In this chapter we consider six senior management teams (SMTs) and the part played by heads, with support from other SMT members, in creating and developing the teams. Headteachers are shown to have used the power accompanying their status in the management hierarchy to adopt a team approach and to work on shaping the culture of teamwork that underpinned its operation. We go on to look at the process of teamwork, focusing on shared decision making within SMT meetings. We discuss the significance of the norm that decisions must be made by consensus and examine how heads delimited the boundaries of joint work. Finally, we examine briefly the criteria used by team members, other staff and chairs of governors in judging the effectiveness of the SMTs.

Creating a team approach

The teamwork process represented the 'state of the art' within the unfolding of each team history, a pattern of working practices in which the heads had been prime movers. As one deputy acknowledged, 'You cannot just wave a management wand and say you've got teams. It doesn't happen that way. You have to do everything you can to create as much of a team as possible.' All six heads had been through significant experiences which had moulded their beliefs and values about teamwork. One head had turned to teamwork after a difficult period in the mid-1980s when teachers had taken industrial action. He had experienced a 'one term training opportunity' (OTTO) where the course leader had advocated a collaborative management style:

---

* This material has been edited and was originally published as 'Team Dynamics'.

The OTTO was most useful as an opportunity to recuperate, rethink, and replan the future of the school. I realised how much I had been wound up at that time when most heads were under considerable stress. I was able to realise that a lot of the problems in my school were not my problems, that I had to shift owner-ship of problems. That was a weakness in the previous system when the head had to take over responsibility for any problem, even down to fixing a lock or looking after a case of child abuse. The system simply was not working . . . I became determined with the appointment of the new deputies to move towards a team approach.

He had since taken every opportunity to appoint senior staff committed to teamwork.

The other heads, who had been appointed to their present post more recently, adopted a team approach from the outset. Their previous experience in senior man-agement positions and the circumstances they inherited affected their decision. Three heads had valued their SMT experience when they were deputies. The two taking up their second headship had different experiences as heads in their previous school. One continued the style of 'collaborative decision making' he had developed in his first headship, assisted by the fact that his predecessor had adopted a consultative style of management and existing SMT members welcomed his approach. In contrast, the other decided that a change was required from her previous style as head of a smaller school. She would be unable to deal with as many management tasks herself in a larger institution.

Each head therefore ascribed a positive value to teamwork. One was fascinated by the part played by leadership in developing teams:

> The buzz is taking a group of people who probably would never wish to go on holiday with each other, find themselves in the same campsite and actually settle down around the same stove. And don't squabble about it but produce a good meal at the end.

The heads used their power to build towards their conception of teamwork within the current institutional context. Some activities were directed towards establishing a cul-ture of teamwork, symbolising the values and practices that they wished others to embrace.

Unilateral action had been taken by one head in expressing his values concerning fairness and openness, to which he expected other staff, including SMT members, to conform. He made public within the SMT what individuals had said to him concern-ing any SMT member, removing the potential for a form of manipulation that had existed in the past:

> It was possible under a former regime to play one person off against another. Access to information being a key factor. That's not possible now because [the head] . . . will actually start the meeting by saying, '[A deputy] came to me a moment ago and said x' – so instantly it's public.

The head had ruled out reference to past incidents or enmities, so paving the way for new alliances among the staff he inherited:

> There's a lot of historical memory within the school. I'm not actually that inter-ested in it . . . there are some people who are very expert at keeping their skele-tons in their cupboards and as far as I am concerned, in many cases, long may

they stay there – or worms in the can. Because once they are out you can't get them back in.

Other staff had convinced another head that his personal style as leader had an impact on the school climate. In turn, he worked to ensure that the SMT was influential in sustaining the professional culture of the school, convincing his colleagues that the SMT's top priority must be high academic standards, and that its operation should be a model for the rest of the staff.

Selection of SMT members

All six heads used opportunities created by staff vacancies to appoint new members to the SMT according to what was needed to build a strong team. Four had expanded the size of the group, either through new appointments or by inviting staff to become members of the SMT. Selection criteria included educational values, competence in the individual responsibility to be undertaken, and the ability to fit into the existing SMT and contribute effectively to teamwork. Four heads had been influenced by the work of Belbin (1981) on complementary team roles, and sought to achieve hetero-geneity in teamworking styles within the SMT. One head was unique in being able to create a team from scratch. He used a typology of complementary team roles to assess candidates during the selection process for both deputies, having become aware of his preferred team role as a result of his recent training: 'I knew where I stood in the team and I wanted people not to be mirror images of myself but to have different qualities so that they could give different things to the team.' In contrast, the departure of a deputy at a different school had only recently provided the head with his first opportunity to make an SMT appointment. He sought to complement existing team members by appointing a 'completer/finisher' who would ideally be female, so reducing the present under-representation of women on the SMT. The suc-cessful candidate was indeed a woman, who commented:

> I learned after I'd been appointed why I'd been appointed. In particular the fact that I was a finisher and completer and task oriented in the Belbin sense was important. I'm always willing to finish a job, get on with it and say, 'What's next?' So I think my personality fits in with personalities in the team.

At another school, the head held an interview with each teacher to find out about staff concerns for the school, then invited an allowance holder into the team who was an ideas person and a good communicator. As existing SMT members left the school, she first invited another allowance holder who was long established and gave strong team support, then appointed a new deputy from within the school who was 'a very good curriculum thinker'. When the next opportunity to appoint a deputy came up she sought someone who had strong 'people skills', whose individual responsibility covered staff development and other personnel issues. This was an external appoint-ment, where the new deputy perceived that the selectors were looking for someone with a 'human touch in dealing with people'.

An important element of culture building was the heads' involvement of existing SMT members in selecting their future team colleagues. SMT members were consulted prior to inviting allowance holders to join a team. Where there was a formal selection process, as in the appointment of deputies, existing deputies were more closely involved than their allowance holder colleagues. They played some part in observing and initial interviewing of candidates. Questions about teamwork were frequently asked.

Some form of practical exercise entailing a team situation was reported in four schools, in three cases consisting of a simulation. In one case, selectors observed a 'goldfish bowl' exercise where each candidate presented a topic for discussion. Criteria for judgement of their performance were not divulged to the candidates. A positive criterion was each candidate's ability to facilitate other candidates in the group in offering their views; a negative one was to identify individuals who dominated. In another SMT, members had a meeting with the final two candidates for the staff development coordinator post which included SMT membership. They were asked to comment on the school development plan and present their plans for staff development. The exercise was designed to represent as closely as possible the working situation which the successful candidate would join.

An equally unintended consequence of SMT involvement occurred in two schools where the successful candidate was not the one preferred by an existing deputy. A difficult period of mutual adjustment followed, where the new SMT members had to work to gain these deputies' acceptance. It appears that in both cases it was difficult for a team member to accept the successful candidate (as teamworking norms required) having legitimately indicated at the selection stage that this person was not her or his first choice of team colleague, although the final decision rested formally with the governing body and was heavily influenced by the head. By contrast, in the three instances where an SMT member was an unsuccessful internal candidate for promotion to another post within the SMT, no friction was reported between this person and the successful candidate.

Team development

SMTs may go through a rapid period of evolution connected with changes in team membership, where old hands and newcomers go through a process of mutual adjustment. *Unstructured development* of the teams was largely subliminal, an outcome of working together. Interdependence grew with experience of support between the heads and their team colleagues. An SMT member (other than the head!) in three schools mentioned how the head's concern for them as people facilitated their own contribution to teamwork, echoing Halpin's (1966) contention that leadership includes attendance to personal needs.

The heads strongly appreciated the support of their SMT colleagues, since it was through them that much of the heads' work was achieved. One head valued having colleagues with whom she could give vent to frustrations. Yet, for the heads, support did not always include development. Two heads mentioned how few SMT members gave them positive or negative feedback on their performance. One commented:

> The one thing I never get from anybody – this isn't sob stuff at all – I never get any comment on my own performance, ever . . . I don't expect other staff to do that but even my closest team won't turn round – they almost feel you actually shouldn't say anything.

Another perceived that lack of praise from SMT colleagues was gender related, stating how the female deputy

> will give me the emotional support if I need it. She will realise what a woman is feeling in some situations. The men probably realise but can't come and support me in that way. She'll come and tell me if she thinks I've done something well or if a parent said the head is from a rotten school – and the others wouldn't do that. The men wouldn't say, 'I thought what you said to the parents was very good.' They won't give the praise, but a woman will to another woman.

Members of three SMTs mentioned how enjoyment of teamwork was nurtured through humour. A deputy remarked that 'a team that can joke together can work together'. SMT experience also offered a diffuse learning experience for individuals. An allowance holder reported how his ability to summarise points made in meetings improved by his noting how the head did it: 'There are times when I think, "I wish I had said that." So simple, so clever and so effective.'

Structured development activities (especially those offered by local authority staff) were variably employed by the teams. One or more individuals from each SMT had attended a training course during the last few years where teamwork had been addressed. In one authority there were courses for newly appointed deputies. This training did not extend beyond individuals, whereas the annual residential meeting supported by another authority was regarded as highly beneficial for development of the whole team. Residentials gave SMT members an opportunity for uninterrupted debate and being in each other's company. As an allowance holder put it: 'Time together to thrash through philosophy and just to relax together on those weekends just brings you together as a team.' The residentials could also provide an environment where tensions within the team could be resolved.

Activities initiated in school which related to the teams' management role included review days, sometimes with an external facilitator; a day's team training delivered by a management consultant from industry; and a seminar given by an industrialist on applying total quality management to schools. One head and one deputy had attended a week-long leadership course offered by the Industrial Society.

Formal induction of new SMT members was largely confined to instances where they were shouldering new individual responsibilities. The staff development coordinator at one school had received extensive support from the head, which included 'weekly meetings, very close monitoring, and complete availability if I needed him'. An allowance holder had found his first residential meeting an 'enormously valuable' induction into the SMT, while a deputy reported how her induction began prior to taking up post. It encompassed attending SMT meetings and participating in staff appointment panels. Her counterpart at another school had benefited from informal induction support from a deputy who was a friend and to whom she could turn for feedback and advice.

There was a marked contrast in how far the SMTs engaged in social activities intended as part of team development, reflecting different values among the heads and other SMT members. In all cases, socialising was an optional extra, rather than an obligatory part of the team approach. [. . .] One head reported how the SMT celebrated together as a group, as a way of reinforcing the culture of teamwork: 'Once or twice a year we have meals together and so on. And they are enormously good humoured. They do a good function and help to smooth over historical memories.

They are a way of giving people time as well.' At another school, SMT members took turns to host a social event at their home for team colleagues and their families. Otherwise, the head avoided social contact with individuals to avoid being 'seen to be having any favourites'. She believed that team leadership entailed paying even-handed attention to other members. Socialising with certain individuals carried the risk of a social hierarchy being formed within the team.

Two SMTs had very little social contact. One head perceived that socialising was not essential for effective teamwork, but would have added a desirable dimension:

> If we were the sort of group that could meet more informally, maybe socially, I think that would introduce a different element into the team. It continues to be . . . fairly formal I suppose. There is not the easy give and take, cut and thrust that I think might come about if you had a group of people who had more in common in terms of age, social life and family background.

Her view was confirmed by three other SMT members. Here the culture of teamwork included an implicit understanding about its limits: socialising was off the SMT agenda.

In sum, the process of team development was multifaceted: both subliminal and structured. The heads played a key part in nurturing their preferred teamwork culture, but it depended equally on the values of SMT members, only some of which were deemed to be appropriately the target of the heads' influence. This culture was strongly expressed within SMT meetings.

Joint work

[. . .]

Team meetings fulfilled, in the main, two purposes connected with the SMT's role: sustaining an overview and decision making. Within their responsibility as managers, heads required an overview of the school. Accordingly, they put items on the SMT agenda so as to gather information from other members, and monitored their progress within their individual areas of responsibility. Other members were less concerned with detailed knowledge of colleagues' work.

As team creators and leaders, the heads used their power simultaneously to promote the possibility of genuine participation in decision making and to keep the potential range of processes or outcomes within bounds that they defined. We suggest that the heads faced a dilemma over how far to foster an equal contribution by their colleagues to decision making. Equal contribution gave the advantage of increasing the range of ideas concerning a management problem. Yet it also opened up the possibility that heads might be outnumbered by their colleagues over a decision for which they alone could be held externally accountable. They protected their interest in avoiding their own disempowerment, which would follow from the empowering colleagues if synergy should fail to be achieved. Heads' safeguards, which potentially set boundaries, related to:

- chairing SMT meetings;
- setting the team agenda, and so delimiting what was to be included;
- making unilateral decisions by excluding them from the SMT;

- establishing the norm of consensual decision making within the team;
- retaining the right to make unilateral decisions by withdrawing them from the SMT arena.

They all *chaired SMT meetings*. Chairing was tied with *setting the SMT meeting agenda*, drawn up by the head in consultation with SMT colleagues.

One head had suggested to colleagues that they rotate the chair and agenda building task, to introduce a more equitable distribution of responsibility for the team meeting process. Other SMT members had resisted this proposal because they were comfortable with his performance and perceived that he was in the best position to do the work. A deputy noted that the head had the greatest access to information which might affect the agenda: 'Most stuff that goes onto the agenda goes on because it has come in through his desk. It's the only desk that everything travels across.' Another deputy added that he was trusted not to withhold items that should be within the province of the SMT. An allowance holder reported how the head informed SMT members about what he intended to keep off the agenda to save them time. Within the dialectic of control within the team, the head bowed to the influence of other SMT members, although he had the authority to compel his colleagues to take a turn at chairing and agenda building. We suggest that to have insisted would have run counter to the belief in consensus decisions, so might have undermined the culture of teamwork.

Equally, heads excluded little from the SMT agenda apart from matters connected with staff members' personal circumstances and issues connected with the performance of individual SMT members which were addressed outside the meetings. Five heads were reported very occasionally to *make a unilateral decision with school-wide implications without putting it onto the SMT agenda*. One head decided to have a school uniform but then invited SMT members to consider the detail of what it should be. Major unilateral decisions by another were largely confined to the early days of his headship, where he had defined the initial size of the SMT and interviewed each member of staff prior to announcing changes.

There was considerable variation over how far the outcomes of discussions within SMT meetings were recorded or disseminated to other staff. At one school, the head or other SMT members wrote items for the weekly 'headteacher's bulletin for staff'; another wrote brief action minutes which were published on the staff noticeboard. Minutes for SMT consumption only were made at two schools, while no formal record was made at the others. Whether a record of meetings was made public to staff outside the SMT affected how far they felt informed about the team's work.

Consensual, democratic, or unilateral decision making?

In all six SMTs, members subscribed to the norm that *major decisions must be made by consensus*, even though, technically, the head might decide. Consensual decision making may be interpreted as expressing the norm within the culture of teamwork that each member had an equal contribution to make to joint work. Adherence to consensual decision making blurred the distinction between consultation (where the decision maker seeks others' views and then makes the decision alone) and shared decision making (where all parties share the making of the decision itself). If consensus could be found after various views had been put forward on a problem, it was immaterial whether the head was consulting SMT colleagues within the framework of a management hierarchy or whether individuals were contributing as equals to making a shared decision.

Consensus seeking as a model of decision making implies adherence to a second norm: that individuals should compromise their view where necessary to reach a 'working consensus' acceptable to all participants. Then unified commitment to implementation of the decision may be expected since implementation follows agreement reached before the decision was made. This model differs from democratic decision making in the point at which compromise is expected to occur. In the latter model, primacy is given to individual views before the decision, needing agreement amongst only a majority prior to the decision. The main compromise comes after the vote, where those holding a minority view are expected to commit themselves to implementing something that they legitimately rejected in contributing to the decision itself.

The major practical difficulty with consensual decision making finding a working resolution of dissenting views prior to the decision where individuals are not prepared to subscribe to the norm of compromising their view. In democratic decision making, dissenting views may remain unsullied, but a major practical problem arises if those holding a minority view are not ready to commit themselves to implementing something in which they do not believe. Rather than revert to democratic decision making (and hence a vote) where agreement was difficult to reach on major decisions, other means were attempted in all the SMTs to find a working consensus – testimony to the strength of the norm of consensual decision making.

One deputy expressed his belief in compromising to reach consensus, implying that the culture of teamwork placed a duty upon SMT members to seek it:

> I think one respects the views of other members of the team. I think one has to, and feel, 'I still have my worries, I still have my doubts, I still might think it's wrong but we wish to try it this way; let's try it this way and see what happens.' Otherwise things would never move on. I think you run the risk of being seen and being tempted to be obstructive. In a place that has to be managed, has to be organised, things have to be moved on, decisions have to be made sometimes, however difficult they are.

According to a deputy at one school, the team had evolved a strategy for determining the extent of consensus as a way of focusing subsequent debate on areas where dissent remained: 'Quite a useful tool we have worked on is to decide how much we can decide. It is possible to go this far without compromising or prejudicing anything else'.

Where there was disagreement, heads could in principle resort to their authority within the management hierarchy to change the rules of decision making by allowing a majority decision (according to the democratic decision-making model). Where other SMT members advocated a course of action which lay outside the boundaries of acceptability to the head, the latter could *withdraw a decision from the SMT and make it unilaterally*. Both strategies would override the norm of consensus which, in turn, was allied to the contradictory belief that each SMT member should be able to make an equal contribution to the decision. Unless the break with consensual decision making was accepted by SMT members other than the head as a legitimate move for heads to make by switching to the perception of a management hierarchy, it risked undermining the culture of teamwork, with its norm of equal contribution to decisions.

The heads were reported as withdrawing a decision on very rare occasions. One head commented that, where she deemed it necessary, she had said to her SMT colleagues: 'I hear what you say, but for the good of the school . . .'. She recalled overriding the unanimous view of the rest of the SMT when the deputies had led an argument that the SMT should respond to unfair press criticism of the school. The head felt it was more prudent to keep quiet. She noted that her colleagues 'had the good grace to turn round and say afterwards: "You're absolutely right".' Their response may be interpreted as an acceptance that in retrospect the head's view was the best, and that she had the right as head to overrule them. An allowance holder in this team commented: 'In some areas we all bow to [the head's] view because she is, after all, head of the school.' [. . .] A more common situation, where both heads and other SMT members had backed down when strong arguments had been presented against their view, indicated the strength of the norm of consensual decision making within the culture of teamwork. One head had acquiesced when his proposal for a new name for the school was argued down by SMT colleagues. During a debate about staff smoking on the premises, a deputy at one school held out for a total ban, whereas colleagues wished to confine smoking to a designated room. Afterwards he spoke to the head, backing down from his position to enable progress to be made.

The example set by heads in backing down symbolised to other SMT members that they practised what they preached within the culture of teamwork. An allowance holder commented how the head's behaviour influenced colleagues' willingness to contribute:

> The fact that we are very open in our discussions, the fact that [the head] doesn't totally dominate things, the fact that sometimes he is in a minority and is prepared to back down, change his view, modify it or say, 'I'm happy to accept that but I don't agree' sets the tone for everybody else.

The norm that the team should be involved in making major decisions did not inhibit only heads. A deputy noted how she held back from making certain decisions alone because colleagues might perceive that they should be team decisions. The culture of teamwork led to the creation of a boundary to be negotiated between individuals' delegated authority to make decisions within their area of responsibility and the authority which rested with colleagues as members of the SMT. Each member could legitimately have an input into the work of others in the team. This distribution of authority contradicted the management structure in so far as individuals (including, to a lesser extent, heads) perceived themselves as accountable to the team, rather than solely to a line manager or to the governing body.

Surfacing of disagreements over decisions, and consequently the need for their resolution, depended on the openness of the SMT debate. The degree of openness, in turn, depended on norms within the culture of teamwork that were to some extent contradictory, depending on how strongly they were held by each member. They included the norms that members should:

- state a view and express it frankly;
- listen to others' views;
- be willing to challenge where views differ;

- be sensitive to colleagues' feelings;
- refrain from making personal attacks;
- confine confrontation to the meetings, if personal animosity does arise.

An important part in fostering this aspect of the culture was played by heads. With the authority as team leader, one head had spelled out the norms she wished other SMT members to adopt:

> Within the confines of the meeting you can say anything you like to me as long as you do it politely. But outside of this room the team must be seen to act coherently. I think it is very unsettling and damaging for groups of people if they sense that their managers are at odds. So any differences can be aired but only between ourselves.

Frankness could lead to strong emotions. An allowance holder mentioned how coping with the emotional consequences of open debate had not been easy for the group to learn: 'Some of the debates do get fiery and we get quite stroppy at times. I think we are getting better at leaving it in the room, no matter how stroppy it gets.' SMT members at another school highlighted the problem posed by an individual's confrontational style that did not conform with the norms of colleagues. They recalled how a past team member had been 'willing to listen and prepared to concede to effective arguments', yet did not appear to take into account colleagues' feelings. Emotional conflict generated in this way could distract team members from disagreement connected with the content of the debate.

[. . .] We have seen how gaining a multiplicity of perspectives on management issues was an important part of the role of the SMTs. Yet the desired openness of debate in SMT meetings appears difficult to achieve where actions according to contradictory norms were expressed among team members. Another deputy speculated whether the cordiality of relationships among SMT members narrowed the range of views brought to bear in decision making: 'Maybe at times we are almost a bit too much at one. While that's good for managing and good for the team approach, I sometimes wonder if we generate enough provocative thought.' Being too ready to compromise might mean suppressing minority perspectives which, if included in the debate, might contribute to higher quality decisions.

Most individuals in each SMT perceived that they made a contribution to debate which complemented that of others. The teams were more than the sum of their parts because the combined contributions of their members were more diverse than that of any individual. In addition to perceptions of adopting a team role related to the work of Belbin (1981), contributions included:

- acting as a devil's advocate and so challenging colleagues constructively (deputy);
- promoting more openness of debate (deputy);
- shaping decisions (head);
- being close to the staff and so able to represent their views (allowance holder);
- being a visionary for the team (head);
- adopting a conciliatory style (deputy).

These contributions related to the perceived need for multiple perspectives, including the reporting of staff opinions, and working towards consensus.

Collective responsibility

Consistent with the model of consensual decision making adopted in the SMTs, a norm variably reflected in their culture of teamwork was that all team members share responsibility for making and implementing shared decisions. The norm carried the expectation that members' first loyalty on SMT matters should be to the team. In the words of a deputy:

> We share in the process of formulating policy and therefore through how we act consistently around the school we must ensure, as best we can, the implementation of policy. So loyalty, consistency, leadership – in whatever domain – are an important aspect and we share responsibility for that. The outcome would be, if you could not accept anything, that you would have to step down from the senior management team rather than to stand out in public against the senior management team. You can argue as much as you like inside the room but if the decision be that we would do otherwise [than you wish], you accept it.

Loyalty to the team was expected by the heads. It implied that a united front be presented to outsiders. Unity gave the team considerable power through the command of information within the dialectic of control between the SMT and other staff. An SMT member could not be 'picked off' by lobbying and so enable other staff manipulatively to influence the work of the team. Heads defined what information could be divulged to other staff and what must remain confidential to the SMT.

A few leaks were reported in two teams: either inadvertent, where an individual did not realise a matter was confidential, or when a team member expressed frustration about what had gone on within an SMT meeting where there had been dissent among members. A few team members other than heads occasionally experienced some conflict of loyalty when reporting back to the team about teachers' performance or when faced with the negative consequences of some SMT decisions. [. . .] A deputy pointed to the symbolic value of admitting to other staff when the SMT had made a mistake, as it exemplified the values that SMT members expected these teachers to hold.

Perceptions of SMT effectiveness

Team members, a sample of other staff, and chairs of governors were asked about the effectiveness of the SMTs. Their responses reflected their different levels of familiarity with the internal workings of the teams. Chairs of governors worked most closely with heads. Staff outside the teams did not normally attend SMT meetings, but those with middle-management responsibility worked with the SMT in consultative meetings and were consequently more familiar with their mode of operation than mainscale teachers. Overall, the six teams were judged from within and without to be quite or very effective. There were no major discrepancies in the judgements made by insiders and outsiders, and areas perceived by other staff as being capable of improvement were matched by the concerns of SMT members. The range of criteria used in making judgements is instructive, relating to many of the topics we have already discussed. It offers one starting point for considering what makes for effective SMTs.

Table 10.1 Criteria for judging effectiveness of SMTs

Positive	Negative
Input: Team members	
Individual	
• Competent in SMT role	• *Weak in SMT role*
Group	
• *Complementary strengths*	• Too large for discussion
• Small enough for discussion	• Two-tier structure
• Single-tier structure	
Process of teamwork	
Internal	
• Protect agenda from external pressures	• Inner cabinet
• Head shares information and decisions	
• Full participation by all members	
• Work hard	
• Positive relationships	
External	
• *Communicate decisions*	• *Fail to communicate*
• *Encourage staff input and respond*	• *Some members inaccessible leading to*
• *All members accessible to outsiders*	*'them and us' perception*
• *Present united front*	• *Expression of dissent or leakage of*
• *Positive relationships with outsiders*	*confidences*
	• *Aloof, unpraising of staff*
Outputs for SMT	
Direct	
• Decisions made	• Fail to follow through
• Decisions implemented	
• Full backing of SMT members for decisions	
Indirect	
• *School runs smoothly in difficult circumstances*	
• *Good educational results*	
• *Happy pupils*	
• *High staff morale*	
• *Within budget*	

We have combined the responses from the six schools into a single list of criteria which is shown in Table 10.1.

The criteria are divided into those which are positive (linked with SMT effectiveness) and those which are negative (associated with ineffectiveness). They relate to:

• inputs to the teams – referring to individual members and the structure and combined talents of the group;
• the process of teamwork – covering the internal operation of SMTs and their external relationships;

- outputs from the SMTs – encompassing those that are a direct outcome of the process of teamwork (such as major decisions) and those perceived to have an indirect link (like the quality of pupil learning).

There was some overlap between criteria used by SMT members and outsiders. The criteria listed in normal type in Table 10.1 were emphasised mainly by SMT members; those in italics were primarily the concern of other staff and chairs of governors. Team members concentrated upon input, internal process and direct output – dealing with areas which were central to the teams' operation. Criteria employed by outsiders related to their experience of the SMT: especially to external relationships, to individual team members; performance (which included liaison with other groups in the area of their individual responsibility), and to indirect outputs. The chair of governors at one school was unique among the chairs at the case study schools in having attended several SMT meetings as an observer. On this basis, he perceived that it worked well as a team. [. . .] Similarly, a teacher with middle-management responsibility at another school gave her impression that the SMT coped well in difficult circumstances and referred approvingly to team members' candidness in relating to the rest of the staff:

> They're handling a difficult situation pretty well. I feel there's a lot going on in the way of initiatives and we've actually taken on a lot of initiatives in the school, and there's talk of innovation overkill. And they are willing to admit they've made mistakes, and do face up to problems.

An example of an insider's view was given by an allowance holder:

> It works excellently as a team I would say. Because all the important decisions relating to the running of the school are made via a procedure which invites consensus and they all have the full backing of the team. And all of the team feel responsible for implementing them.

Most judgements about ineffectiveness are consistent with concerns such as the perception that some individuals were more competent as team members than others, or the inhibiting effect of a team with a two-tier structure or 'inner cabinet'. Those relating to external relationships may be characteristic of permanent 'top teams' where a central aspect of their group role, as in the case of SMTs, is to work with and through the people in the institution who are accountable to them.

Effectiveness is mainly about instrumental ends. SMTs are ultimately concerned with promoting the education of pupils through the work of staff. Yet despite the perception of a large majority of team members that their team approach soaked up a large amount of precious time, most also reported a range of intrinsic benefits for themselves. We have already noted how mutual support was valued by heads and other SMT members alike. For several SMT members, teamwork was valued as a way of spending their professional lives. According to an allowance holder the SMT was

> terrific fun to work in. There's lots of humour and lots of answers. It's always enjoyable. One always feels it has been a good hour or two hours [in SMT meetings]. You enjoy it, as well as achieve something, and relax with a good conscience.

In this chapter we have looked at six SMTs: continually evolving entities with varied structures and working practices, fulfilling a broadly similar role in managing the school. We have glimpsed how heads were instrumental in using their power to build a team, fostering the culture of teamwork that they valued. They may have been 'first among equals', but we have also seen how the first actually depended on the equals – other SMT members, who also used their influence to help shape this culture. We explored how the contradictory norms relating to a management hierarchy and equal contribution by members of a team, and certain gender-related factors, were built into each SMT structure and process of teamwork.

References

Belbin, M. (1981) *Management Teams: Why They Succeed or Fail.* London: Heinemann.
Halpin, A. (1966) *Theory and Research in Administration.* New York: Macmillan.

11 | Headship and effective teams in the primary school*

JOHN JOHNSTON AND SUSAN PICKERSGILL

Introduction

Central government's thrust for quality assurance has induced a changed and changing climate of expectation for schools and the management of them, and makes it imperative that managerial behaviour is centred on leadership for collegiality.

Successful primary school heads have received the messages being sent by central government and others to primary schools about how they should operate; they have had the personal and professional determination, clarity of vision, courage and personal and interpersonal skills to interpret and use the considerable powers and duties of the office wisely. In being able to bring these qualities to the development of a managerial stance, they have succeeded through and with other staff in moving their schools in the direction of collegial structures and processes and to practice that is grounded in co-operative teamwork. The translation of this stance into practice involves the interaction of personality, experience, values, dispositions, attitudes and coping strategies. Where the difficulties have been accommodated and/or overcome for the greater good, both the head and other staff have been willing and able to cope with and adjust to the plethora of changes arising from educational reform.

Arguably, a significant proportion of schools have not had the managerial impetus to make the necessary changes, despite rhetoric to the contrary. Although this may be because their heads have been unable to construct an achievable mission for the school, the evidence from Pickersgill's (1990) study of primary heads' perceptions comprehensively points to the difficulties heads report in conveying that mission to others and in attaining a commitment to it. Exactly what the specific problems are and what the solutions to them in any particular case might be would require detailed information on the individual school, its environment, traditions, how it operates and

* This material has been edited and was originally published as 'Personal and interpersonal aspects of effective team-oriented headship in the primary school'.

the people involved. This is because of the uniqueness of each school context and because the people who staff schools typically call upon varying degrees of resilience in the face of adversity, experience different degrees of approval needs and differ in the extent to which their 'on-the-job' experience acts as a stimulus to their job satisfaction and their growth and development. Moreover, individuals vary in their need to resort to defence mechanisms and resistance as strategies for coping with the exigencies and pressures of their work. This means that it is not just a question of examining managerial stance or the managerial practice in which it is expressed, but also of how colleagues individually and as a group interpret and respond to it. Although this makes for enormous variation and for unpredictability, it underscores the extent to which the personal and interpersonal skills and behaviour of the head are now, more than ever, crucial dimensions of leadership.

For schools and particularly heads to have been expected to accommodate the significant degree of change, without substantial emphasis being placed on their being adequately skilled and resourced to do so, is to underestimate the nature and structures of feeling and practice which any head and all school staffs embody. It was to address such issues, that a central thrust of the Primary Guidelines Initiative in Northern Ireland (NICED 1984) was to encourage a new kind of professional dialogue and the development of structures for collaborative processes in schools generally. Although much has been achieved in moving towards establishing not just the artefacts but also the processes for creating and managing collegiality, it appears not to have been without substantive and avoidable cost for heads. The development of collegiality, insofar as it has been achieved, has affected the adults in schools, because its pace has disturbed both formal and informal group processes. It has left heads confused, because on one hand they can see more enlightened practice having ensued, while on the other, as the result of educational reform, they are now facing another set of major requirements which appear to threaten the more open processes which they have had to accommodate. They fear that the gains, which have been made through their efforts to change attitudes, alleviate teachers' fears and establish healthy and dynamic teamwork, are in danger of being lost (Pickersgill 1990).

This fear alone is enough to deskill them in terms of the personal and interpersonal competence which they can bring to their managerial practice. To the extent that such deskilling induces felt-perceptions of diminished efficacy, loss of confidence or uncertainty, it is likely to inhibit the head's exercise of entrepreneurial leadership flair and his or her energy for taking risks and making decisions. This is because, although change inevitably brings with it uncertainties, the substantive move towards collegiality and away from hierarchical managerial conceptualisations and structures additionally brings risks as well. It is also because differences in practice and philosophy among colleagues are in many cases avoided by heads, because they are convinced that they cannot (or would not) cope with the turbulence created by facing them and talking about them (Southworth 1987: 71).

How the primary head perceives, adjusts to, and uses the legal, financial and referential powers associated with the role as it changes, do affect the face of the managerial behaviour which occurs and may be thought of as playing a significant part in distinguishing effective leadership. Although these powers are basically coercive in nature, their impact on the staff depends largely on how they are handled by the head. Used sparingly, they can help to retain leadership when the head is under pressure or threat. If too much is made of them, inauthentic behaviour may be induced in teachers, pupils and parents, even to the point of servility in the short term. The climate of defensiveness, formality and even fear which can be produced by this is likely to be detrimental, not only to the spirit and work needed in the primary school, but also managerial practice to facilitate it. Thus the head's managerial stance, and the practice which expresses it, must act as a filter through which the official or legislative powers of the head are translated, if the active involvement of staff in responsible cooperative and creative teamwork is to be achieved through persuasion. Successful filtering is demanding, for it must overcome not only perceptions about the role, but more importantly it must take on board the conflicts and contradictions which are inherent in the head being accountable for the success of democratic processes to what, in many ways, is external bureaucracy.

A 'high-risk' context

Heads in primary schools are being severely taxed by the differentiated nature of the role and by its susceptibility to externally determined changes. Their perceptions are that the work of headship is increasingly lonely, isolated, undervalued and inadequately resourced in terms of training and support. Many heads are anxious about their ability to meet the very diverse expectations for their behaviour (Pickersgill 1990). They genuinely feel a strong sense of responsibility for much, if not all, of what happens in 'their' school, and because of this they typically make enormous investments of 'self' in their work. For the individual, this creates a high-risk context in which the returns are generated in the form of 'success', acknowledgement, recognition and judgements of worth among members of the role set. It is likely to be against these and other similar criteria that evaluations are made by the head. If sufficient evidence is not forthcoming or the evidence is incongruent, the loneliness, isolation and the lack of boundary may reverberate on the role holder to create doubts as to the efficacy of the effort expended, the commitment made and the personal attachment felt.

   If these doubts are not dealt with, in time the primary head may experience acute levels of ontological insecurity as defined by Laing (1969). This could be experienced as a degree of anomie or debilitating anxiety, a loss of confidence or reduced personal and professional security. This insecurity may have direct implications for his or her managerial practice and, because the head is the focal role holder, eventually for school effectiveness.

Towards teamwork and collective responsibility

Heads must understand that their perceptions of the role as a changing one require that they make appropriate alterations and adjustments to their managerial practice and their approach to it. These include a willingness to move away from the persistent acceptance of schools as being hierarchical organisations requiring a top-down approach to management and leadership. In turn, this means that the head must reject the taking of sole responsibility, in favour of the collective responsibility appropriate to membership of a team of professional colleagues. The corollary is that the school's accountability must derive from ownership or professional accountability by each individual member of the team rather than be the burden of the head alone.

Achieving this requires team-oriented leadership and presupposes that heads reject unilateral or authoritarian behavioural dispositions in favour of those conducive to collaboration and participation. Skilled delegation, communication, consultation and group management are essential elements of the latter and, if they become clearly visible in all facets of managerial practice, can lay important foundations in eliciting the co-operation of staff. This requires heads to know when to take the lead and when to confirm the leadership offered by their colleagues.

To do this, the head needs detailed knowledge in four main areas. He or she must have a clear *understanding of the task* and this requires a coherent conceptualisation of the aims of primary education and the responsibilities of the school. The head must have a thorough *knowledge of the situation*, including an understanding of the school as an organisation and of its environment. Thirdly, he or she must *know the people* through and with whom this must be achieved, and most importantly this means knowing the teachers both individually and as a team. Finally (s)he must *know himself or herself* in terms of values, behavioural dispositions and interpersonal skills. Moreover, the head must be able to bring his/her knowledge in each of these areas to the network of interaction between them, through his/her managerial practice as leader of a professional team. The premise of this chapter is that the latter places the focus firmly on the head's personal and interpersonal behaviour in managing for quality processes within various contextual constraints.

Constraints

One of the most basic problems for the head is that of resistance to change. People, and therefore the organisations they create, often resist change and their resistance may be greatest when they feel that they have some investment in the original design, or when their response behaviour has become a habit. Schön (1971) takes this a little further in suggesting that resistance can be particularly strong when a change is perceived to threaten any 'stable stage' which shapes and maintains identity. In Schon's terms, primary schools and those who staff them, perhaps paradoxically, can be viewed as having a strong sense of 'stable state'. Part of the reason for this is that heads themselves as well as the other staff are all products of the education system of which the school is part. Because of this, they may have a considerable investment, in terms of their personal as well as their professional identity, in the school being, if not resistant, certainly slow to change.

In such situations, Schön's thesis would suggest that managerial practice cannot depend solely on traditional problem-solving or scientific approaches. The intent of such approaches is to predict accurately and with consistency, whereas the primary head faces a situation in which, de facto, many variables cannot be controlled or predicted. Hence what is called for is managerial practice which aims to maintain a stable process rather than a fixed outcome. The stable state is sustained in this situation, not by controlling the outcome, but rather by using a process in which what can be fixed is the knowledge that the head has about both the prevailing 'conditions' and 'stance'. Here, 'conditions' consist of those facts which may be known such as history, culture, resources available, structure, relationships and so on. 'Stance' includes attitudes, values, beliefs, expectations and assumptions. Although both of these are likely to alter over time, their importance for managerial practice is that they are identifiable at the point at which a decision is being made and therefore provide a basis for distinguishing alternative courses of action and for making choices between them that have a greater likelihood of being implemented. A latent advantage accrues from this for managerial behaviour if, as is often the case, plans have to be altered or new conditions have to be incorporated. Because other possible ways of acting have already been generated, the head and his or her team are not taken by surprise and thrown off stride by the need to adapt planning.

A second problem is that, for managerial processes firmly characterised by teamwork, the head must seek to develop and maintain collective responsibility. This must be done through practice which is designed to elicit acceptance. The concept of team being used here is of a group of people working together to achieve common objectives and being willing to forgo individual autonomy to the extent necessary to achieve those objectives. The school staff team is only as strong as its weakest interpersonal relationship. Where there is unprocessed or unresolved animosity between members of the team, there is potential for divisiveness and a threat to team cohesion.

Managerial practice can be governed by the misconception that it is the head's job to take sole responsibility for interpersonal relationships in the team and for ensuring that people like each other. The responsibility for developing a satisfactory way of working together and for refraining from destructive behaviour in collaborative contexts primarily lies with the individual team member. If this is not understood and accepted, not only may effective team work be prohibited, but the role of the head can be debilitated, in extreme cases, to the point of becoming untenable.

In any case, the frustrating thing for the head as leader of the team is often that nobody can really do much about the conflict except the contestants themselves and they may be unwilling or unable to do so. Thus the head must seek to place responsibility for managing the relationship constructively with the individuals themselves.

[. . .] For autonomous teamwork to operate, the head must expect on occasions to have to take a leading role in creating clarity in the team about individual roles and responsibilities and in delineating territorial boundaries. In addition to dealing directly with interpersonal problems as they arise, team members also need to provide feedback on how they relate to each other on a more general basis. When things are going well, people tend to take relationships for granted. Regular periodic reviews on a semi-formal basis can help to keep a relationship in perspective and provide useful learning opportunities for both parties. It requires initiative and discipline from the head to ensure that this takes place, because the pressure of the event-driven nature of roles in the primary school can mean that day-to-day events often seem more urgent.

Identification of the positive features of a relationship provides perspective for any possible improvements and is critical to the constructive climate of a review. Both the head and teachers need to know what they are doing well, but the evidence is that heads frequently experience either feedback deprivation or feedback imbalanced in favour of the negative. If positive feedback is not available to the head, and negative feedback is habitually highlighted by members of the role set, there are likely to be significant consequences for the heads' confidence and self-esteem, and therefore for managerial practice.

Developing personal and interpersonal skills: some considerations

The criticism of management courses is that where they recognise the centrality of the head's role in achieving and sustaining teamwork and the management of people, their emphasis tends to be more on 'knowing that' rather than 'knowing how' and on role requirements. The emphasis needs to be more centrally located in developing the head's personal and interpersonal skills. The climate of relationships in a school has an important influence on growth, development and productivity within it, and this places a premium on specific training for skilled functioning on the part of the head, as the pivot of the organisation's teamwork.

Being at ease with himself or herself is a prerequisite for being at ease with colleagues, and being able to put others at ease is an asset of inestimable managerial worth in the primary head. However, teaching prowess, which contributes significantly in the appointment of heads, has not in the past readily lent itself to the cultivation of skill in dealing with adults. Also, for teachers as members of the head's role set, the years of working life spent in teaching children may be at the expense of not working constantly with adults, particularly peers.

Often in-service support has not been specifically directed at helping heads and their teachers to develop interpersonal skills. Teachers have had to take on board major new roles as curriculum developers and co-ordinators. These bring them into quite different types of contact with the head and with each other, often without them having the skills necessary for effective coping. Heads are acutely aware of the onus this places on them and their felt perception is that their behaviour and managerial practice must be conducive to ameliorating any problems which may ensue.

Heads report that they endeavour to achieve this through developing and maintaining a close working proximity with and among staff, the active encouragement of co-operative teaching and, where appropriate, high levels of participative involvement by staff in the general management of the school. At one and the same time, however, they often feel they must keep some controlling distance between themselves and their colleagues. This would seem to be a manifestation of a lack of trust in their own ability and that of others to process interpersonal professional contact in healthily open and productive ways. A belief that one is doing the 'right' thing may be helpful in motivating or generating action. On the other hand, if the head is unsure he or she may find it difficult to act in a decisive way and find that considerable energy is consumed in the process of living with competing or conflicting perspectives. Much self-confidence and perhaps even courage may be required in such circumstances and if, as is the case, heads feel pressurised by a multiplicity of externally precipitated changes, confronting interpersonal issues may be unnecessarily taxing.

Pointing to inadequacies in heads' skills in relation to 'people management' clearly shifts the focus onto the provision of training experiences specifically directed at dealing with frequently occurring problems in interpersonal relationships in schools. Although this would inevitably be a costly and a slow process, it is one which cannot any longer be avoided. It must start from a phenomenological perspective which assumes the uniqueness of the individual, rather than from a position that assumes shared experience and an external reality, common to everyone. When heads are helped to understand this, they can progress towards effectively managing the vagaries of the human behaviour which they encounter on a daily basis.

Heads need awareness training in the interpretation of all channels of human communication including the non-verbal. To be adequately skilled communicators they need to be alert to the use of body language, paralinguistics and the plethora of auditory, visual and kinaesthetic channels of communication. Decoding skills, together with active listening skills, can be learned. Opportunities must be made for heads to acquire such skills in group processes which maximise the learner's control over, and responsibility for, his or her own learning.

For the head in the present climate of rapid change, probably one of the most often-demanded interpersonal skills is that of managing immediate emotional reaction in such a way that the probable constructive intent behind it can be explored. If this behaviour can be sustained, it can create a calm and positive emotional climate for teamwork and may save endless time and energy being wasted in unnecessary wrangling. Its effective exercise calls for a high degree of emotional maturity in setting a leadership example. Of course, the problem for the head facing responsibility for demonstrating this behaviour is that there is no inevitable direct correlation between positional power and emotional maturity.

For the head to improve his or her encounters and relationships with others, and to provide practice which enables others to do the same, requires attention to improving the more visible aspects of talk and action. However, the management of social interaction additionally requires the acknowledgement, analysis and modification of more deeply rooted feelings and beliefs, if behaviour is to change. This would seem to embody the possibility that some degree of personal change, and willingness to countenance the latter, may be required. The problem here is that there may be a 'chicken and egg situation', in that the climate of trust and openness which would facilitate this may not be in existence and may have to be created by an improvement in social interaction itself. In this kind of situation, the question is how the intervention can or should be made and by whom. Traditionally, the expectation has been that the head, as the major power broker and focal role holder, is best placed to take the initiative. While in many contexts this may be a reasonable proposition, there is no guarantee of its validity, nor is it entirely justifiable.

Heads perceive limitations in the contribution which 'learning on the job' can make to improving managerial performance. To accept the proposition, however, would be to deny the potential efficacy of experiential learning and the contribution it can make to ensuring that managerial practice is attuned to the special circumstances prevailing in the particular school at a given time. In the sense in which it is being used here, experiential learning refers to that which is rooted in doing and in experience, and which illuminates experience in providing direction for the making of a judgement as a guide to choice or action.

Principals and heads often think of their work as dealing with people locked into habitual expectation and report that they find difficulty in modifying this. Part of the problem may be that they themselves also fall into the same category, for it is often typical of those in this situation to be convinced that the problems are caused by a scarcity of resources, a diminishing degree of control for them to exercise and by somebody else not doing what they should be doing. Equally heads give the impression that their behaviour depends upon being grounded in verifiable facts to a degree which is inconsistent with both the context and the content of primary school management. In such circumstances, experiential learning under their own steam may not be sufficient because their underlying assumptions and expectations (i.e. stance) may be particularly difficult for heads to identify and may require an outside facilitator and some practice, for them to be able to help themselves. Equally, heads may need help in articulating the elements that they take for granted, such as ways of perceiving a situation, the expected outcome or what they feel they already know and do.

Making room for personal and interpersonal skills development

Given the state of morale among heads about their role, it is unlikely that the head's efforts and managerial practice alone, however skilled they may be, can cope success-fully with personal and interpersonal skills development. Additional resources in terms of support for teachers as well as heads are clearly imperative if existing percep-tions of responsibility and accountability are to be altered, existing skills refined and adapted, and the necessary additional teamwork skills developed. In many cases this process could begin with the development of a wider perspective, which would enable both heads and their staffs to step outside their insularity and pursue greater clarity of vision and perspective regarding what a primary education should be, how it is to be managed and how they can, as members of a staff team, make a more effec-tive contribution to its delivery.

How this may be effected in any particular school is a problem which may defy easy or quick solution. In conventional problem solving, action is determined by a goal or objective and evaluation is usually tied to measuring how closely the stated goal has been achieved. In the work of headship, heads report an awareness that frequently not only is there likely to be a degree of ambiguity in goal statements but also an element of 'loose coupling' in the context in which attainment of goals is sought. The latter primarily relates to the concept of professional autonomy and just where the boundaries lie, between the power of the primary head and the teacher's right to expect to exercise his or her own professional judgement in relationships and beha-viour with the child as client. Moreover, the degree to which many of the objectives of primary education and its management have been attained is often not readily amenable to measurement. Many of the issues here may only be capable of resolution through reference to the situationally specific context, in terms of personnel, their resources for personal and professional functioning and their capacity for growth and development.

Effective time management

Heads report their awareness that inefficient use of time could be symptomatic of in-effective management, yet feel either that it is a problem beyond their control or that they cannot do much about it because of the nature of headship. They genuinely believe that additional secretarial help would be the panacea they need to relieve them of involvement in much of the minutiae of school life. While undoubtedly addi-tional resources in this or other respects could be ameliorative, one suspects a ten-dency to oversimplify a problem that has much deeper roots. It may be that, irrespective of the demands of headship, primary heads are typified by the ad hoc nature of their approach to planning their use of time and that it is this, as much as the nature of the role per se, which often results in their behavioural orientation being variously or dominantly reactive, hyperactive, proactive or inactive.

Undoubtedly, there is an event-driven dimension to the role which often dictates that heads operate by moving from one crisis to the next. As Everard and Morris (1985) point out, it is often very easy to be busy doing the wrong thing, because the threat involved in doing the right, yet more taxing thing, is displaced or reduced. Thus those who are endlessly racing against time may not necessarily be those who are most effective.

The manifestations of this type of event-driven behaviour are frenetic activity both mental and physical, even to the point of hyperactivity. No issue great or small escapes the notice of the hyperactive head and he or she needs to become directly and instantly involved. The outcome of this can be that colleagues feel threatened and pressurised and the head himself or herself becomes overburdened and increasingly debilitated by the time pressure this exerts on the more legitimate and consequential aspects of managerial practice.

It is also possible for apparently proactive behaviour to be unproductive if it is merely a response to insecurity and, as such, is characterised by continuously fearful anticipation and planning for eventualities which may not necessarily materialise. Since this is not really proactive behaviour, but rather reactive behaviour, it can account for the expenditure of considerable energy and for the creation of time pressures.

One suspects that a degree of inactivity may sometimes accompany this behavioural orientation. Human behaviour in response to situational demands often imbues the philosophy of 'not doing today what can be put off until tomorrow, by which time it may be forgotten about'. The best way to see the consequences of this is from a 'today' perspective, because only then can what was not tackled yesterday, when it should have been, be seen to carry forward to pressurise the time and space for what is rightfully today's business. Many heads take recourse to some combination of these behavioural orientations in their use of time. This is understandable but, if such behaviour predominates it may act as a negative model for other members of the team.

The most prevalent impression of headship in the primary school is of the fragmented ad hoc nature of the head's day. [. . .] Ferner (1980), among others, suggests that the easiest way to gain a realistic picture of a typical day is by keeping a time log which records the activities engaged in and the amount of time spent on each. If such a log is kept for a period of a week or so, the time spent on each activity can be totalled to provide a picture of relative use of time and the likely places where it can be saved. It may then require a relatively small step to spending more time on establishing priorities.

However, when heads become concerned about their use of time, the evidence is of responses which include remedial action in the form of resorting to either working harder or trying to work more quickly. Working harder, which normally means working longer, can be beneficial in many respects. Work done off-site is less pressurised and creates a feeling of confidence through being prepared for the next day or term or whatever. But it can also be counter-productive by reducing the amount of time available for private life. Working 'smarter' by working more quickly may be an option open to those of a more casual or easy-going disposition. But for those of a different temperament, it may create additional pressure and stress similar to that induced by working inordinately long hours.

Working selectively and differentially

A productive approach is for the head to respond by working more efficiently, more selectively and more differentially. Working more efficiently means planning and prioritising. Many heads insist that it is too time-consuming to plan their work, when in fact exactly the reverse is the case. Daily planning, and adherence to it, is an effective means of achieving control over time rather than letting events, people and crises of one kind or another take control.

As the role of the head becomes more onerous, it is imperative that the head works selectively. As many duties and tasks as possible should be delegated, and the burden for which the head undertakes total personal responsibility should be stringently but prudently regulated and monitored. Although the heads interviewed in Pickersgill's study (Pickersgill 1990) were somewhat less reluctant to delegate since the Guidelines Initiative and the introduction of the October 1987 Conditions of Service, in some instances the principle of 'relative indispensability' still prevailed in their managerial practice. Heads admitted to an apparently unnecessary amount of double checking of the work of others and to resorting to completing duties assigned to others, lest they might not be done. This endorses the view that not only must prudent initial delegation be accomplished, but the head must allow it to be implemented and see that it is. This provides one substantial avenue for making much more effective use of those members of staff with so-called 'middle-management' allowances. It might also mean that not only could a more substantive role be required of the deputy, but in the longer term this would be a more realistic preparation for his or her eventual headship, than hitherto has often been the case.

It is also of significance, for the managerial performance of the head, that he or she learns to work differentially. This means accepting that different standards of work output, across the range of activities, is not only acceptable but necessary for efficiency. Clearly many tasks and duties have to be carried out to the highest possible standard, but it is equally true in other aspects of the work that for this to be less so is of no real or serious import. Many heads seem to be incapable of recognising that some jobs need only be done adequately. Choosing which tasks have a high impact on school effectiveness, and according them priority, is thus prudent management, as is the development and maintenance of effective communication networks supportive of interpersonal interaction. The latter is easily enhanced through having streamlined data storage, retrieval and transmission systems, and, with the increasing availability of low-cost microcomputer technology, this has come closer to being realisable.

Controlling 'interruptability'

Observations made on visits to schools underline, time and time again, the extent to which heads make themselves 'over-available' for interruption. This suggests that heads must devise strategies and mechanisms for reducing their 'interruptability'. Alongside this, it might be wise time-management practice for heads to insist on short periods now and again for reflection and regrouping, and during which it is acknowledged that they cannot be interrupted, other than in cases of emergency.

[. . .]

The advantages which are likely to accrue from such practices could mean that the head finds that time becomes available. This could create new space for focusing on the issues of major import in creating a more dynamic teamwork environment. Staff development, curriculum development and the development of teamwork and interpersonal interaction could be approached in a more coherent and a less frenetic and ad hoc manner. The outcome of this is likely to be that a more appropriate or healthy balance could be achieved between the nomothetic and idiographic dimensions of school management, which would not be to the detriment of either.

[. . .]

Conclusions

There is clearly a need for a more systematic approach to the training of prospective heads than merely relying on the observation of role models (or anti-models) and learning 'on the job'. Whilst such experiential learning is important, it is less appropriate in developing the personal and interpersonal managerial skills required by the fundamental change taking place in the education system of the late 20th century. It tends to be associated with a rather static and somewhat restricted form of learning, to be time-consuming and unsystematic, and to be more appropriate in responding reactively to problems than being proactive in ensuring effective schooling. For all these reasons, this type of learning is of limited value in the development of effective management.

Formal management training interspersed throughout the head's career would seem to be imperative.

While existing management conferences and other opportunities to take refresher courses are clearly felt by heads to be arousing their awareness and creating networks of contact through which they gain support, much more is required and still has to be achieved. The inherent nature of the role, developments connected with it in the recent past and the outworking of major legislative change, singly and together, make this a matter of urgency.

It is indeed vital that the system supports its headteachers through enabling them to refine and develop their skills. If heads are less than effective in the interpersonal role which is required of them by so many and on which dynamic primary school processes so fundamentally depend, primary education cannot have the leadership it merits and requires.

However, until such times as primary school processes are solidly founded in teamwork and individual professional responsibility and accountability, it is likely that the onus will remain on the head to make the initial investments. Where the head cannot make these first moves, they may have to be initiated by a third party or through skill-training courses which develop the head's personal and interpersonal competence and thus facilitate his or her ability to manage social interaction.

Typically, intervention must approach interpersonal behaviour modification both through interpretation and insight, and through action. The former of these two elements produces the understanding which is necessary for people to realise what changes they need to make. Action, on the other hand, must be aimed directly at changing behaviours through helping people to do this for themselves, in a process in which the emphasis is firmly on self-management. For it to be other than this would be inconsistent with notions of professional and personal autonomy, with the taking of responsibility for one's membership of a team and with the shift to more demo-cratic processes, in which the head is more than ever colleague and team member.

References

Everard, K. B. and Morris, G. (1985) *Effective School Management*. London: Harper and Row.
Ferner, J. D. (1980) *Successful Time-Management*. New York: Wiley.
Laing, R. D. (1969) *The Divided Self*. London: Penguin.
Northern Ireland Council for Educational Development (1984) *Guidelines for Primary Schools*. Belfast: Stranmillis College.
Pickersgill, S. (1990) 'Perceptions of the primary head', unpublished MA(Ed) thesis. School of Education, Queen's University, Belfast.
Schön, D. A. (1971) *Beyond the Stable State*. New York: Norton.
Southworth, G. (ed.) (1987) *Readings in Primary School Management*. Lewes: Falmer Press.

12 | Managers communicating*

COLIN HARGIE, DENNIS TOURISH AND OWEN HARGIE

Introduction

All organizations, including education organizations, now operate in a turbulent environment of constant change with little indication that such pressures will be reduced in the near future. This is forcing them to re-examine their functions, structures and internal/external relationships. As a result, effective communication has been identified as a significant factor influencing the ability of organizations to achieve their objectives (Young and Post 1993).

However, research into managerial communication practices is at an early stage. A review of the literature on managing innovation (Henry and Walker 1991) and managing change in organizations (Carnall 1990) shows that little attention has been paid to the role of communication as a variable in innovatory change. Within the UK, until recently, there has been little empirical research into the nature, flow and functions of communication within organizations (Hargie and Tourish 1993). However, there is growing interest in the role of communication as a significant variable in determining organization success (Clampitt 1991; Whetten and Cameron 1991).

In particular, there is a growing emphasis on the importance of interpersonal communication. This arises from the realization that the greatest challenges to management are not problems of setting objectives or making decisions but rather those of implementation. Successful implementation, it is argued, depends to a large extent on effective use of interpersonal communication skills (Schein 1983). The challenge of implementation is therefore a major reason why there needs to be a much greater emphasis on the role of interpersonal communication within organizations. It is now widely recognized that as an organization becomes more complex greater demands are made on the interpersonal skills of its members. Interpersonal communication is

* This material has been edited and was originally published as 'Managers communicating: an investigation of core situations and difficulties within educational organizations'.

thus central to contemporary organizational life, especially to the role of the manager. Consequently, enriched interpersonal skills have a very large contribution to make in improving organizational relationships. The argument for promoting interpersonal competences within organizations depends not only on the volume of interaction which is necessary but also, more crucially, on the impact of such competences on the effectiveness and efficiency with which organizational objectives are achieved (Guirdham 1990).

Within this context the central purpose of this study was to identify the types of situations facing educational managers which cause them the most communication problems, the types of people involved in these situations, the communication skills which they felt were most necessary to overcome the problems and the types of problems common to their roles as education managers.

Methodology

Study group

The study was carried out within the framework of an interpersonal communication module which formed part of an MSc programme for in-service education managers in Northern Ireland. Eighteen managers took part in this investigation. Details of the sample are provided in Table 12.1. As can be seen from this table, the participants came from a range of educational environments and included school principals, vice-principals and heads of department, as well as executives from the field of educational administration. Almost all of the sample were under the age of 50 years and two-thirds were male. The minimum length of service was 11 years, while over 72 per cent of the managers had been in the education sector for over 15 years. Eleven out of the 18 had received little or no training in communication and none had received extensive training in this field.

Procedures

The study was conducted within the consultative research paradigm (Caves 1988) using an expert systems approach to knowledge elucidation. Here subjects are recognized as having expertise within their own area and are facilitated by the researcher to employ this expert knowledge in an analysis of their work situation. In this way subjects are required, in a sequential set of steps, to formulate and identify component elements of the field of enquiry under analysis. Three such stages were involved in this investigation. First, participants individually completed forms which required them to itemize the following four dimensions:

1 those managerial situations where interpersonal communication difficulties most frequently arise;
2 the types of people who cause most difficulties within the above situations;
3 the key interpersonal skills required to perform their managerial role most effectively;
4 the most common problems they faced in their role as managers.

Second, these forms were analysed and collated in order to formulate the total series of elements as expressed by all of the managers. This resulted in the compilation of

Table 12.1 Details of the sample

Males	Females		
12	6		
Age range			
31–40	41–50	Over 50	
9	8	1	
Length of time within education sector			
11–15 years	More than 15 years		
5	13		
Position currently occupied			
Head of department	Vice-principal	Principal	
5	5	2	
Education board	Other		
4	2		
Amount of communication skills training received			
No training at all	Little training	Some training	Extensive training
4	7	7	0

four inventories comprising 19 difficult managerial situations, 23 types of people who caused difficulties, 19 key interpersonal skills and 20 common problems. The third phase of the research involved presenting these four inventories to the subjects and requesting them to rank each list of items in order of their importance *in their own situation*. Thus, they ranked the 15 most important managerial situations, the 15 people who caused most difficulties, the 15 most important interpersonal skills and the 15 most common managerial problems. Again, this final stage was completed by each person individually.

Results

The data were analysed in two ways. First, each element was scored in terms of the total number of times it was selected regardless of rank. Second, all of the items were weighted in terms of the rankings they received by allocating a score of 15 to each item ranked first in order of importance, a score of 14 to each item ranked second, and so on down to a score of 1 for an item ranked fifteenth. The results are presented in Tables 12.2–5.

From Table 12.2 it can be seen that situations which require participative management scored most highly in terms of weighted importance and were second in relation to total number of mentions, while in the context of the latter criterion listening to staff was most frequently cited. The next two situations viewed as important were motivating staff and delegation of tasks. Within these situations, opinionated or aggressive parents were weighted as most difficult to deal with, while awkward colleagues received most mentions, with dominant individuals and people frustrated by change filling the other top four places (Table 12.3). In Table 12.4, listening emerged as the most important interpersonal skill area, being both listed and given a high weighting by all of the participants, followed by the skills of handling aggressive indi-

Table 12.2 Most frequently reported managerial situations where interpersonal communication difficulties arise

	Weighted totals		Frequency totals	
Participative management	173	(1)	14	(2)
Motivating staff	142	(2)	13	(3)
Listening to staff	137	(3)	15	(1)
Delegating tasks	118	(4)	14	(2)
Conflict management	118	(4)	10	(5)
Personal encounters (e.g. dealing with resource requests)	105	(5)	14	(2)
Chairing meetings	92	(6)	13	(3)
Staff development/training	91	(7)	10	(5)
Keeping relevant staff informed	85	(8)	11	(4)
Meetings with senior management team	81	(9)	8	(7)
Timetabling	81	(9)	8	(7)
Resource/budget allocation	69	(10)	8	(7)
Raising controversial issues	68	(11)	9	(6)
Evaluation processes	67	(12)	9	(6)
Participating effectively in meetings	63	(13)	8	(8)
Curriculum committees	63	(13)	7	(8)
Discussion of a teacher's performance	60	(15)	7	(8)
Staff selection	59	(16)	7	(8)
Dealing with parental complaints	59	(16)	7	(8)

viduals and being decisive, and then a range of skills which were given similar weightings, including showing empathy, chairing meetings, persuading and negotiating. Table 12.5 shows that, in terms of more general managerial problems, time management received the most mentions and the highest weightings, followed by excessive workload, making the right decision and difficulty in delegating.

Discussion

The results indicate a clear correlation between frequency and weighted rank of perceived communication problems: those items which were most frequently cited tended to attract the highest rankings. In other words, certain issues were consistently regarded by these education managers as being of key importance. This consistency within the context of individual ranking would suggest that the items listed can serve a number of purposes. First, by highlighting central problem areas, management training can be targeted more precisely to meet identified difficulties and needs. Second, the situations and difficulties identified suggest areas for further research.

The situations, people and problems reported by the study participants where interpersonal communication difficulties arise are to a large extent internal to the organization (Table 12.2). The most frequently mentioned difficulties are mainly those dealing with staff in a variety of different contexts. Listening to and motivating staff, delegating tasks, managing conflict and personal encounters are all ranked highly as examples of where interpersonal communication difficulties arise. So, too, are staff

Table 12.3 Most frequently reported types of people where the most communication difficulties arise

	Weighted totals	Frequency totals
Opinionated/aggressive parents	257 (1)	13 (5)
Awkward staff	208 (2)	17 (1)
Dominant individuals among staff	178 (3)	16 (2)
Staff frustrated with change	163 (4)	14 (4)
Staff determined not to be overburdened	160 (5)	15 (3)
Incompetent staff	149 (6)	11 (6)
Principal	81 (7)	10 (7)
Pupils	69 (9)	10 (7)
Whole staff as a group	58 (10)	8 (9)
NI School Exam and Assessment Council	55 (11)	5 (11)
Parents	47 (12)	8 (9)
Inspectorate	43 (13)	8 (9)
Senior management team	38 (14)	5 (11)
Vice-principal	38 (14)	4 (12)
Local education authority officers	32 (15)	5 (11)
Administrative staff	34 (16)	6 (10)
Ancillary staff	33 (17)	5 (11)
Advisers	32 (18)	4 (12)
Heads of departments	26 (19)	5 (11)
Members of department	24 (20)	5 (11)
Year teachers	24 (20)	5 (11)
Prospective employees	22 (21)	4 (12)

Table 12.4 Key interpersonal skills required to do job effectively

	Weighted total	Frequency totals
Listening skills	227 (1)	18 (1)
Handling aggression	156 (2)	16 (2)
Decision making	149 (3)	13 (4)
Empathy	136 (4)	16 (2)
Chairing meetings	135 (5)	13 (4)
Persuading skills	133 (6)	14 (3)
Negotiating skills	130 (7)	16 (2)
Assertiveness skills	125 (8)	13 (4)
Delegating skills	106 (9)	13 (4)
Oral skills	103 (10)	12 (5)
Time management	103 (10)	11 (6)
Informing	99 (11)	11 (6)
Counselling skills	98 (12)	13 (4)
Keeping calm	94 (13)	11 (6)
Appraisal skills	93 (14)	11 (6)
Speaking effectively as a group member (not leader)	86 (15)	10 (7)
Interviewing skills	76 (16)	11 (6)
Explaining skills	59 (17)	12 (5)
Encouraging staff to acquaint managers with their problems	47 (18)	10 (7)

Table 12.5 Most frequently reported managerial problems

	Weighted totals	Frequency totals
Time management	129 (1)	13 (1)
Excessive workload	115 (2)	10 (3)
Making the right decision	102 (3)	13 (1)
Difficulty in delegating	80 (4)	9 (4)
Staff resistance to ideas/legislation	78 (5)	11 (2)
How to be truthful but kind	68 (6)	9 (4)
Enthusing staff where there is no immediate personal gain	65 (7)	9 (4)
Unrealistic expectations	63 (8)	7 (6)
Conflict management	62 (9)	8 (5)
Negotiating assertively	61 (10)	8 (5)
Team building	60 (11)	6 (7)
Overloading other staff	59 (12)	7 (6)
Persuading staff to undertake tasks	57 (13)	8 (5)
Post-holders need to be pursued to carry out tasks	57 (14)	8 (5)
Teacher performance/finding best way forward	56 (15)	8 (5)
Disciplining a colleague	53 (16)	5 (8)
Red tape/inflexible management structures	45 (17)	7 (6)
Formulating/deciding on budget allocation	39 (18)	5 (8)
Feeling that others aren't on same wavelength	39 (19)	5 (8)
Being forceful but not rude	38 (20)	6 (7)

development/training and keeping staff informed. It is noticeable that, while discussion of teacher performance and appraisal are indicated as sources of communication difficulties, they figure much lower in the ranking. These reported situations are in turn closely associated with the types of people who cause the most communication difficulties. Staff characterized by this sample as awkward, dominant, incompetent, frustrated by changes and those determined not to be overburdened are the staff groups which feature prominently in this regard.

Interestingly, organizations tend to conceptualize the notion of a communication strategy as referring to external relationships. The data here (Table 12.3) suggest that, in fact, managers within education organizations currently experience most difficulties mainly with internal communications. It might therefore be useful to first expend effort on clarifying and resolving such difficulties, so that the whole organization can then direct its attention to communication relationships with its external environment.

The two main groups of people with whom most communication difficulties arise are parents and staff (Table 12.3). Opinionated and aggressive parents are seen as the most serious source of communication difficulties. However, while such parents are reported to create the greatest difficulty by the study participants, dealing with parental complaints, interestingly enough, is ranked relatively low in terms of the most frequently reported situations where interpersonal communication difficulties arise. By contrast, it is in dealing with staff that most of the communication difficulties are generated. This reinforces the point suggested earlier: it may be that managers and organizations require much more of a focus on their internal communication relationships than they have been used to in the past.

One of the major problems identified by most of these education managers relates to the excessive workload that they feel they have to carry (Table 12.5). This in turn creates severe time management problems for them. The problem of time management is highlighted by the fact that a large proportion of the managers found difficulty in delegating responsibilities to others. This problem is exacerbated by the difficulty many experience in persuading staff to carry out tasks. Post-holders, in particular, have to be persuaded by many managers to carry out their responsibilities. At the same time many managers are also concerned that they might overload other members of staff. Excessive workload and problems of time management are reflected in the concern expressed by most managers over making the 'right' decision.

A large number of the problems that education managers encounter centre on inter-personal relationships, especially those involving other staff. Staff resistance to new ideas and to legislative changes is seen as posing a significant problem. Trying to enthuse staff in the present climate where there is little prospect of personal gain is seen as difficult by managers, while dealing with 'unrealistic expectations' and being 'truthful but kind' create problems which they have to address.

The study participants identified a range of key interpersonal skills which they felt were important in order to do their job effectively (Table 12.4). The broad variety of skills deemed necessary highlights the many different facets of education management. These fall into two broad categories of activities that managers engage in, initiating and responding. Foremost among the skills indicated is that of listening, which was rated highest by all the education managers. This is very much in keeping with the growing awareness that listening should be regarded as a central aspect of the man-agement role, particularly during periods of rapid change (Thomson 1992). Listening is an important responding skill which can be effectively employed for different pur-poses. It is central to the use of counselling skills which the study participants indicate to be a significant dimension of their role as managers. So, too, is the skill of empathy which is rated highly as a key management skill.

A range of initiating skills which also show the diversity of the management role are identified. These include the interpersonal skills required in chairing meetings, decision making, delegating and conflict management together with those of negotiation and persuading, all of which feature high on the list of managerial situations where com-munication difficulties arise. Interviewing and appraisal skills are also seen as import-ant along with those of explaining and informing.

The varied demands of being an education manager are reflected in the fact that handling aggression, keeping calm and time management skills are all rated as very important by the participants. Skills such as persuading, negotiating and assertiveness are also seen as very important. These are, indeed, the kinds of skills which would be most useful in dealing with issues relating to those staff indicated in Table 12.3, such as 'awkward staff'; 'staff frustrated with change'; and 'staff determined not to be overburdened'.

Conclusion

Given that the study group was small, this investigation into managerial situations and difficulties represents a first step towards charting and clarifying the range of commu-nication problems, issues and perspectives which impinge on the role of education managers. Much more extensive research is required in order to gain as full a picture as possible of the range of interpersonal communicative factors that impact on the changing role of managers within education organizations. It is only by conducting concerted research that the content of training programmes for educational managers can be validated and tailored specifically to meet their training needs within their organizations.

The methodology used here is one means of assessing managers' own understanding of day-to-day communication practices within organizations. A complementary approach, capable of building on these initial findings, is the use of communication audits. This method of communication analysis is one which is proving increasingly to be of value in studying organizational communication. A communication audit has been defined as 'a thorough analysis of the nature, structure, flow and practice of communication within an organization' (Wolvin and Coakley 1991). The idea that organizations should examine actual internal communication practices is relatively recent in the UK. Most organizations still lack any effective instrument for assessing their interpersonal communication systems (Tourish and Hargie 1993). There is, however, growing evidence to suggest that for the effective functioning of the organization the effectiveness of communication systems should be evaluated at regular intervals (Smith 1991).

Effective communication skills are a crucial necessity within contemporary organizations and are essential to organizational success. The quality of interpersonal communication is a critical variable affecting the level of organizational success, since the foundation of all managerial and organizational success is the ability to work with and through others (Hamilton and Parker 1990). The effective use of interpersonal skills, therefore, forms the basis of good management practice. It is through communication that managers gain and offer the information required to make successful decisions within organizations. 'Interpersonal skills' refers to those aspects of communication that managers need to employ successfully in direct person-to-person contact. Education management, therefore, can be regarded as a highly interpersonal activity in so far as most of the activities in which such managers engage involve relating to other people. In practice, managers spend a large part of their time meeting and talking with others. The effective use of interpersonal skills enables the individual to manage working relationships more effectively. One distinguishing factor between successful and unsuccessful management is the degree of interpersonal competence displayed. Individuals who are able to manage the way in which they relate to others are much more successful in terms of achieving their objectives. Research indicates that managers consistently underestimate the effect which their behaviour has on how other people behave and, consequently, on the attainment of organizational goals (Hayes 1991).

Interpersonal communication skills involve subtle and complex forms of human interaction which can be acquired and developed. Interpersonal skills training programmes have been constructed for a large variety of different types of trainee groups in order to develop a range of communicative competences. Such programmes are flexible and are tailored to cater for the particular requirements of a specific group. Specialist skills can be identified around which the actual training programme is then developed and implemented. There are a number of levels at which interpersonal skills training should be focused. First, education managers need to explore the constraints that limit the effective use of these skills. Managers generally often overrate their own communicative effectiveness. They need to develop an insight into their own interpersonal competence so as to be able to recognize whether they are able to use these skills effectively within their own organization. It is important that managers within education organizations know when and why to use particular interpersonal strategies and how to manage the effects which these produce. Education managers need to acquire and develop specialist communication skills and learn how to apply these skills to particular situations within the organization.

References

Carnall, C. (1990) *Managing Change in Organizations*. Englewood Cliffs, NJ: Prentice-Hall.

Caves, R. (1988) Consultative methods for extracting expert knowledge about professional competence, in R. Ellis (ed.) *Professional Competence and Quality Assurance in the Caring Professions*. London: Croom Helm.

Clampitt, P. (1991) *Communicating for Managerial Effectiveness*. Beverly Hills, CA: Sage.

Guirdham, M. (1990) *Interpersonal Skills at Work*. Englewood Cliffs, NJ: Prentice-Hall.

Hamilton, C. and Parker, C. (1990) *Communicating for Results*. Belmont, CA: Wadsworth.

Hargie, O. and Tourish, D. (1993) Assessing the effectiveness of communication in organizations: the communication audit approach. *Health Services Management Research*, 6 (4): 276–85.

Hayes, J. (1991) *Interpersonal Skills: Goal-Directed Behaviour at Work*. London: Harper Collins.

Henry, J. and Walker, D. (1991) *Managing Innovation*. London: Sage.

Schein, E. (1983) SMR Forum: improving face to face relationships. *Sloan Management Review*, Winter: 43–52.

Smith, A. (1991) *Innovative Employee Communication: New Approaches to Improving Trust, Teamwork and Performance*. Englewood Cliffs, NJ: Prentice-Hall.

Thomson, P. (1992) Shaping strategic change – the case of the NHS in the 1990s. *Public Money and Management*, 12(3): 33–42.

Tourish, D. and Hargie, O. (1993) Don't you sometimes wish you were better informed? *Health Services Journal*, November: 28–9.

Whetten, D. and Cameron, K. (1991) *Developing Management Skills* (2nd edn). New York: Harper Collins.

Wolvin, A. and Coakley, C. (1991) A survey of the status of listening training in some 500 corporations. *Communication Education*, 40: 152–64.

Young, M. and Post, J. (1993) Managing to communicate, communicating to manage: how leading companies communicate with employees. *Organizational Dynamics*, 22: 31–43.

13 | Communication in educational management*

COLIN RICHES

Communication and theory

Communication is an everyday experience which we all claim to know something about but, in fact, is a quite complex activity. Without communication, all that we think of as human experience would cease to exist for it is a vital component of all spheres of life. Management could not take place without communication, and organizations could not exist without it. It is a common complaint within organizations that communications are unsatisfactory and need improving. Mistakes are often made because communication is not seen as a two-way exchange, but as a directive from above, without any consideration of those for whom the communication is intended, or of *their* views. Negotiation in communication is often vital if the message is to be fully received, accepted by the parties concerned and acted upon. Successful organizations, and schools and colleges are no exception, need good communications. Because so many changes are taking place in educational institutions, effective communication is more than ever critical for their effectiveness.

Among the significant changes are:

- an increased *complexity*, both in structure and technology, even in the smallest primary school
- the *market forces* which are operating within education highlight the need for effective communication between the organization and clients (potential and actual) and within the organization itself
- Government education and general *legislation*, e.g. with regard to employment law, has brought about so many changes which require careful communication if misunderstandings are to be avoided and if colleagues are to take 'ownership' (if they can!) of such developments

---

* This material has been edited and was originally published as 'Communication'.

- increased complexity in the organization of schools and colleges highlighting the importance of both *vertical* and *horizontal* (e.g. within departments) two-way communication
- an increasing concentration on *efficiency* and *effectiveness*, arising partly out of LMS and competition within the education service, points up the need for communicating this with clarity and sensitivity to all staff within organizations.

Of course all this begs the question, 'What is communication?'

What is communication?

A straightforward definition of 'communication' is that it is an activity which takes place when a message is transferred satisfactorily from one party to another so that it can be understood and acted upon if necessary. It has been defined (by Rasberry and Lemoine 1986: 23) as 'sorting, selecting, forming and transmitting symbols between people to create meaning'.

For communication to take place there has to be a *source*, *transmission* through *channels* and a *receiver*. Communication involves the meeting of minds through the ebb and flow of actions, reactions, questions and answers. Windahl *et al.* (1992: 221) have defined it in a rather more comprehensive way as 'The exchange and sharing of information, attitudes, ideas and emotions'. This emphasizes that communication is not confined to written or oral exchange of simple messages only but embraces the collective activity of sharing an experience at a variety of verbal and non-verbal levels. Modern thinking about the subject has moved away somewhat from thinking about a linear model of communication as a movement from a *source–sender–message–channel–receiver* model to the notion of communication as shared experience. While much of the discussion which follows is within the linear model of communication it is a very useful corrective to think of communication as very much a two-way experience involving whole *personalities* to varying degrees.

We have been considering the outline nature of communication in general up to this point but it is useful to think too of a classification of the activity into different spheres of communication. These are:

- *basic mechanical aspects of communication:* the use of mechanical/electronic devices to transmit (encode) and receive (decode) messages. Systems theory has also been used to make sense of how communication inputs are transformed through management functions like planning, organizing and leading into outputs
- *interpersonal communication:* this concerns the behaviour of people when transferring information etc. from one to another, and involves verbal, non-verbal and listening behaviour. Teaching has its roots in such communication
- *organizational communication:* this recognizes the fact that within an organization all the members are sending and receiving signals simultaneously in dynamic interaction with one another. In other words there is a *network* of communication experiences and all within that network (and outside it) influence the process. Analysis of these processes is important in schools and colleges.

Communication takes place for a variety of *reasons* and through a variety of *methods*. Reasons for communicating might be to inform, explain, persuade, reprimand, encourage, thank, appraise, propose, consult, apologize or praise (and one can think of many others). Methods might be *written* in the form of letters, memos, reports, minutes, telex, telemessages, *oral* through conversations, face-to-face casual encounters, interviews, meetings, conferences, telephone, teleconferences, or *visual* in the shape of diagrams, graphs, illustrations, slides, VDU, video, television, body language (Smithson and Whitehead 1990).

Communication models

The simple communication model

This is made up of three elements: the source (or sender), message, and receiver. The source may be an object, e.g. a book or a person; the message may take many forms such as a question, an appeal, or even a smile. The receiver is the person to whom the message is directed. The characteristic of the receiver will influence the way she/he perceives the message and interprets it. In communication the three elements can take many forms. The message may have wider implications than we intend because we communicate more than the spoken word. This simple model makes a fundamental conceptualization, even if it is not sophisticated enough to understand the intricacies of most communication in organizations (Figure 13.1).

The general communication model

A more complex model is encapsulated in Laswell's statement that communication is really about the five Ws: 'Who says What, to Whom, in Which channel, with What effect' (Laswell 1948). The variables here are as follows: starting with the information source (the sender), the message, filtered by the sender, is encoded into words, gestures or postures as the case may be. These are transmitted along various channels, which can be blocked by noise (i.e. distractors). The receiver picks up these audio-visual stimuli, which are then decoded into understandable meanings or ideas. The communication destination is reached when there is a shared understanding between the sender and the receiver. By means of feedback the sender will know that the receiver has interpreted the message correctly (Lopez 1965) (Figure 13.2). If, in this case, for example, the information source is the drama teacher, the message is filtered by the sender and encoded in her perceptions that the school play is the most important event at the moment, and indeed this is demonstrated in the enthusiastic tone of her memo and by every gesture when she meets those involved. A general atmosphere exists in the school so that many channels are being used to convey the message that 'the play's the thing'. However, some staff literally make a noise while others put blocks on the activities surrounding the production, thinking, for example, that many members of the cast should be concentrating on study as public examinations draw

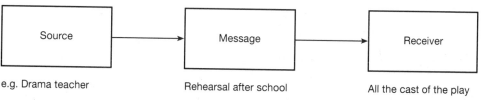

e.g. Drama teacher   Rehearsal after school   All the cast of the play

Figure 13.1 A simple communication model

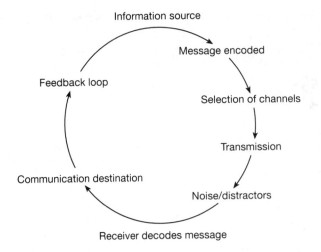

Figure 13.2 A general communication model

near. Others have never liked the idea of a school play anyhow, believing it allows a few to shine instead of concentrating on developing interpersonal communication through drama! The receiver picks up the message having filtered it (decoded) through her/his own perceptions and maybe conveyed to those concerned with a special twist of elation or irony. The communication reaches its destination and there is some joint understanding of it by the sender and receiver which is fed back from the latter to the former at a convenient moment. Processes like this example happen many times daily in a school or college situation.

Using slightly different working Rasberry and Lemoine (1986) have produced a diagram (Figure 13.3) which introduces other variables influencing the communication process – and adding to its complexity. The significant new variables referred to here emphasize the influences on *meaning* which affect the way messages are encoded and decoded, the fact that there are competing messages (they cause 'noise'), the process takes place over *time* and *space* in a situation of existing *relationships*. In short, communication takes place within an *organizational environment*. One could apply this model to teacher appraisal, for example.

Research on *source* credibility indicates that high-credibility sources have a greater potential for influencing behaviour than low-credibility ones. The content of a message is often interpreted according to the source. Other research has shown, more interestingly, that source credibility has no effect upon the *attention* of the receiver (Secord and Backman 1964). A source can gain credibility by using a high prestige medium to carry the message.

The *channels* of communication (which in the literature generally refer to both the methods and paths of communication) can be enormously varied. They can be both formal and informal. The choice of channel to be used will depend on personal preference based on the sender's knowledge of the receiver, experience and the environment. [. . .] Formal channels are related to a hierarchical chain of command and are usually connected with official activities like meetings, formal memos, reports and so on. Informal channels operate unofficially through 'the grapevine', which can often be a

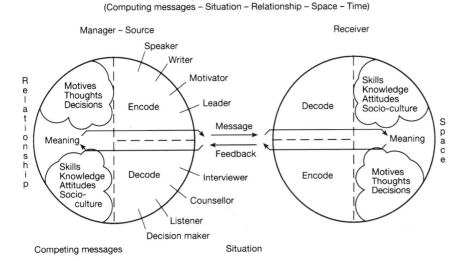

Figure 13.3 A model for effective managerial communication
(Rasberry and Lemoine 1962)

speedy way of helping the official channels convey a message or correct the misinformation of a previous message through a formal channel. However, the grapevine can be a vehicle for unwarranted gossip, scandal or rumour – and a sign that managers have been indiscreet in the way they communicate or have failed to inform people when they should have been informed.

In *decoding* it is helpful if there is an 'understanding' between the sender and receiver, say because they are of similar status or background, i.e. 'they speak the same language'. The major point to be made about the receiver is that she/he will perceive a communication in the manner that is consistent with previous experiences, and communications that are not so will tend to be rejected.

Feedback completes the cycle of communication and shows that the model is not restricted to one direction. It takes the linearity away from the model and suggests the reciprocal and sharing aspect of communication. Feedback can be verbal, non-verbal or in written form. The sender of a message might observe one of four possible reactions to the message: agreement, partial acceptance but a wish to negotiate its meaning, disagreement or apathy. Speed of feedback will have an influential effect.

The term *noise* can be taken literally but in communication theory is usually used to mean conceptual noise, that is those differences in individuals which confound and complicate the ability of individuals to understand one another. Noise, or distortion, can operate at each stage of the communication process, but the sender or receiver are specially vulnerable to it.

Barriers to communication

There are various barriers to communication which may be broken down into a number of sources of distortion:

Language or semantic problems: words and symbols may mean different things to different people and jargon can be confusing. We each interpret messages in terms of our own backgrounds, needs and purposes and in relationship to the particular context or situation. Also disorganized ideas and the use of the wrong word or phrase may lead to poorly expressed messages which confuse rather than enlighten.

Attitudinal problems: participants in communication can easily have different values, which may reflect deep emotions, beliefs and prejudices, and refuse to recognize and understand other people's viewpoints. This affects the way in which messages are represented and interpreted and can be a fundamental barrier to communication, particularly in the sphere of interpersonal relations.

Different perceptions of the problem

Undue emphasis on status: we speak of people 'standing on their dignity' and remaining so aloof and superior that easy exchange becomes difficult.

Excessive selective perception: hearing what we expect to hear, related to our experience and background and/or what we know or believe. For example, if a person is favoured, the 'halo' effect operates in which everything is seen in a favourable light; and if the opposite is the case the 'cloven hoof' perception takes over, and all is seen unfavourably.

Selective retention/rejection: a failure to hear (and see) what is being heard (or shown) and forgetting what has been told. This can happen because of lack of interest (the passive receiver) and concentration. Perhaps there are physical barriers contributing to this as well, such as fatigue, discomfort, excessive comfort, and a stuffy environment; or the barriers of indifference or prejudice.

The withholding of information: because knowledge is power.

Premature evaluation of what is being said: one's mind is made up without hearing the full message.

An artificial wall of silence has developed between the sender and the receiver: which clearly prevents a full communication exchange.

Poor choice of communication channels: the failure to select the right medium to convey the message.

Natural reserve, fear or lack of confidence: which tend to silence people.

Effective communication is learned through training and experience. We learn to communicate more effectively by having the appropriate techniques or skills, having the opportunity to practise them and having our performance reviewed by experienced commentators in a non-threatening environment. We have to realize that it takes two *willing* communicators to make full communication possible. A clear flow of communication within an organization can greatly aid its effectiveness.

Communication flow

Downward communication

Communication flows within three main directions in the typical organization: downward, upward and horizontally. *Downward communication* is crucial to the function of an organization; it concerns messages and information sent from senior management to other staff. On organizational charts the flow normally follows the formal lines of authority downward from position to position. This is usually the strongest flow of the three major ones. Management has the power to put messages in motion and start them on their downward journey – either to be received or not, or to arrive distorted, or late.

The common reasons for poor downward communication are as follows:

- *growth of an organization causes isolation:* face-to-face contact is less frequent, formal lines of communication are established and individuals tend to isolate themselves so that close contact between the various levels is lost
- *clearly defined objectives are missing:* management is sometimes confused about the information it thinks its subordinates need and want to know. This confusion is seldom sorted out
- *when management does not audit its communication techniques:* established habits are rarely examined and ineffective communication practices continue unquestioned
- *confusion arises as to who is responsible for what communication activities*
- *segregation between senior and other levels in the organization:* a non-participatory management style can isolate managers from the wants and needs of staff and devalue the downwards communication.

Downward flow can be improved by establishing objectives about what the manager wishes to communicate and the content of the messages to be communicated.

Upward communication

Upward communication flows from subordinates to superordinates and depends on the trust and confidence felt by the former towards the latter. Effective upward flow is premised on the assumption that participation of staff is accepted within the organization. Reasons for poor upward communication include:

- *size and complexity of an organization:* the larger the organization the more common the barriers to upward flow
- *unrealistic assumptions* that others are listening and understanding the messages in the correct way
- *filtering and distortion:* each step upwards allows for a filtering and consequential distortion of messages
- *the manager–staff relationship:* this can affect the free flow of messages as staff feel inhibited by those with status in the organization
- *others in the hierarchy can create bottlenecks:* e.g. a gatekeeper such as a deputy or a secretary, a status seeker within the organization who uses the information for his/her own benefit, the promotion rival who keeps information that could help others to obtain promotion.

Horizontal communication

Lateral or horizontal flow of communication is beneficial because it acts as a coordinating device across departments and units at the same level, for people who are working for the same objective but are performing differentiated tasks. Horizontal flow of communication is the most frequent because individuals at the same level usually talk to each other about work-related events, management and personal matters. It is a flow which is strongly associated with group and team activities. Poor horizontal communication can divide a team, whether it be a managerial team or any other type. Departmental rivalries and personality clashes and conflicts are often felt in the lateral flow of messages. Improvement depends on developing inter-departmental contacts and developing communication skills like conflict management.

Communication networks

A more sophisticated perspective on communication flows is the study of the relative effectiveness of various communication *networks*. There are specific flows (or networks) which exist within the broad categories discussed above.

Beginning in the 1950s, many research studies have been conducted to test the importance of various networks on the effectiveness of communication (e.g. Guetzkow and Simon 1960). The most frequent networks examined have been the circle, all-channel, wheel and chain, although there is also the pattern both upwards and downwards (Figure 13.4). The circle corresponds to a group working in a physical arrangement so that they can communicate with their immediate neighbour but not with others. The all-channel network is analogous to communication patterns in a task force or functional team. The wheel arrangement corresponds to a manager at the hub with the subordinates on the periphery obtaining information from that one source, while the chain describes the one-way downward communication process of a heavily hierarchical organization.

There are conflicting views about the evidence obtained but the general consensus is that for performance on simple tasks the wheel and all-channel networks have the best scores and the circle the worst. When complex tasks are performed the all-channel network tends to score highly. The chain network is useful only on simple tasks and morale is low at the end of the chain! Lewis (1975) has elaborated on these findings in diagrammatic form (Figure 13.5).

One should approach these findings with some caution because there is evidence that other factors influence the communication process, such as the powerful influence of the task structure within the group on performance. Once the structure has been set up the task is more readily achieved irrespective of the basic network set up. But undoubtedly there is enough evidence to say that communication networks influence the communication process in a significant way. There is also sufficient evidence to challenge how a school, for example, does its networking as an organization and to analyse the sub-networks which exist, say within departments. One can also ask the question about how effective the respective networks are as vehicles of communication. Does the network exclude those who should be included?

Communication content

The purpose of examining communication from a content perspective is to look at what research has taught us about the potential for various types of content for changing attitudes. The value of one-sided communication, i.e. communicating the favourable side of an argument only as against a two-sided communication which gives a

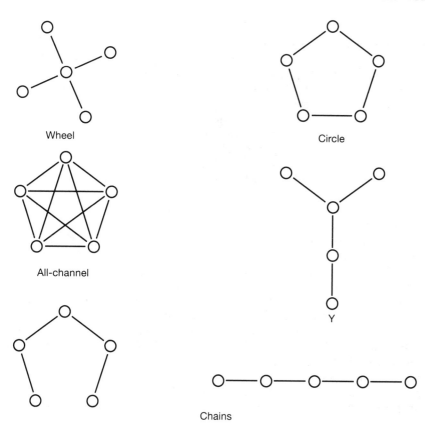

Figure 13.4 Patterns of networking
(Mullins 1993: 203)

Characteristic	Circle	Chain	Wheel	All-channel
Speed	Slow	Fast	Very fast	Slow/fast
Accuracy	Poor	Good	Good	Poor/excellent
Morale	High	Low	Very low	Very high
Leadership stability	None	Marked	Very pronounced	None
Organization	Unstable	Emerging stability	Very stable	Unstable
Flexibility	High	Low	Low	High

Figure 13.5 Communication and organization structure
(Lewis 1975: 86, quoted in Rasberry and Lemoine 1986: 108)

rounded picture of the issue, appears to depend largely on the level of knowledge possessed by the receiver prior to the communication. Given a relatively low level of knowledge, both types produce about the same kind of attitudinal change in the receiver. However, if the initial knowledge is high the one-sided communication is less successful. Thus in managerial terms, putting both sides of an issue is likely to decrease resistance to attitudinal change in most circumstances.

Two points of view exist with regard to the ordering of communication content, one arguing for primacy (the message received first is the most persuasive) and the other for recency (the message received last having the greater influence). Two factors seem to favour recency over primacy in that it leaves no time for unfavourable messages to be put across and it will be easier to recall.

A final issue with regard to content is the comparative appeal to emotion and reason. The divisions are not in practice as clear cut as this in that the same message may be seen in different ways by people. For example, a manager may announce that staff are to be made redundant in the college and the emotional reaction might be, 'I wonder if it will be my turn next'. In handling change both elements need to be addressed. Emotional resistance to change has to be met at an emotional level as well as at a rational one.

The issues of content cannot be entirely separated from that of communication flow. For example a 'leaked' communication may be more effective than a formally presented one. Perhaps the deciding factor in the content/flow issue is the importance and relevance of a communication to the receiver. Information that does not have such a direct effect on the receiver could be sent through formal channels, but if it does have a direct effect then a multi-channel approach may be preferable.

Communication skills

Examining the communication process from a skills perspective has problems. First, it is difficult to generalize about the effectiveness of a given skill because skills are individual in nature and can be practised in many different ways. Secondly, the list of communication skills is so vast that we can never be sure that we have covered them all. For these two reasons little is known scientifically about communication skills. Also the teaching of a skill may be limited because of the personality involved, particularly if it is a skill requiring some modification of personality.

Of the vast field of communication/inter-personal skills we have chosen to select three exemplars for limited analysis: effective listening, non-verbal communication and negotiation. Collectively they have a contribution to make to developing skills in the more specific area of interviewing (selection, appraisal, counselling and so on) where communication skills are so important.

Effective listening

Carl Rogers and Fritz Roethlisberger (1952) argued that ineffective listening is the greatest barrier to effective communication. Too often we say in communication with a person, 'Go ahead, I'm listening' when, although we hear a voice, the words are not listened to and the *mind* is not engaged. Listening is a most difficult skill to learn. Perhaps this is because, throughout our lives, we develop improper listening habits and become expert in the art of not listening when appearing to listen; having an interested expression when all the time we may be thinking about something entirely different!

Real listening is *active* in the sense that what is said is taken in, thoughtfully considered and, if relevant, shapes future exchanges. A good listener listens with understanding, looks for what is actually meant through inflexions and words that could be clues to hidden and double meanings. Active listening requires getting inside the sender's point of view. However, we have to recognize from the outset that effective listening is never total; when we listen we engage in selective perception. Because we are all different and have different purposes in our listening we will listen to different stimuli and, although we have 'heard' the same message we are likely to assign a different significance to it.

Listening involves the *filtering* of a variety of stimuli. For a two-person model of communication exchange, Hunt (1980: 67–8) has identified seven basic factors which influence a receiver's power to listen:

1 *auditory and visual:* the ability to see and hear with acuity
2 *concentration:* the ability to focus exclusively on the communication exchange
3 *situational constraints:* such as external factors and the physical environment
4 *the history of the relationship:* between the sender and receiver
5 *the perceived purpose of the communication exchange*
6 *the perceived degree of difficulty of the message:* without understanding attention will slacken
7 *the perceived usefulness of the message.*

As the receiver, in particular, we need to engage in in-depth listening. We must go beyond words to discern their real meaning.

Non-verbal communication

One dimension of listening which has not been emphasized, as yet, is the non-verbal behaviour associated with it. We will certainly be aided in our listening, and in the whole process of communication, if we can understand to the full the non-verbal communication signals that are sent out by senders and receivers, either deliberately or involuntarily: 'Probably more feelings and intentions are communicated non-verbally than through all the verbal methods combined' (Tortoriello *et al.* 1978: 23). However, there are problems of interpretation in seeking to understand specific pieces of non-verbal communication (NVC). In the first place NVC is culturally conditioned. Secondly, we can never be absolutely sure that we attach the same meaning to other people's bodily cues as we do. Thirdly, not all NVC is intentional; there is a fair amount of our NVC which 'leaks' through to the other person in spite of oneself. A final difficulty is that although for purposes of discussion and analysis we draw a distinction between verbal communication (VC) and NVC, they are all of a unity. The whole of this behaviour may be subsumed under the term 'body language'.

The functions of NVC may be broken down into the following categories:

• *repeating* what a person has said in a NV gesture
• *contradicting* words through NV behaviour
• *substituting* a clear NV message for a word

- *complementing* when VC reinforces NVC
- *relating* and regulating: i.e. giving a signal
- and *accenting* or putting a NV emphasis on a word that is spoken.

Each of these functions can help or hinder communication flow between people. There is a good deal of evidence that when verbal cues and non-verbal cues are contradictory the non-verbal ones win (McMahan 1976).

Communication and negotiation

One arena where the spoken word and NVC are closely married is in negotiation, particularly if conflict has been part of the process! In such a situation a wide variety of communication skills will be called into play. Negotiation has been defined as

> a way of reconciling interests and reducing conflict in situations where people have to interact with one another but where no side is powerful enough to impose its will. All human relationships have an element of cooperation and competition and negotiation is lubrication between these two tendencies.
>
> (Lowe and Pollard 1989: 120)

By argument and compromise, in a close and concentrated communication exchange, a mutually acceptable outcome is hopefully arrived at.

We must not suppose that negotiators start from equal positions of strength; indeed it is common to hear it said that so-and-so starts from a strong or weak negotiating position. The factor of differential power cannot be ignored: *position* power where a person(s) controls resources, *personal* power through the force of personality, and *negative* power, possessed by everyone, can fuel the conflict. Both groups and individuals, consciously and unconsciously, spend time and energy developing these sources of power. Lowe and Pollard suggest that the effectiveness of negotiators is dependent upon the frame of mind adopted by the negotiator, the procedures used and the process of interpersonal communication. Pennington and Gooderham (1987) provide a useful map of the process (Figure 13.6). So interpersonal communication becomes vital in a negotiation scenario.

Negotiation calls for the exercise of general skills, but there is also a specialized language of negotiation which has its own specific central speech-acts, or words and phrases. Mulholland (1991: 186) has classified these as:

(a) call for agreement
(b) give reasons why there should be agreement
(c) compare and contrast options
(d) judge or evaluate ideas and options
(e) clarify and test the views expressed
(f) assess the strength of feelings
(g) establish and reiterate goals.

Non-linguistic behaviours play an important part in this process, but talk has a major function and any speech acts which bring about conflict, obstruction and obstinacy are inappropriate.

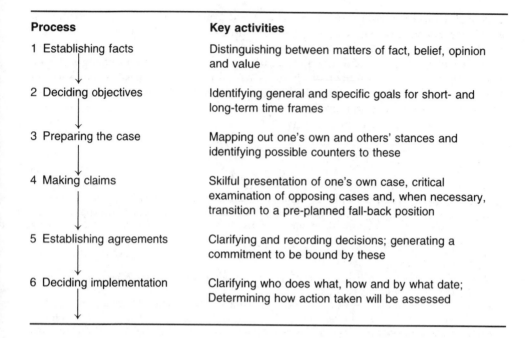

Process	Key activities
1 Establishing facts	Distinguishing between matters of fact, belief, opinion and value
2 Deciding objectives	Identifying general and specific goals for short- and long-term time frames
3 Preparing the case	Mapping out one's own and others' stances and identifying possible counters to these
4 Making claims	Skilful presentation of one's own case, critical examination of opposing cases and, when necessary, transition to a pre-planned fall-back position
5 Establishing agreements	Clarifying and recording decisions; generating a commitment to be bound by these
6 Deciding implementation	Clarifying who does what, how and by what date; Determining how action taken will be assessed

Figure 13.6 Negotiation: a model of a process
(Pennington and Gooderham 1987)

Conclusion: some managerial implications

This chapter has covered a wide range of concepts, theoretical positions, and strategies involved in the communication process, but it has been by no means comprehensive. The reader will have observed many points which are relevant to educational management. Effective management has to start from a full understanding of the details of how the communication process impacts on every management activity and be as precise as possible on the way that communication theory can be translated into effective practice.

All schools and colleges would find value in examining the stages, content and processes of communication discussed above in relation to their own internal and external patterns of communication. For effective communications, whether written, oral or non-verbal, managers in schools and colleges would benefit from an audit of formal and informal procedures, and any barriers they engender. They should establish a positive communication policy, based on sound theory, making sure that this policy is *communicated*!

One major improvement in communications might be to achieve more empathy, i.e. understand more closely the receiver's needs, attempt to predict the impact of a message on the receiver's feelings and attitudes and adjust it to attune with his or her vocabulary, interests and values. For example, bluntness which is acceptable to one teacher (or student) may well be anathema to another. School and college managers need to know their staff and customers. A second area of improvement might be

through feedback to ensure that a communication has been accurately transmitted. Other strategies might include using simpler and more direct language, making sure that the message is really the one intended, attempting to break down the levels of communication in a hierarchical organization (a difficult task without changing those structures) and using a number of channels to ensure that the message is conveyed fully. The methods should be matched to the needs and circumstances of the school or college. Effective communication in school and college management is never a luxury but always an absolute necessity.

References

Betts, P. W. (1993) *Supervisory Management* (5th edn). London: Pitman.

Guetzkow, H. and Simon, H. A. (1960) The impact of certain communication nets upon organization and performance in task-oriented groups, in A. H. Rubenstein and C. J. Haberstroh (eds) *Some Theories of Organizations*. Homewood, IL: Dorsey Press.

Hunt, J. W. (1980) *Managing People at Work: a Manager's Guide to Behaviour in Organizations*. London: McGraw-Hill.

Laswell, H. D. (1948) The structure and function of communication in society, in L. Bryson (ed.) *The Communication of Ideas*. New York: Harper and Bros.

Lewis, P. (1975) *Organizational Communications* (2nd edn). Colombus, OH: Grid.

Lopez, F. M. (1965) *Personnel Interviewing, Theory and Practice*. New York: McGraw-Hill.

Lowe, T. J. and Pollard, I. W. (1989) Negotiation skills, in C. Riches and C. Morgan (eds) *Human Resource Management*. Milton Keynes: Open University Press.

McMahan, E. M. (1976) Non-verbal communication as a function of attribution in impression formation. Paper presented at the Speech Communication Convention, San Francisco, December.

Mulholland, J. (1991) *The Language of Negotiation, a Handbook of Practical Strategies for Improving Communication*. London: Cassell.

Mullins, L. J. (1993) *Management and Organization Behaviour* (3rd edn). London: Pitman.

Pennington, R. C. and Gooderham, D. G. (1987) *Negotiation in Schools*. Middlesborough: Department of Management Studies, Flatts Lane Centre.

Rasberry, R. W. and Lemoine, L. F. (1986) *Effective Managerial Communication*. Boston, MA: Kent Publishing.

Rogers, C. R. and Roethlisberger, F. J. (1952) Barriers and gateways to communication, *Harvard Business Review*, 30 (July–August): 44–9.

Secord, P. F. and Backman, C. W. (1964) *Social Psychology*. New York: McGraw-Hill.

Smithson, S. and Whithead, J. (1990) *Interpersonal Skills, a Handbook for Management Trainees*. Kingston upon Thames: Croner Publications.

Tortoriello, T. R., Blatt, S. J. and DeWine, S. (1978) *Communications in the Organization: an Applied Approach*. New York: McGraw-Hill.

Windahl, S., Signitzer, B. and Olson, J. T. (1992) *Using Communication Theory*. London: Sage.

14 | Effective teambuilding*

JOHN ADAIR

Teambuilding applies when you are building a team in the first place or amalgamating two teams or organisations to form a new entity, or completely reconstituting and revitalising an old team. Few leaders have the luxury of building their own teams in this second sense. Usually they inherit a team from someone else. The latter kind of team may include individuals who would not be there if you could start again and choose your own people. How do you transform an assembly of individuals into a team?

That challenge may not be on your agenda now. But you never know when you might be asked to recruit and train a team for a particular task. It is bound to happen at least once – perhaps many times – in your career as a manager. Are you ready for it?

In this chapter I assume you are the leader and can select or build your own team. But the higher up the corporate ladder you climb the more you will be involved in building teams where you are not a member. The key appointment, of course, is then the leader. It is useful to remember when making it that the team leader has very distinctive responsibilities which more or less define the role. The team leader:

- may be responsible for selection; if not, ought to be involved in it;
- is responsible for ensuring that the standards and discipline of the team are such that high performance through interdependence happens;
- allocates special responsibilities and controls the use of resources;
- directs the formation of team strategy and plans;
- has more to do with the team's interface with other groups and individuals involved in its performance;
- will have to make considerable demands on the team as a group and on individual members.

* This material has been edited and was originally published as 'Teambuilding'.

Selecting the team members

The importance of choosing the right people as team members from the collection of possible members is the first principle of team success.

There are degrees of choice. There are constraints on the pool of people from whom the choice must be made, as well as constraints of time.

Occasionally, if there is genuinely a missing piece in the jigsaw puzzle, the leader can look to another part of the organisation or even outside the organisation itself. But compromises will almost certainly have to be accepted. Few good leaders have quite the team they would wish for – just as few good teams have quite the leader they would desire.

Shelves of books have been written on the subject of interviewing and choosing people for jobs. With the requirements of high performance teamwork in mind, their contents can be simplified into the three key factors:

- technical or professional competence
- ability to work as a team member
- desirable personal attributes.

Of course it helps if you already know the people well. Sometimes the larger group from which selections or substitutions must be made is just a list of names; at other times this supply group can be a very familiar reserve clearly involved with the current team and often considered to be not only a reservoir but also a training group – in effect, already a part of the team. The leader or selector starts with a fairly large number of people and eliminates potential members by a process of interviewing and testing.

Technical or professional competence

What is this person going to bring to the team? The first and most pressing require-ment is that s/he should possess the skill or knowledge that is needed in the team.

As a leader you are most probably a generalist yourself. It may therefore be difficult for you to gauge the degree of professional ability of the person before you. Arguably, if you are aspiring to lead in that field, you should have *some* knowledge for making a judgement. The modern heresy that a management science exists that can be trans-ferred from one industry to another has bred shallow managers, those who cannot assess the competences of those who work for them. A leader in any field should still have sufficient knowledge to be able to assess the professional worth of the team mem-bers. [. . .]

Given that two candidates are equal in specialist competence (and as desirable team members) preference might well be given to the person who has something else to offer. Many people have some other professional experience or technical expertise which is secondary to their main interest but could be highly relevant to the team in certain contingencies. You are seeking flexible people, not narrow specialists; those who can turn their minds and hands to a variety of problems with confidence.

Ability to work as a team member

Your selection process should discover those who are not motivated – they do not *want* to achieve, they do not strive to be in the team, and they will not work hard in

'Nobody's perfect but a team can be'

How to design and construct a team that simultaneously meets the requirements of both functional and team roles constitutes one of the most intriguing aspects of teambuilding. This is also one of the most critical factors determining the fortunes of management teams in industry. It is here that the Marks and Spencer experience of team work offers the most valuable insight.

In a significant sense the effectiveness of the M & S management teams linger on the company's success in enabling most of its staff to have a relatively high degree of versatility in terms of functional as well as team roles. The M & S staff are to a considerable extent 'generalist' in both dimensions. This makes it possible to combine and recombine teams. This is perhaps another aspect of what Robert Keller has referred to as the 'inimitable magic' of M & S. But if our analysis has been substantially correct, then maybe it is not as mystic as the word 'magic' implies – though nonetheless 'inimitable'.

The M & S investment in training and in creating the conditions for effective team work has been gigantic and amazingly long term, but the payoff, as we have seen, is equally spectacular. In practical business terms it enables the company to acquire a unique competitive edge which goes a long way to explaining the enviable record of the company's success.

(Tse 1985: 86)

harness or as individuals. Such individuals will have a bad influence on the rest of the group. Some people may not appear to be well motivated. However, others can inspire or motivate us and it is important to find out if the potential is there before you discard someone on the grounds of motivation.

The second sort of person to leave on one side are those who will not make good team members because they are disruptive. Harmony in groups is fragile. The key question to ask yourself and others relates to this factor: is this person capable of functioning as a member of a high-performance team? If the person is essentially a loner, or so highly individualistic that they cannot subordinate their egos to the common good, you will be wise to leave them out of the team.

It is not easy or necessary to analyse too closely what constitutes this general capacity for working with others. So much depends upon the other people involved in *this* team. You have to be sensitive to the chemistry of the group. The concept of *balance* is important here.

Once you have eliminated the non-starters you should learn as much as you can about each individual. Then make your judgement in terms of the chemistry and balance of the group.

Interviews are a fairly blunt instrument for such team selection. It is infinitely preferable, if it can be arranged, to see the person in action with other members of the proposed team. If that is not possible you can possibly see them at work in another team, or at least talk to someone who has witnessed them working in groups. The best people to tell you about someone's capacity as a team member are those who have worked in harness with them.

Desirable personal attributes

So far you have thought about the person in terms of their technical or professional ability and their fitness for the role of team member. In both areas you are looking for a certain standard. If you have in mind the formation of an exceptional team, as opposed to a merely ordinary one, you will be seeking technical skills of a high order, ones which interlock with the contributions of other members of the team.

By now you will also have eliminated those with the roots of two kinds of problems in them. Those who lack the basic motivation to work hard are bound to become problems for you, because team members – intent upon high performance – will turn against them. If you select those who have a tendency to put up people's backs by their manner, conversation or behaviour, you can be sure they will cost you a great deal of time later on. Apart from the thankless task of trying to develop them, you will expend time reconciling and harmonising.

What are the desirable extra attributes you should look for? S/he will be someone who can contribute to the *process* skills of achieving the task – especially in the areas of decision making, problem solving and creative or innovative thinking – not merely contributing from a knowledge-base to the *content* of those decisions.

Desirable attributes include the ability to listen to others and to build on their contributions. This implies a flexibility of mind. The person who is too possessive about their own 'territory' or information is setting limits to their own and to the group's growth as a team.

Such flexibility implies a certain lack of suspicion. The ability both to give and to inspire trust is related to integrity, which may be defined as wholeness of character and adherence to standards – professional and moral – beyond oneself. If you appoint someone to your team who lacks integrity, whatever their professional competence or superficial social 'interactive skills', you are taking a big risk.

Last on the list, but still desirable, come such factors as likeability or popularity of a person. Members of teams are able to suppress quite intense personal dislikes for each other over the duration of the team's working life, and being likeable to everyone is not essential. But evidence suggests that children learn better from teachers they like. On that analogy it seems fairly obvious that adults will work better with colleagues they like.

Checklist: have you selected the right team member?

Task

	YES	NO
Has s/he an alert intelligence?	☐	☐
Where applicable, has s/he a high level of vocational skills?	☐	☐
Do his or her knowledge/skills complement those of other team members rather than duplicate them?	☐	☐
Is s/he motivated to seek excellence in results and methods of working together?	☐	☐
Does his or her track record really bear out the scores given above?	☐	☐

Team

Will s/he work closely with others in decision making and problem solving without 'rubbing people up the wrong way'?	☐	☐
Does s/he listen?	☐	☐
Is s/he flexible enough to adopt different roles within the group?	☐	☐
Can s/he influence others – assertive rather than aggressive?	☐	☐
Will s/he contribute to group morale rather than draw cheques upon it?	☐	☐

Individual

Has s/he a sense of humour and a degree of tolerance for others?	☐	☐
Has s/he a certain amount of will to achieve ambition, tinged with understanding that s/he cannot do it all alone?	☐	☐
Will s/he develop a feeling of responsibility for the success of the team as a whole, not simply his or her own part in it?	☐	☐
Has s/he integrity?	☐	☐
Does s/he have a realistic perception of his/her strengths and weaknesses?	☐	☐

Teambuilding exercises

[. . .]

A crucial event in the movement from being a group to becoming a team can be the teambuilding exercise. This can be based upon either (1) a substitute team task (for example, a business case study or a few days of out-door activities) or (2) a real task (for example, going away for a weekend to plan strategy).

There are pros and cons to both approaches. The advantage of a substitute task type of event is that success or failure is not of paramount importance. Nor are there any technological or professional challenges to meet, so that people can concentrate on the essential issue of learning how to work more effectively together as a team. The disadvantage is that the activities during the event can be perceived as games with little or no relevance to the job in hand. Moreover, at a certain level of seniority, managers become less willing to learn through this medium.

The real task has the obvious advantage of reality and immediacy. But the danger is that people become so immersed in it that the training objective is lost.

How does a leader, having assembled individuals into a new group, turn them into a team? For a team has to be grown or built through the experience of working together.

If time allows, the leader can run training sessions for the group, which will have as one objective learning to work as an effective team. The tasks in these sessions may well be of the 'substitute task variety', but they should never be trivial or totally irrelevant. They should also be seen as introductory to tasks which closely resemble the actual tasks which the group will be called upon to tackle together.

Reviewing

In teambuilding exercises careful briefing about the object is vital. Then the key part played by the *review* after the trial runs needs to be stressed. This can be unstructured. You can simply get the group together and ask 'How did the job go? Could we have worked better as a team?'

More often than not, with able managers or staff, the general discussion that follows such open-ended questions will cover all the points that the leader already has in mind. The process of reflection, digesting experience and relating it to principles, has begun. The important point is to build into the programme opportunities for this unhurried reviewing or looking back on the day's work together.

A more structured approach can be followed, using questionnaires or checklists which individuals complete and then discuss. These certainly have a place, if used appropriately, in getting a group to think critically about itself. They are especially useful if a group is unaware of the real level of its performance, or is disguising itself from some of the problems within its life it can and should be solving. The results of a checklist can then provide it with some hard evidence to discuss.

The *reviewing* phase in the teambuilding activity is not temporary. A highly effective team is characterised by its tendency towards regular and searching self-evaluation of performance. Reviewing is an essential part of the process of being a high-performance team. It should establish the facts first. What was our objective? Did we in fact achieve it? If we did not, in what ways did we fail?

Then you can come to *diagnosis*, introduced by the question *why*. 'Why did we succeed or not succeed?' Analysis of the reasons for success or failure will start in the task circle. Was the goal clear? Did we have a workable plan? Was it communicated? Did we act flexibly, possibly altering the plan, in the face of serious difficulty? And so on.

Then you should ask questions about the teamwork circle. 'How well did we work as a team?' Here questions-and-discussion should range over co-ordination and co-operation, group standards (technical and social), communication, atmosphere, changes in morale, the presence or absence of mutual encouragement.

Thirdly, any deficiencies in individual skills should be explored to identify training which will remedy them. You should be careful, as a general rule, not to criticise individuals in front of the group. Remember that you are *appraising* performance, not acting as a negative critic, so you will point out the good as well as the not-so-good points.

Teambuilding exercises, especially if they involve one or two nights away together, provide opportunities for *developing* informal relationships. Over a drink in the bar or the meal table, team members can get to know each other better. They compare their different as well as similar perspectives. Such discussion allows members of a team to see the *complexity* of the different strands of wisdom and desires of the team and allows that complexity to be ordered or negotiated through careful discussion.

It is important for the leader to set a high standard of listening in these informal sessions. Reflections on issues and careful exploration of individual views implies a philosophy of teamwork which is far removed from the various 'instant teamwork' recipes offered on one-day courses to managers. In many organisations people are encouraged to have as few meetings as possible and to get on with the 'real work'. But work which ignores individual values and perspectives can lead to superficial activity. In such low-performance teams, members are not committed to the activity, and the quality of the team's life is not enriched by the range of experience available within it.

The role of consultant

In teambuilding exercises there is no doubt that the right consultant can play a significant part as a catalysts. He should not usurp the role of the leader, the person who owns the problem of developing *this* group into a team. The role – as an outsider – is complementary to the leader's one.

Why, then, are consultants not more widely used to develop the effective teams that industry, commerce and the public services need?

Generally, consultants in this field have approached teambuilding from a background of T-group or sensitivity training. They have imported all the assumptions of the Group Dynamics movement into their work, including some faulty assumptions about leadership. Inevitably this has led to a resistance to their message from practical managers, followed often by an outward rejection of what appears to be the old group dynamics approach. However, in an article entitled 'Second Thoughts on Team Building', two British consultants, Bill Critchley and David Casey, questioned the value and assumptions which underlie what is often called teambuilding and ultimately their usefulness in certain settings:

Teambuilding: at what price and at whose cost?

We were running a teambuilding session with a top management group and something very odd began to appear. Our disturbing discovery was that for most of their time this group of people had absolutely no need to work as a team; indeed the attempt to do so was causing more puzzlement and scepticism than motivation and commitment. This wasn't the first time our teambuilding efforts had cast doubts on the very validity of teamwork itself, within our client groups.

We admitted that we had assumed that good teamwork is a characteristic of healthy, effectively functioning organisations. We had been assuming that the top group in any organisation should be a team and ought to work as a team. We further assumed that a properly functioning team is one in which:

- people care for each other
- people are open and truthful
- there is a high level of trust
- decisions are made by consensus
- there is strong team commitment
- conflict is faced up to and worked through
- people really listen to ideas and to feelings

- feelings are expressed freely
- process issues (task and feelings) are dealt with.

It had always seemed logical to us, that a teambuilding catalyst could always help any team to function better – and so help any organisation perform better as an organisation. Better functioning would lead the organisation to achieve its purposes more effectively.

Reality was, however, at odds with this cosy view of teams, teamwork and teambuilding. In truth the Director of Education has little need to work in harness with other chief officers in a county council. He or she might need the support of the Chief Executive and the Chair of the elected members' Education Committee, but the other chief officers in that local authority have neither the expertise, the interest, or the time, to contribute to what is essentially very specialised work.

Even in industry, whilst it is clear that the marketing and production directors of a company must work closely together to ensure that the production schedule is synchronised with sales forecasts, they don't need to involve the *whole* team. And they certainly do not need to develop high levels of trust and openness to work through those kinds of business issues.

On the other hand, most people would agree that *strategic* decisions, concerned with the future direction of the whole enterprise, should involve all those at the top. Strategy should demand an input from every member of the top group, and for strategic discussion and strategic decision-making, teamwork at the top is essential. But how much time do most top management groups actually spend discussing strategy? Our experiences, in a wide variety of organisations, suggest that 10 per cent is a high figure for most organisations – often 5 per cent would be nearer the mark. This means that 90–95 per cent of decisions in organisations are essentially operational; that is decisions made within departments based usually on a fair amount of information and expertise. In those conditions, high levels of trust and openness may be nice, but are not necessary; consensus is strictly not an issue and in any case would take up far too much time. There is therefore no need for high levels of interpersonal skills.

Why then, is so much time and money invested in teambuilding, we asked ourselves. Perhaps the spread of teambuilding has more to do with teambuilders and *their* needs and values rather than a careful analysis of what is appropriate and necessary for the organisation? We each wrote down an honest and frank list of reasons why we ourselves engaged in teambuilding. We recommend this as an enlightening activity for other teambuilders – perhaps, like us, they will arrive at this kind of conclusion; teambuilders work as catalysts to help management groups function better as open teams for a variety of reasons, including the following:

- They like it – they enjoy the risks.
- Because they are good at it.
- It's flattering to be asked.
- They receive rewarding personal feedback.
- Professional kudos – not many people do teambuilding with top teams.
- There's money in it.
- It accords with their values: for instance democracy is preferred to autocracy.

- They gain power. Process interventions are powerful in business settings where the client is on home ground and can bamboozle the consultant in business discussions.

All those reasons are concerned with the needs, skills and values of the *teambuilder* rather than the management group being 'helped'. This could explain why many teambuilding exercises leave the so-called 'management team' excited and stimulated by the experience, only to find they are spending an unnecessary amount of time together discussing other people's departmental issues. Later on, because they cannot see the benefit of working together on such issues, they abandon 'teamwork' altogether.

We began to see that there is a very large proportion of most managers' work where teamwork is not needed (and to attempt to inculcate teamwork is dysfunctional). There is at the same time a very small proportion of their work where teamwork is absolutely vital (and to ignore teamworking skills is to invite disaster). This latter work, which demands a team approach, is typified by strategic work but not limited to strategic work. It is any work characterised by a high level of choice and by the condition of maximum uncertainty.

Although there are tasks that do not strictly demand teamwork it does make a difference if they are tackled by a team. In other words, if there is a team it will approach these tasks in a different way from a mere collection of individuals. Although the task may require a certain structure in the group, so also the nature of the group (especially if it is working as a team) will affect the perception, definition and ultimately the accomplishment of the task. A good consultant can help a group see possibilities of at least a degree of teamwork in what seems to be a mere assemblage of individual tasks or contributions. [. . .]

In conclusion, the first objective in teambuilding is to choose the right people in the light of the team's purpose. Then you should aim at developing a group identity. Giving the team a name and a base or place to meet are important steps in that direction. In the early meetings it is helpful to remember that the new members – who may know you well but not each other – are coming with the following questions in mind:

- Why are we in this group?
- Do we need to work as a team?
- Even if it is not necessary would it benefit us to do so?
- Are we going to collaborate or compete?
- Are our objectives realistic?
- How are decisions to be made?
- How is our performance to be appraised?
- How are we going to grow in effectiveness?

Points to consider

Teamwork is required by many tasks; even where it is not strictly needed, working as a team can transform performance and enhance job satisfaction. Good teams are not the products of chance. As a leader, one of your three major responsibilities is to build the team.

If you are assembling a new team, concentrate on selecting individual members who will use complementary skills, techniques and knowledge and also build up the common life. Look for those with extra qualities of personality and character mentioned above.

Within the first year of its life try to get your team away for a day or two on its own. With the help of a varied programme of tasks and events – practical activities followed by review – identify with them the strengths and weaknesses of the team, listing the areas for improvement. Return home with an action plan for moving from low- to high-performance team levels.

The power of a team to accomplish its mission is directly related to how well the leader selects and develops its members.

References

Tse, K. K. (1985) *Marks and Spencer: Anatomy of Britain's Most Efficiently Managed Company*. Oxford: Pergamon.

Index